Family Stories in French-Canadian History

Migrations

Judy DePue

Migrations: Family Stories in French-Canadian History
Copyright © 2023 Judy DePue.

Produced and printed by Stillwater River Publications.

Visit our website at **www.StillwaterPress.com** for more information.

First Stillwater River Publications Edition

ISBN: 978-1-960505-57-6 (paperback), 978-1-960505-99-6 (hardcover)

Library of Congress Control Number: 2023913501

Names: DePue, Judy, author.
Title: Migrations : family stories in French-Canadian history / Judy DePue.
Description: First Stillwater River Publications edition. | West Warwick, RI, USA
    : Stillwater River Publications, [2023] | Includes bibliographical references and
    index.
Identifiers: ISBN: 978-1-960505-57-6 | LCCN: 2023913501
Subjects: LCSH: DePue, Judy—Family. | DePue family. | French-Canadians—
    United States—History. | LCGFT: Family histories.
Classification: LCC: CS71 .D417 2023 | DDC: —dc23

1 2 3 4 5 6 7 8 9 10
Written by Judy DePue.
Cover and interior design by Elisha Gillette.
Cover photo courtesy of Nicolas Gagnon.
Author photo courtesy of Joan Shirley.
Published by Stillwater River Publications, West Warwick, RI, USA.

To all of my family.
For those who came and left this earth before me, I hope I honor your legacy. For my brothers, nieces, nephews, and cousins, including those I haven't met, I hope you will find this history intriguing. It tells how some of our ancestors came to be on this continent. It also tells of building blocks that are part of who we are. We inherit the legacy of our ancestors. What can we learn from them?

LIST OF FAMILY TREES

Chapter 3
William and Mary Jane's children

Chapter 4
John and Catherine's children
Frederick Dupee's ancestors, 4 generations

Chapter 5
Isadore and Mary's children

Chapter 6
Allor-Allard family line back to France,
from Isadore Allor back to Jacques Allard
Isadore Allor's ancestors, 5 generations
Mary Frances Furton's ancestors, 5 generations

Chapter 10
Norbert and Genevieve's children
The Poirier line
The Leroux line
Norbert Dupuis' ancestors, 4 generations

Chapter 11
The Dupuis line back to France (Norbert to Martin)

Chapter 12
Travels of Sylvain Dupuis, his parents and siblings, from deportation
Travels of Françoise Leblanc, her parents and siblings, from deportation

❧

Table of Contents

❦

INTRODUCTION

A TYPICAL GENEALOGY SEARCH PROVIDES A LIST OF ANCESTORS, who married whom, and the names of their children across multiple generations. This is not that type of book. It's a collection of stories. I was initially interested in learning about my father because my parents were divorced when I was an infant. Who was he, and what shaped him?

As a psychologist, now retired, I spent decades helping others heal from their personal or family distresses, yet I knew almost nothing about my father or his family. I only knew that he was a very troubled man. My training as a counseling psychologist emphasized understanding the whole person, their personal and family history, and their strengths and weaknesses before considering options for any treatment. My father is now deceased, but my curiosity about what shaped him has not waned.

Genealogy can be used to answer such questions. With genealogy tools, we can all be sleuths for uncovering family mysteries, often from the comfort of our homes. My career also utilized research skills, as I sought to disseminate and evaluate strategies designed to reach more people by offering innovative health services in various community settings. This required understanding the context in which the service would be placed. Now, I could transfer those skills to genealogy research. In a genealogy search, like any other detective work, you find and verify clues, examine the contexts of those clues, and piece together the evidence. The process drew me in. After I found information about my father, I kept going. I searched my father's paternal (DePue-Dupee-Dupuis) and maternal (Allor-Allard) lines back in time, more than 400 years and ten generations, to when these ancestors came to

1

North American shores from France and elsewhere. I discovered I have a French-Canadian heritage, which I knew very little about. Gradually, my ancestors moved westward. Some of them moved on to Michigan. I learned to put the tiny bits of information together, like puzzle pieces, to tell their stories. What I found was surprising.

My ancestors were not famous people, but they were no less interesting. I discovered that they were real actors and pioneers in history. Thus, their stories may belong to many families who traveled these or similar routes as they migrated westward from the shores where they landed.

I found my grandparents at the outbreak of the Detroit automotive boom. A great-uncle was a beloved parish priest. There was a newlywed couple who set out to walk from Pennsylvania to the Mississippi River when they were taken hostage by Indians. My family tree includes soldiers who were part of Cadillac's expedition to settle in Detroit. There were "*voyageurs*" who traveled by canoe over the 650 miles from Quebec to Detroit and beyond. I found *Filles du Roi* (Daughters of the King), who were brought to Quebec from France to marry the local bachelors and help grow the colony. I found family members among the first settlers of Quebec. Other family members were among the early settlers in Acadia (present-day Nova Scotia), and they braved the numerous wars in Acadia between England and France, buffeted by changing rulers every few years. There are many amazing stories you will read about. Many of these stories still have relevance today.

I also hope these stories spark an interest for readers to explore other family stories and find family actors in other history. Research is always an evolving process. Genealogy is a collaborative sport! Hopefully, the documentation provided here will offer stepping stones or inspiration for others as they do their own research.

Judy DePue
July 2023

1

Looking for a Better Life

"We have always held to the hope, the belief, the conviction that there is a better life, a better world, beyond the horizon."
—Franklin Roosevelt

Leonard

⚜

PAULINE'S JOURNEY TO MICHIGAN

MY MOTHER, PAULINE, WAS IN HER NINETIES WHEN SHE TOLD ME about her experiences growing up and how she met my father. Before then, she was always busy, it seemed. She would typically be found baking, making jam, canning fruit, or making meals for others on the farm, like her mother and other generations before her. Farm life meant rarely sitting still. There was always work to do. Now, she was stooped over with arthritis and had difficulty getting around. So, she was a captive audience for my questions.

We sat at the dining room table at my brother and sister-in-law's home in Kansas, where my mother was then living. With her grandchildren and great-grandchildren in and out, there were happy distractions. Despite her physical aches and pains, she seemed more content at this stage of her life than ever. Her face was softly framed with curly white hair. In her mid-nineties, her eyes still had their sparkle. She had many wrinkles on her face, but when she smiled, which was often, all of her wrinkles curled upward. Her whole face smiled. She usually loved to chat with anyone, family or strangers. She would freely share stories about me and my siblings, about what she was proud of, including embarrassing details that we'd prefer she'd keep to herself. Her conversations were about the everyday details of her day, to which others could relate: about family, food, weather, and the natural world. I marveled at her ability to identify flowers and the local birds from their songs. You had to be careful saying you admired something she made, such as her baking, because she would go out of her way to make it for you again as a gift. Even her pharmacist and hairdresser benefitted from her gifts. This gave her joy. Most people found her likable.

When asked to look back on earlier experiences, however, she was not often self-reflective, except to use time-worn sayings. One of her favorites was, "It's a great life, if you don't weaken." In fact, her strength was often tested during her lifetime. But now, when pressed with my questions, she was less talkative than usual. Her memories from seventy years ago were sparse, like small threads I tried to pull on to gather more details. Her voice became tentative, but it was unclear if this was because of the long distance of time to recall clearly or because she was hesitant to go there. I already knew she typically evaded questions about my father. Her usual evasion tactic was changing the subject or latching on to any distraction. I knew how to persist, but my techniques didn't always succeed. Therefore, the stories I gathered were patchy. Some of the details I gathered with my own research.

My mother told me it was in the summer of 1936, when she was twenty years old, that she decided to leave home. She had never traveled before, nor had any of her siblings. It was the middle of the Great Depression. Her mother, Olive, was born in Michigan,[1] and Pauline still had relatives there that she wanted to visit. So, it seemed that Michigan became an idea in my mother's mind, like a shiny beacon on the horizon to set her sights upon.

I already knew that my grandmother Olive had been adopted.[2] It was in the 1890s, after her own mother, Minnie, was widowed with four young children to care for. Minnie was destitute. Widows had few options at the time, especially if they were poor. Minnie's sister had her own family and could take in only one child, so she took five-year-old Tom. Minnie decided to keep her two youngest, an infant and a toddler. Olive was the oldest child at age seven. Minnie heard about a family without children who would adopt an older child to help out. Thus, Minnie "let go" of Olive. It is difficult to imagine the circumstances when loving your child could lead to giving them away for a better life than you could provide. This new family would take Olive with them to western New York, far from her biological family. Olive's new family was not wealthy, although they were better off than her own and they were kind to her. With her adopted parents' blessing, Olive kept in touch with her original family. I found a box of Olive's letters when we moved my mother out of the farmhouse at age ninety. Olive had corresponded with her brothers and cousins but rarely with her biological mother. It must have been hard to forgive a mother who had given her away. Some of this family had made the trip from Michigan to western New York to visit Olive. It was these cousins that Pauline sought to visit.

At age twenty, Olive married a local farmer, Ray Dewey,[3] who would be my grandfather. He was a good man. They started with a rented farm and later bought their own place. They had eight children together, Pauline being the fourth. It wasn't a prosperous farm. Things were difficult for the family even before the Depression. They barely got by. Despite this, Olive believed in education; she was active in the school committee that established the one-room schoolhouse in their rural neighborhood. This school went through the eighth grade. All of their eight children went on to high school, walking the three miles to town. They all had chores on the farm but also worked extra jobs to earn money needed for school supplies. Their clothes were homemade. My mother told me she had only one dress for school and one for her chores at home. She couldn't afford to mess up either one of them.

When my mother graduated from high school, she was very proud of her accomplishment. She told me she had a boyfriend at the time. But she decided to leave anyway. So, she decided that Michigan would be her destination to start a new life for herself. What she didn't say explicitly was that she could see what her life would be like if she stayed. It would be a farmer's wife, like her mother's. But she wanted something more. Many people were on the move during the Depression, looking for hope on the horizon.

To pay her way, Pauline got a waitress job on a Lake Erie passenger ship between Buffalo and Detroit. She remembered a few details about the ship she took. However, I was able to find descriptions online from this era. The Great Lakes steamers were reminiscent of wealthier times. They would soon be phased out due to the greater use of cars, buses, and truck shipping. In 1936, I imagine a country girl might become awestruck. The ship "City of Detroit III," running between Buffalo, Cleveland, and Detroit, was one of these. It rivaled ocean liners in luxury.[4] It could carry 5,000 day-passengers and 1,500 for an overnight voyage, in addition to its freight transport. As they boarded, passengers entered a wood-paneled lobby where they were faced with the grand staircase. At the top of the stairs was the grand salon, with its mythology-themed murals. The dining room, with its window walls at the back of the ship, seated 350. Patrons paid $3.50 (about $35 in today's money) for the Buffalo to Detroit trip, with an extra dollar for an overnight stateroom.[4] This was a high price for many people during the Depression. "I had many offers," my mother told me, of her customers' advances and proposals on the ship. My mother always had a warm smile, so this wasn't surprising. But she kept her focus on her work and her destination.

The Detroit riverfront, where the steamships docked, was a busy transportation hub at the time, even while the Depression had dramatically slowed the passenger and freight businesses.[5] This was where goods from ships were moved onto the railroads. Pauline stepped off the ship as planned, into the unknown city. She had the bills and coins from her earnings and tips in her pocket. The bustling city was no doubt noisy and confusing, a whirl of new and exhilarating sights, sounds, and smells, much more thrilling than anything she had seen before. Nonetheless, she found her way to the bus station.

At the bus ticket window, she said she realized her cousins lived some distance from the city. Her earnings from the ship would only cover part of the way. She bought a ticket for as far as she could afford and got off near a cherry orchard. Michigan is known for its beautiful orchards that were originally planted by the French settlers when it was still part of colonial New France. The cherry-picking earned her enough to pay the rest of her bus fare. I had to admire her resourcefulness. After reaching her destination, she strengthened relationships with her Michigan cousins, with whom she kept in touch for the rest of her life, following Olive's correspondence tradition.

Pauline's adventure didn't end there. She went back to Detroit and found another waitress job. It was on this job that she met Leonard, who was a regular customer at the bar. I asked what attracted her to him. What was he like? "He was a talker," she said, leaving it at that. I waited a few moments. She looked out the window but kept her silence. I decided to honor her reticence. Apparently, he charmed her. Or, she simply got caught up in the new relationship's momentum. They married a short time later. I found her marriage certificate online; it was April 1937.[6] Their daughter, my sister Loretta, was born in November that year. Suddenly, she was fully immersed in her new life in Michigan.

Before long, Pauline's sister Edna followed her to Detroit. And soon, Edna also found a husband and settled down to a life in Michigan. I don't know what prompted Edna's journey. While Edna was two years older than my mother, I often sensed a rivalry between them, at least on Edna's side. I suspect Edna would not have wanted it said that she "followed" Pauline at anything. She wanted to be first. While my mother was usually kind and accommodating, Edna could be opinionated and a bit prickly. Maybe Edna sought Pauline's company, like Ying seeking Yang. She needed the balance. I'm sure they were a support to one another in Michigan. It was interesting that Edna's husband, Onnie Lehto,[7] who came from a large Finnish family, was very easy going and gregarious. I remember him as often the life of any party. Edna seemed very happy when they were together. Onnie was a good counterpart to Edna as he could soften her harder edges. I wondered how my mother's personality fit with Leonard's. Could he reinforce her qualities? Could she stand up for herself?

STARTING A NEW FAMILY IN DETROIT

It was not an easy start to family life. It was still the Depression, and Leonard had a hard time finding work. They shared an apartment with a friend, his wife, and their two children. The 1940 census shows Leonard

My father, Leonard, with Loretta
and David at the Holden Street house

and Pauline,[8] with my sister Loretta, age two, and my brother David, age nine months, living with Gerald and Nilda Hanna, along with their two children (Marie, age two, and Gerald Jr., age three months). The address was 5924 Lincoln Street. The census states that Leonard was Gerald's "brother-in-law," but Pauline told me they were just friends. The apartment was near the bar where Gerald was a bartender. At this same bar, Pauline still waited on tables. They needed her income. Leonard's work was sporadic. He told the census he had worked only fourteen weeks that year. Pauline remembered washing diapers in the bathtub of that apartment. With four small children, there were a lot of diapers. The apartment was crowded and noisy. The bar was a respite in contrast.

As Pauline remembered, they later rented the first floor of a house on Holden Street for $40 a month. A streetcar ran out front. There was a front porch and a backyard where Pauline could hang her wash outside. This was a relative luxury.

Pauline was more comfortable recounting stories about her children. My brother Richard was born in February 1942. Richard was still a baby when two-year-old David got his arm caught in the ringer of the washing machine. Leonard wasn't home. Fortunately, the Henry Ford Hospital was within walking distance because they had no car. Pauline said she got a neighbor boy to stay with Richard and rushed David to the hospital. She was told that the doctors would not see David without payment. My mother said she had only $8, but luckily, this was just enough to treat him.

As Loretta and David got older, they went to a Catholic school nearby. It was within walking distance, and the kids came home for lunch. However, money was tight, and it was difficult to come up with enough for both lunch and dinner. "Dinner was often pancakes," Pauline recalled.

Leonard was often unable to support his young family. My mother did tell me they had been evicted more than once for rent nonpayment—their belongings put out on the curb. She didn't tell me she had to endure Leonard's heavy alcohol use. Those pieces of the story were gleaned from others. My brother David remembered when he was about five years old, seeing Leonard in a limp heap passed out on the bathroom floor. He also remembered hearing his parents arguing with voices raised. He said he didn't know what to make of either of these events at the time. Years ago, my aunts had whispered to me about my mother's hardships, that my father was a drinker and abusive, which is why my mother left him. My mother never talked about this part of her marriage. Even in her 90s, this part was still walled off. Now, I recognize this silence as typical of someone who may have been physically abused, traumatized, and ashamed. Women too often believe it is their fault for being in this situation.

In the early summer of 1946, Pauline found her strength. She had the courage to go alone once again, now with her three small children, and make her way back to western New York. She left quickly while Leonard was at work. She told no one except her sister, Edna. Edna and her husband drove Pauline and the children back to the New York farm. Pauline left everything behind. By then, she must have thought it was the horizon behind her, back home, that was the best one to pursue. She didn't know she was pregnant when she left, but I was born in western New York in October of that year.

Many years later, I found my baptismal certificate. It was dated October 24, 1946, at St. Dominick's Church in Detroit. Apparently, my mother traveled back quite soon after giving birth to settle her divorce, and she took me along. As she recalled that trip years later, she told me that she found the apartment she had left was empty, and everything was in storage. She didn't have enough money to pay the storage fee. Again, she had to leave the pieces of her life behind. With four young children on her own, she had few options. But unlike Olive's mother, Pauline had a family who would take her in, along with all her children. My mother lived most of her life back on the family farm where she had grown up. She raised her children there and cared for her aging parents amidst her extended family. My mother died in 2017 at age 101.[9] I am proud of her strength to get out of a difficult marriage, for herself and for us. While my siblings and I grew up without a father, we had our grandfather and several uncles nearby. Together, they provided a patchwork of paternal roles.

But what about Leonard? Who was he? It was clear I wasn't going to learn about him from my mother. I would have to look elsewhere. I came to learn that he, too, had been looking for a better life, and he sorely wanted a family of his own. His pain was now compounded.

2

RIPPLE EFFECTS

Lillian and Fred's wedding photo in 1909

❧

LEONARD'S FAMILY

My siblings and I had minimal communication with our father, Leonard, as we were growing up. He sent us letters and cassette tapes as spoken letters. These were difficult to read or hear because they were filled mostly with his rants, in free associations that went on and on. He lamented the plight of the poor with a government and society that seemed not to care. He seemed to be a disturbed and broken man. In my twenties, I wrote and asked him about his family. He replied in one of his few lucid letters, at least in parts, in between his commentaries on society. He told me his father Fred had bred, broken, and trained horses for plows and buggies. He also had a string of trotters and raced them in sulky races. In 1910, Fred sold the farm to go make autos in Detroit when manufacturing was becoming the wave of the future.

Later, with my genealogy pursuits, I learned that Frederick Dupee and Lilliam Allor were married on Feb 9, 1909[1]; Fred was twenty-seven, and Lillian was twenty. They were married in Saint Clair, Saint Clair County, Michigan. They had both grown up in St. Clair County, about thirty miles north of Detroit. This wedding photo, found on Ancestry. com, is the only photo I have seen of Fred. His WWI draft record described him as medium build, medium height, and with gray eyes and brown hair.[2] Lillian appears kind and attractive.

The U.S. Census confirmed my father's report. Fred moved to Detroit around 1910 for the opportunities the city offered. When the 1910 U.S. Census was conducted on April,[3] Fred was living in a Detroit boarding house and working in an auto factory. But by June, Lillian had joined him. Their son Edward was born on June 8, 1910, in Detroit.[4] Their second son, Alvoy, followed in February 1912,[5] and then Leonard was born in December 1913.[6] All three boys were born in Detroit. It must have seemed like a promising future at the time. However, Lillian died within a month of Leonard's birth, on Jan. 2, 1914.[7] Her death record shows the cause of death was "labor pneumonia." It saddened me that Lillian didn't get to see her children grow up or meet her grandchildren. My grandmother Olive died when I was eight years old, so I didn't get to know her very well either. Sadly, such maternal deaths were not unusual then; there were 610 maternal childbirth-related deaths per 100,000 in 1900-1920, compared with 17.1 such deaths in 2018.[8] Yet these statistics all have real-life ripple effects for the families involved.

NAME CHANGE FROM DUPEE TO DEPUE

Sometime after Fred and Lillian's marriage, they changed the spelling of their name from Dupee to Depue. Why they made this change is unknown. None of Fred's siblings used this new spelling. Fred and Lillian's marriage record shows the spelling as Dupee, and Lillian's death record in 1914 shows the spelling as Depue. Their children's actual birth records have not yet been found; it is unclear if that spelling was used at the time of their births. The use of a capital P with DePue seems to vary. Some of the Depue brothers and cousins capitalized it as adults, and some did not. Most official records show a lowercase p, although that may have been the record keepers' choice. Fred's remarriage documents show the spelling of his name as Depue. However, in the 1920 census,[9] Fred's family, including all three of his boys' names, are listed with the old spelling, Dupee. This change in spelling can cause confusion when looking for official records and family genealogy. But I would learn this was not the first change in the spelling of our family's name.

FAMILIES DEALING WITH LOSSES

With three very young boys to take care of, Fred went home to Columbus, in St. Clair County, to be near his original family. Fred remarried on June 26, 1917, to Elizabeth Snoblen.[10] They married in nearby North Branch, Lapeer County. Elizabeth was from North Branch, from a farming family. She was age thirty, and Fred was thirty-six at the time of their marriage. The boys and Fred were starting over. This family of five was shown in the 1920 census, in January of that year,[8] when the boys were nine (Edward), seven (Alvoy), and six (Leonard); Fred was then age thirty-nine, and Elizabeth was thirty-two. According to that census, Fred was a farmer, and the family lived in St. Clair County, Columbus District, Michigan. Fred owned their home, with a mortgage at the time. But sadly, Elizabeth died in June of 1920.[11] She died shortly after giving birth to their daughter Marian, who also died around the time of her birth.[12] This left Fred widowed again following childbirth, and his boys were left motherless again.

Soon, Fred found another new wife, Frances Wikowski/Miller/Blum, whom he married on August 24, 1921, in Detroit.[13] Fred was then age forty, and Frances was thirty-four. Frances's Polish-born parents had changed their name from Wikowski to Miller sometime during Frances' childhood.[14] Therefore, her records show both names, making it confusing. When she married William Blum in 1907,[15] she was Frances Miller. I discovered that Frances and William Blum had four daughters together (Frances,[16] Dorothy, Lucy,[17] and Blossom Blum). However, their daughter Frances died as an infant.[16] William Blum died in 1919,[18] leaving Frances widowed. Then, five-year-old Lucy died eighteen months later on January 3, 1921.[17] Therefore, when Frances married Fred DePue in August 1921 in Detroit, they certainly had deep losses in common! Frances brought her two remaining daughters, Dorothy, then age eleven, and Blossom, then two years old, into her new family with Fred and his three boys.

In his own memoir, my cousin Roger Depue,[19] described his father

Alvoy's childhood. He said that Fred's third wife, Frances, wasn't very happy about suddenly being saddled with three rowdy boys. After a while, "to settle the friction in the household," Fred sent the three boys out to work as farm hands in exchange for their room and board. This practice was not unusual in those days. Poor families who could not afford to take care of their children did this more often. As mentioned in Chapter 1, my other grandmother Olive's adoption is an example of her mother letting go of children due to hardship. It must have been a convenient outlet for unhappy stepmothers as well. Child labor laws were not passed until the mid-1930s. But even then, child labor was permitted on farms. Fred must have felt in a bind. He made a decision to keep his wife happy, but how did it feel as a dad to send his sons away? It was three strikes for the boys: they lost their mother and their first stepmother, and then they were sent away from home. Did my father ever have the opportunity to bond with a maternal caregiver? Now, his father also abandoned him. This is important for healthy development. These losses at such a young age would certainly have an impact. But it was about to get worse.

On the farm, there would have been hard work. Physical punishment was probably used to keep the boys in line. Many years later, my cousin Kathleen, Edward's daughter, told me that her father said conditions on the farm were very harsh. He didn't like to talk about it. Nonetheless, she said the effect on him was lifelong, as he was often withdrawn and distant. The boys were very young when they were cast out of their home to live on the farm. Edward, as the oldest at age eleven or twelve, was placed at the same farm as Leonard, who would have been age eight or nine at the time. Alvoy was placed on a different farm. It is unclear how long the boys stayed on these farms. But the deep pain they endured would persist.

Leonard's alcohol abuse as an adult was likely a symptom of his lingering pain. Any physical abuse inflicted on my mother may have been prompted because he was physically abused himself. Research in the 1990s showed that with an increase in adverse childhood events (ACEs), there is a greater risk for negative outcomes in health, well-being, and life opportunities as adults.[20] As I learned more about Leonard's adult behavior, I could see the far-reaching effects of his childhood experience with loss, neglect, and abuse.

By 1930, Fred and his wife, Frances Depue, were shown in the federal census living in Detroit with Frances' daughter, Blossom, age eleven, in the house.[21] Frances' daughter Dorothy had married in 1928.[22] The census showed that Fred was then employed as a repairman in the auto industry. They owned their home at that time, valued at $5000. But the boys were not living there.

STUMBLING INTO ADULTHOOD

While searching for where my father went next, I found his name in a 1930 census record, at age eighteen, residing at the Wayne County Training School in Northville, Michigan.[23] Residents were described as "scholars at this institution." What was this place? It was alternately known as the Wayne County Training School for Feeble-Minded Children or the Wayne County Child Developmental Center (renamed in 1966) for children with developmental disabilities. It opened in 1926 on 1,040 acres for this purpose, with thirty-eight buildings, including eighteen dormitories, four classroom buildings, a hospital, and a fire station. At its peak in the 1930s, it held 700 children (ages six to eighteen) and staff who also lived on this campus. It closed in 1974.[24] I knew that such state-funded schools were all around the country. There was one in my hometown in New York state. While they aimed to provide appropriate education and skills training, the large institutionalized settings were later disfavored in lieu of smaller community group homes. In 1930, my father would soon have aged out of this setting. But how did he come to be there?

In one of his letters, Leonard told me his formal education ended around fifth grade. It's unclear when or where he got this education.

While he might have been intellectually disabled, more likely, the trauma and emotional scramble of his childhood would have made it difficult for him to learn. This mindset would also make it difficult to assess his intellectual ability. I don't know how intelligence was tested in the 1920s, but we now know the biases inherent in intelligence testing, including quality of education, learning disabilities, and mental illness. Children with learning disabilities like dyslexia were sometimes institutionalized. Children with traumatic backgrounds may also exhibit behavior problems in school. He might have run away from the farm, was picked up on the streets, and was later sent to the training school. Any or all of these explanations are possible. He said he was living on the streets, doing any kind of work he could to exist. He never mentioned living in this institution, however. He said he shined shoes, sold papers, worked in gasoline stations, and many other things. The street life may have occurred after he left the institution, as many people were living on the streets during the Depression. As an adult, he reflected that living on the streets is how he got to know the plight of poor people and the downcast. These injustices, his own as well as others, preoccupied his attention for the rest of his life.

It is unclear how this background influenced his behavior by the time he met my mother. He evidently liked to drink and hang out in the bar where Pauline came to waitress. He liked to talk, she said. He had difficulty holding a job. Could he get along with employers and other authority figures? Could he focus on his work? His emotional background likely played a part in his drinking and his inability to hold a job, as well as his family life.

Later in his life, he sent me a brief profile written about him by a friend, Agnes Wagner, titled "Profiles of the Retired." Apparently, it was for a newsletter for a community he was part of. This filled me in on the middle parts of his life after the divorce. He told Agnes that he fought the "system" that would break up his home and take his children with all the strength he had, including seven court appearances and five judges. But he lost that fight. He also said he made enemies when he spoke out in support of unions. He wrote letters to the mayor and heads of corporations and spoke out about the need for better treatment for the downcast in Detroit. Eventually, he said he was "blackballed" by industry for his union activity and couldn't find work. He moved from Detroit to New Orleans and on to Texas. He was ordered out of Texas because he was a "communist agitator," as union protesters were then called. He seemed to focus his anger on all authorities. People were afraid to help him, he said. He often went days without food. Once, he caught a roll that bounced off a bakery truck, the only food he had in three days.

He told Agnes that he often slept in bus stations, empty buildings, and once in the snow near a church. He was arrested for vagrancy and put into jail. He gave a former address so that he could vote. Eventually, he made his way back to Detroit, where he got a job as an elevator operator at the Whittier Hotel in Detroit. There, he helped organize the Service Employees International Union. One winter day, when the temperature was ten degrees, Leonard met the California actor Fred McMurray on his elevator. Mr. McMurray told him the temperature in California that day was seventy degrees. Leonard looked into his union records and was pleased to learn that his union had a branch in Southern California. Around this time, the elevator operators were being phased out for automation, so it was a good time to make a move. Leonard saved a little money and bought a plane ticket to Los Angeles. There, he went to work for a local 399 union contract. He worked seven years with the Farmers Market and fourteen years as a janitor for United Artist Theatre. He retired in 1976, after which he gave this interview to Agnes Wagner. She also described him as a "man of letters," as he had trunks of letters from presidents, mayors, senators, and VIPs he had written to all of his life, but she said his rhetoric was "a bit over the heads of ordinary people." This also characterized the letters he sent to me and my siblings.

When I was in my early twenties, I visited Leonard briefly in Los Angeles, traveling from my home in Boston with my husband. We met in a hotel lobby. It was decorated with tropical plants, and the sun shined in brightly from the windows. My father's face seemed to be beaming in the sunlight when I saw him approach us. He was about five foot five inches tall, with a light build. He wore a print shirt over loose pants, fitting our tropical setting. He had a shy half smile, matching my own.

I'm sure he was happy to see his long-lost daughter. But he couldn't make eye contact with me. As in his letters, he rambled on about injustices everywhere without a coherent sentence. As much as I tried, I couldn't bring his attention back to the present to talk about himself or even the weather. He didn't seem to know how to connect in conversation, at least not with me. In turn, I became befuddled and could no longer speak myself. Fortunately, my husband was there to calmly take over. It became clear that Leonard was never going to be the father I had wished for. I had fanaticized about having a father who would be as interested in hearing about my experiences as I would be in listening to him. I imagined we would share in conversations, keeping up with one another's lives over time, even as adults. However, this man seemed to be walled off, using his cascade of words as a shield, unable to listen or engage. I was disheartened.

When I recovered, I also felt sad that for someone who had especially yearned for a family, he wasn't able to hold on to one. Only now that I have put some of the pieces together can I begin to understand the upheavals in his life that shaped him. I can even understand his need for that shield to protect him from further pain. I also came to respect that, after all of his setbacks and debilities, he managed to get by. In time, he was able to hold a job. He lived alone. He earned a small union pension after he retired. He kept up his letters of protest about the unfair treatment of the poor. He used part of his small pension to buy supplies to help those less fortunate than himself. He dropped these off on his regular rounds. Despite his misfortunes, he built a life that turned his hardships into a purpose of sorts. The union's brothers and sisters became his new family. He had a kind heart. He died at age eighty of colon cancer.[25]

My siblings and I were fortunate to grow up without the direct influence of my father's trauma. As adverse childhood experiences (ACES) greatly impact the child's adult behavior, they can also be passed on to the next generations. The American Psychological Association describes intergenerational trauma as when a descendant of someone who was traumatized expresses emotional or behavioral reactions similar to their ancestor. These effects can be passed on not only from living with a family member who is experiencing traumatic pain but also through DNA modifications, so it becomes genetic for future generations. This biological process is referred to as epigenetics.[26] It is interesting that I chose to pursue a career in mental health work. It wasn't a conscious choice based on knowledge of my father's trauma, as I didn't know his full story at the time. But in my career, I have worked with individuals who had been traumatized and needed help with healing so that their trauma would no longer control their own or their family's lives going forward.

WHERE IS HOME?

Although they grew up initially in the same household, and all had been sent off as children to work on farms, Leonard's brothers grew up with different stories.

In the 1930 census, brothers Edward and Alvoy were both living with their grandparents, Isadore and Mary Allor, at 1342 Holden Street in Detroit.[27] At that time, in April 1930, Edward was twenty and working for the auto industry. Alvoy was working at a Creamery. I also found a record for a border crossing in May of 1930, when Alvoy was en route to Edmonton, Alberta, Canada.[28] He listed his occupation then as a farmer and his nearest relative as his grandmother, Mrs. M. Allor. Apparently, none of the three boys were inclined to revisit their father and stepmother's home.

According to Alvoy's son Roger's book,[19] Alvoy was able to cope with working as a child laborer on the farm by going to Catholic Mass. When his boss told him he couldn't go, he snuck out a window and rode his bike several miles to the church in town. He also coped with hardship through exercise and by being physically strong. He was five foot nine inches and had solid muscle, "built like a tree trunk," his son Roger said.

After returning to Michigan, Alvoy went back to the Creamery to work as a laborer, the occupation he also reported at the time of the 1940 Census.[29] He married Viola Westrick in 1933 in St. Clair, Michigan.[30] In another record in 1942,[31] Alvoy said he was a "pasteurizer," apparently, this was his role at the creamery. But by the mid-1940s, he was working in the police department in Roseville, Michigan. He eventually retired at the rank of Inspector after 27 years in the Roseville Police Department.[32]

His son Roger said that his father used this strength in his eventual role as a policeman; he could be intimidating without ever drawing his gun, but he also had a reputation as a fair man.[19] After retirement, Alvoy and Viola moved back to St. Clair, Michigan. They were married sixty-one years, until Viola's death in 1995[33] when she was age eighty-one. Alvoy and Viola had five sons. Alvoy died Sept. 25, 2006, in St. Clair, Michigan at age 94.[34]

In his book, Alvoy's son Roger described how he grew up as the son of a policeman and went on to become Chief of the FBI's Behavioral Science unit. Roger became a pioneer in developing the process of profiling a criminal's background to help solve their crimes. They pursued many of the nation's most violent killers in this way. Thus, he saw the worst effects of how a person's trauma plays out on their subsequent behavior. Roger's account also described the toll he endured from doing this work, as he was immersed in the worst of human deeds.[19] Clearly, Roger's choice of career was influenced by his father's career. But was his deeper pursuit of psychology in policework influenced by his father's earlier trauma? If so, he found a constructive way to apply any intergenerational trauma to policing and later to his own healing.

Leonard's other brother, Edward, was found in the 1940 census,[35] living on Kentucky St. in Detroit. He was in a home he owned, valued at $4000. Edward was then twenty-nine, living with his wife Helen, age twenty-three, and their three-year-old daughter Patricia. He and Helen Miller were married in 1936.[36] My mother and Helen became good friends during her time in Detroit, married to brothers. They corresponded for many years after.

My brother Dave said that Edward excelled at all sorts of mechanics, especially at welding. He worked for the Ford Motor Company and became a trusted "right-hand man" for Henry Ford himself. Mr. Ford had a cot put into Edward's work area so that he could sleep there and be available whenever Henry needed him. At one point, he fixed a problem with the factory's machinery while the assembly line was still running. He was able to weld a crack in a main shaft as it turned, as the gears and belts moved. If he hadn't been able to address this problem quickly and keep the assembly line going, the consequences could have been disastrous; some workers could have been injured, and hundreds of workers would have been idled.

Dave also relayed that Edward often put a signature of sorts, perhaps his initials, on his work. During the war, the Ford plant was converted in order to build tanks for the war effort. One of the tanks later had been blown up in battle, but the piece that Edward welded remained intact. Someone found that piece of tank on the battlefield and sent it back to the Ford Company. Edward's signature was still visible on the part. I also found a very short newspaper article, dated August 22, 1975, that had been reprinted in several newspapers around the country. It said, "Edward DePue, a 65-year-old welder, retired from a motor company in Detroit after 40 years and 7 months without missing a day at work."[37] In one sentence, it said a lot about him. His ability to focus intensely at work may have served him well there, but it served him less well for his family life.

Edward was married twice and had two families. He and Helen had four children. Edward and Helen divorced sometime after Pauline left Detroit. As his daughter Kathleen indicated, the effects of his childhood played out in his family life, as he was often withdrawn. Helen later remarried Rev. Walter Julien, a Nazarene minister, and they settled in Olathe, Kansas. Helen and Walter were married thirty-three years before Walter's passing in 2000.[38] Helen died in 2011.[39] Edward married his second wife Doris in 1961 and had three more children. Edward died in Franklin, Oakland County, Michigan, in 2001 at age ninety-one,[40] and his widow Doris died November 12, 2013,[41] at the age of eighty-two.

All three of Fred and Lillian's boys carried emotional scars from their childhoods. Yet they all had a strong work ethic, and family was important to all of them. Edward hosted some of the many family reunions at his home (see Chapter 4). Leonard attended some of these, even visiting from Los Angeles. The boys seemed to seek out family other than Fred and their stepmother, Frances.

My grandfather Fred and his wife Frances continued to live in Detroit. The 1940 census indicated that Fred was working as an assembler in a factory,[42] but he only worked thirteen weeks in 1939; no doubt this was due to the effects of the Depression. Fred reported he had a fourth-grade education (similar to his siblings, as they grew up on a farm). Frances had completed high school. In 1940, Frances worked full-time as a cook in a high school, working thirty-two weeks that year.

Frances died in Detroit in 1952 at age sixty-one.[43] Once again, Fred was widowed, and again, after losing his wife, he moved back to St. Clair to be nearer his own family, the Dupees. By then, three of his four siblings were still alive and living in St. Clair County, along with many nieces and nephews. Family was important to him as well. Fred was living in St. Clair, in a nursing home, when he died in 1954 at age seventy-three.[44] Fred was buried back in Detroit in Mount Olivet Cemetery,[45] where both Frances and Lillian had been buried.

There is a recurring theme among my grandfather's and my uncles' stories, and that is the pull of St. Clair County. It was home—where they went after their losses and at retirement. What was this place?

Transitions

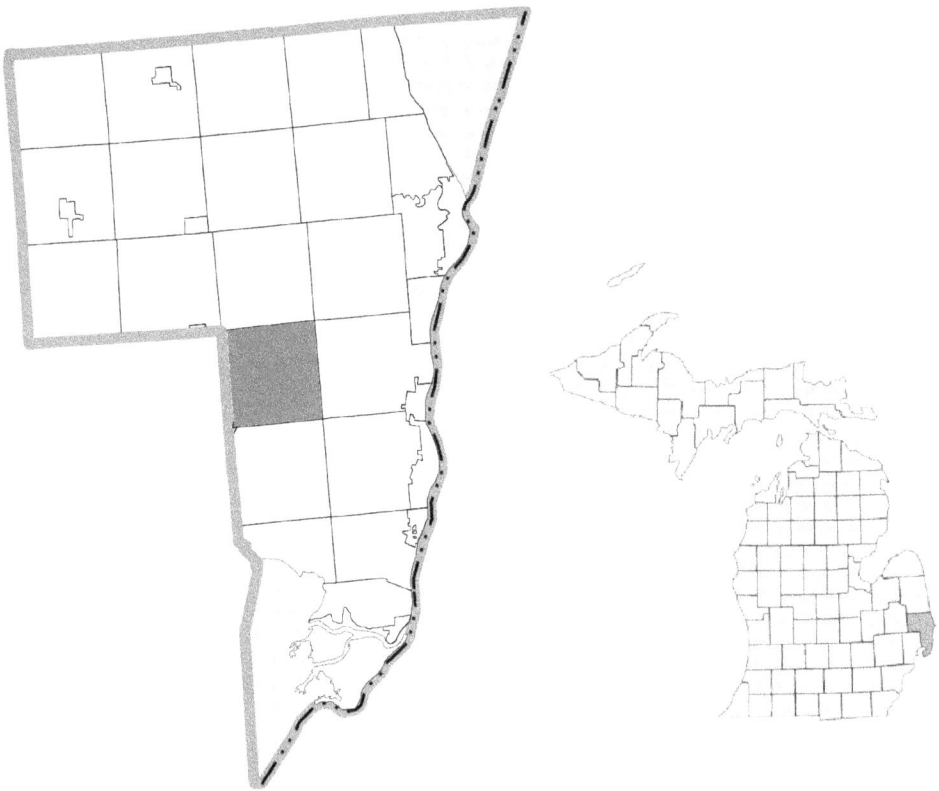

Columbus township is shown at left, shaded within the outline of St. Clair County, Michigan. At right, St. Clair County is shaded within Eastern Michigan's "thumb"

❧

THE DUPEES IN ST. CLAIR COUNTY, MICHIGAN

WITH MY GRANDFATHER FRED'S GENERATION, FROM THE LATE 1800s through the 1950s, I discovered a story of family and home during a time of major transitions.

For Fred, I learned that coming home meant the town of Columbus, in St Clair County, Michigan. The adjacent townships of Columbus and St. Clair, both in St. Clair County, are about thirty to forty miles North of Detroit. Fred grew up in Columbus, while Lillian's family lived in St. Clair. Some of Fred's family moved to the neighboring town of St. Clair as well. St. Clair County remains primarily a farming area even today, with a 2022 population estimate of 160,151.[1] The heart of the area seems to be St. Clair City, on the St. Clair River, with its own 2021 population estimate of 5,477.[2] This city has a population the size of many villages that I know. There must be more to this story.

This county is within the "thumb" of eastern Michigan, with Lake Huron in the North, the St. Clair River in the east, and Lake St. Clair in the south. All types of ships regularly traversed the St. Clair River between Lake Huron, connecting to Lake St. Clair, then the Detroit River, and Lake Erie. Yes, St. Clair is the name of a city, a township, a county, a river, and a lake.

With the benefit of town historical resources online,[3] I could "see" St. Clair something like it was when my grandfather Fred and his siblings were growing up. This was a shipbuilding and lumbering region in the nineteenth century with eight lumber mills beside the St. Clair River. Tree cutting made way for farming. The oak and pine trees also contributed to the shipbuilding. By the 1860s, when Fred's father moved to the area, most of the lumbering industry had moved further North in Michigan. The junction where the Pine River runs into St. Clair River was the shipbuilding center for all types of wooden vessels that sailed on the Great Lakes. This junction was full of sailboats, yachts, large commercial steamers, and even tugboats that held up there for the winter. The shipmasters' club was over the hardware store. There were many sailors in the area because their captains lived in St. Clair City. The captains' houses were made of bricks using clay from the banks of the Pine River, and those bricks were formed in the many local brickyards.[3] Most likely, St. Clair City's population was much larger during the nineteenth century and more like a city at that time.

Another major industry was the Diamond Crystal Salt Company, which started in 1887, drawing on the large underground salt deposits. Those salt deposits also contributed to mineral baths. By the turn of the twentieth century, the city became a resort, bringing visitors on passenger boats to the large Victorian hotels and their mineral baths.[3]

The Dupee siblings could ride their horses and buggies on St. Clair City's cedar block pavement, a surface that must have sharpened the sound of horse's hooves, clop clopping along. They could tie their horses on a hitching post and walk the plank sidewalks to do their shopping. The city held all the services the townsfolk and area farmers might need. The brick-front shops included a variety of department stores, a millinery, tailor and barber shops, blacksmiths, butcher, grocer, lunchroom, and saloon. They likely knew most of the shop keepers who knew their family as well. At the docks, a grist mill shipped flour up and down the various river ports. Coal, hay, straw, and grain would also be shipped to and from here. St. Clair City is where the Dupee siblings might have brought their friends and sweethearts to the ice cream parlor or the bowling alley. There was also a good swimming beach nearby.[3]

Fred's parents were farmers. William Roy Dupee Sr. (1846-1922) came to Michigan from Huron County, Ontario, Canada, in 1862 at age sixteen.[4,5] He grew up across Lake Huron, opposite of Michigan's "thumb." Initially, William worked as a farm laborer in Columbus.

WILLIAM & MARY JANE'S CHILDREN

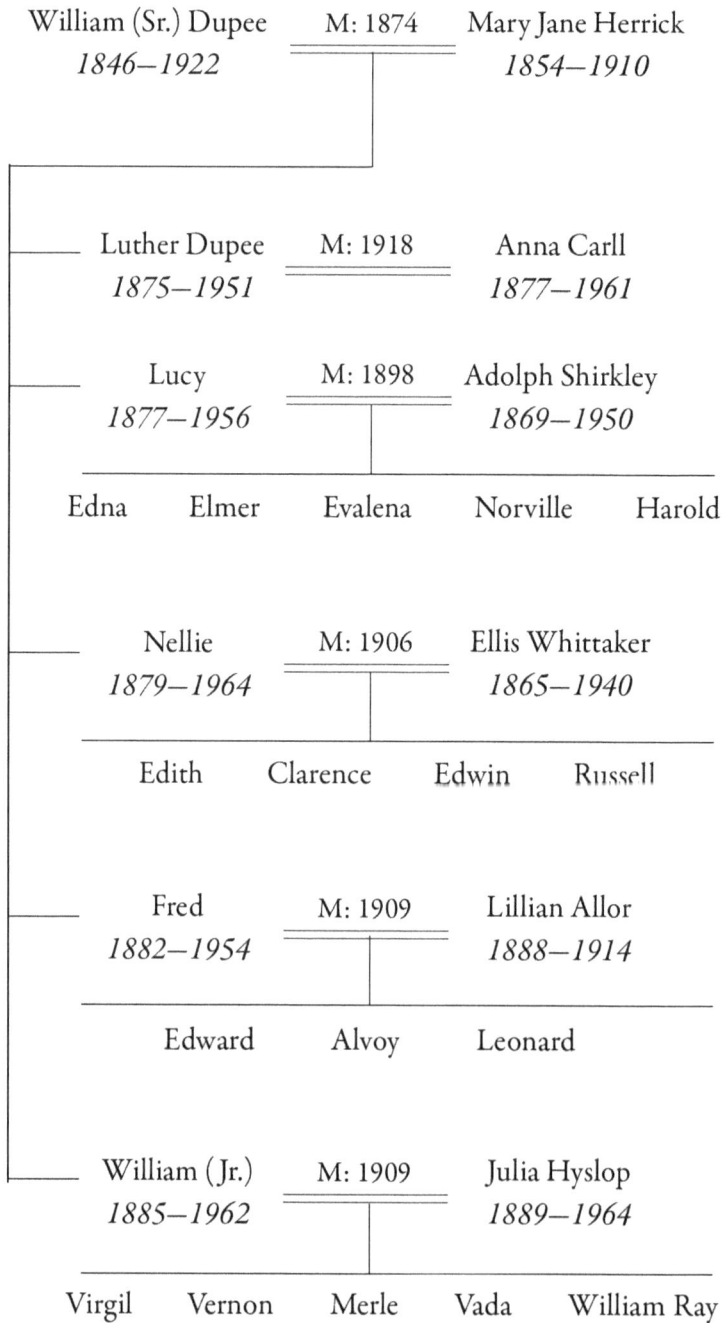

William (Sr.) Dupee   M: 1874   Mary Jane Herrick
1846—1922   *1854—1910*

Luther Dupee   M: 1918   Anna Carll
1875—1951   *1877—1961*

Lucy   M: 1898   Adolph Shirkley
1877—1956   *1869—1950*

Edna   Elmer   Evalena   Norville   Harold

Nellie   M: 1906   Ellis Whittaker
1879—1964   *1865—1940*

Edith   Clarence   Edwin   Russell

Fred   M: 1909   Lillian Allor
1882—1954   *1888—1914*

Edward   Alvoy   Leonard

William (Jr.)   M: 1909   Julia Hyslop
1885—1962   *1889—1964*

Virgil   Vernon   Merle   Vada   William Ray

There, he met Mary Jane Herrick (1854-1910),[6] whose family lived at a neighboring farm. They married in 1874 when William was age twenty-eight and Mary Jane was twenty. By 1880, they were living on their own farm where they raised their five children.[5] William was eventually known as a thresherman,[7] suggesting he had the equipment, albeit horse-drawn in the day, and he could be hired for this service. A threshing machine was used to separate the seeds or grain from the straw. Both outputs were valuable to farmers. He had become an enterprising man of his times.

Among William and Mary Jane's five children, Fred was fourth. In age order, they were Luther (also called Luke),[8] Lucy,[9] Nellie,[10] Fred,[11] and William Roy Jr.[12]

The girls were the first to marry. Both Lucy and Nellie married farmers from nearby. Lucy married Adolph Shirkey in 1898.[13] Adolph and Lucy started on a rented farm in St Clair,[14] and by 1920,[15] they moved to their own farm on Shirkey Road in St. Clair township. Nellie married Ellis Whitaker in 1906.[16] Ellis was widowed with four children when he married Nellie, who was fourteen years younger.[17] Ellis's first wife Dorothy,[18] was the sister of Lucy's husband, Adolph Shirkey. Ellis Whitaker owned a large farm in Columbus just a little south of the Dupees, as shown on a 1916 Map of Columbus.[19]

The boys married a bit later. As noted in the last chapter, Fred married Lillian Allor in February of 1909.[20] Before he married, he had his own niche business, training horses for buggies, plows, and sulky racing. Fred's younger brother, William Jr., married Julia Hyslop in June of 1909.[21] The oldest, Luther, was the last to marry. He married Anna Carll in 1918.[22] Both Luther and William Jr. acquired property next to their father; the 1916 map of Columbus shows their three properties side-by-side.[19] Thus, all the Dupee siblings were initially involved in farming or related work. However, by 1910, major changes were underway.

DETROIT BOOMS, BUSTS, AND BOOMS AGAIN

Auto manufacturing began in Detroit after the turn of the twentieth century, but demand was high when Henry Ford produced the Model T in 1908. Surely, this is what drew Fred to Detroit in 1910, followed by William Jr. The first Model T plant was on Piquette Street. But to meet demand, Ford commissioned a new factory at Highland Park, which would become a model for factories worldwide. It was designed for Ford's innovation of the assembly line, which would open up many new jobs for unskilled workers. The Highland Plant opened in January 1910, and they began using the assembly line in 1913.[23,24] Fred's boarding house in 1910 on McClellan Street was not far from the Highland Park Plant. He may have worked at this plant, or he would at least have seen firsthand the excitement it produced.

Ford's vision with the assembly line was to break down and simplify operations into component parts to standardize the process and maintain quality. He foresaw that by producing cars more efficiently and reliably and thus lowering costs, demand will follow. Moreover, when workers are paid a higher wage, they can become consumers themselves. Then, by increasing the number of consumers and adapting production to meet it, further consumption will follow reciprocally.[25]

Ford came to this full realization gradually, however. Initially, output was much lower than expected, with high absenteeism and turnover. The assembly-line jobs were monotonous and repetitive. Absenteeism averaged ten percent per day. This meant managers had to hire 1,300 to 1,400 extra workers to keep the production system in operation. The yearly turnover rate was 370 percent. Worker discontent also brought a flurry of union activities.[26] Because of all this, in 1914, Ford revolutionized labor relations further, as he announced he would pay five dollars per day, double the rate of his rivals. This was not just a pay raise; however, it was social engineering by Ford. It was a form of profit sharing meant to inspire not only work habits suitable for assembly line production but also to promote his vision of American values that included personal habits, social discipline, and living conditions. The Five Dollar Day came in two parts: wages at about $2.40 per day for an unskilled worker and a share in worker's profits at about $2.60 per day. Workers would only receive their profits if they were "worthy," had appropriate habits and lifestyles, and lived in proper homes. Pamphlets were produced to teach these values, especially to their new immigrant workers.[26] Fred DePue was widowed on January 2, 1914, and would have left Detroit by the time the Five Dollar Day policy was implemented, so he missed any immediate effects of this dramatic change on the industry.

The policy had the desired effect, however, as it stopped high turnover rates, raised productivity, lowered overall labor costs, and helped propel Ford to industry dominance, at least initially. While Ford invested millions into his Highland Park Plant and doubled the wages of thousands of workers, he was also able to reduce the Model T price from $800 to $350 by 1919, and he became the world's first billionaire.[26,27] By 1927, Ford opened his expansive River Rouge plant in Dearborn. This vast self-contained production complex sprawled over two square miles, including a man-made deep-sea harbor, ninety-four miles of railroad track, the world's largest steel foundry, stamping, assembly, and glass-making operations. Ninety thousand workers were employed there. It became another new model for industrialization.[28]

In 1918, Fred reported on his WWI draft record that he and his wife, Elizabeth, were living at 1013 Harper Avenue in Detroit,[29] which was in the middle of the Milwaukee Junction area, which was considered the cradle of the Detroit auto industry from 1890 into the 1920s.[30] Over the years, Fred's census reports gave other addresses in the same area—Piquette Avenue (1930) and Harper Avenue again (1940)[31,32]— and these censuses indicated he worked for the auto and auto parts industry. In 1918, Fred reported he as doing fine assembly work for Detroit Electric, which produced electric cars at that time.[33] In fact, electric cars were very popular from 1907 until their peak in 1916, but they continued selling into the 1930s. Even Clara Ford, Henry Ford's wife, drove one. Compared to the dirty, often unreliable gasoline cars at the time, electric cars were clean and easy to operate, as they didn't require a crank to start. They could travel eighty miles on a single charge and reach a speed of twenty-five mph, which was good for city driving at the time. Once the electric starter came along, easing the operation of gasoline-powered vehicles, and as gasoline car prices dropped, the electric car's popularity started to wane.[33]

Fred's 1954 obituary stated that he worked thirty years for Briggs Manufacturing Company, rising to become a foreman.[34] Therefore, the bulk of Fred's work history was in the same place, apparently starting there in the 1920s and going until his eventual retirement. This put him in the center of the action, producing auto parts for several of the auto companies. The Briggs Company, in 1910, was providing upholstery for a number of car manufacturers, when they agreed to provide interiors for 10,000 Model Ts, leading to a long relationship with Ford. Briggs expanded from interiors to auto trim and auto bodies in the 1920s. They built auto bodies for Ford, Chrysler, Packard, Hudson, and many others. In 1926, Briggs became the largest independent producer of auto bodies in Detroit and the richest. They remained very profitable, even during the Depression. Their investors did well, but their employees struggled during these years.[35]

Briggs workers mounted a major strike in 1933 after a fifteen percent wage cut was announced. While Ford paid a dollar per hour to their assembly-line workers during the Depression, a comparable worker at Briggs earned as low as ten cents an hour. There were 10,000 to 14,000 Briggs workers on strike, which in turn caused a shutdown at Ford and other auto companies because they couldn't get the auto bodies they needed. There were picket lines thousands strong at the various plants. After fifty-two hours of picketing, the pay cut was rescinded, and other demands were met. It was the first victory for strikers in Detroit since 1920. There were further cutbacks in the years leading up to World War II, as Briggs's main customers—Ford, Chrysler, Packard, and Hudson—set up their own design departments.[35] Fred reported working only thirteen weeks in 1939.[32]

Detroit, Michigan and Griswold Streets, circa 1920

Fred and his son Leonard may have been estranged during those years, but interestingly, they may have had some union activity in common, assuming that Fred went out on strike with his coworkers in 1933. Accounts of the 1933 strike in the news coverage accused the strikers of being communists, which the strikers strongly denied. Leonard's union activity may have been in the late 1940s and 50s, but communist accusations were also prevalent during those times. The unions did bring power to the auto industry workers and helped bring these blue-collar workers into the middle class.

William Jr. also had one main employer during the auto industry boom and during his work career. His obituary stated he was employed for twenty-eight years at General Motors.[36] He likely started at GM in the 1920s and worked there until his retirement. William's census reports indicated that he worked as a polisher (1930) and buffer (1940) in an auto factory.[37,38] The General Motors Company started out as a holding company in Flint, Michigan, for Buick, Cadillac, Oldsmobile, and many others. But in the 1920s, the company moved to Detroit, and it was reorganized into a single enterprise with five divisions (Pontiac, Chevrolet, Buick, Cadillac, Oldsmobile). GM then pioneered annual model changes along with innovations in consumer financing. By 1929, GM had overtaken Ford as the leading passenger car manufacturer in the United States.[39]

With the increased labor demands and benefits, Detroit's population nearly doubled each decade between 1900 and 1930, drawing from the farming communities around Detroit, immigrants, and elsewhere in the country, including African Americans escaping the South's Jim Crow laws.[28] Both Fred and William Jr. were back and forth between Columbus and Detroit during this surge, but they were in Detroit long enough to see the dramatic changes in the city. Detroit streets became jammed with more and more autos and more and more people. By 1930, the population had become almost 1.6 million, making Detroit the fourth largest city in the U.S.[28]

The brothers had returned to Columbus due to family concerns. While Fred was dealing with the losses in his own family, William Jr. was helping his parents at home. Fred and William's mother, Mary Jane Dupee, died in April 1910 from stomach cancer.[6] Newlyweds William Jr. and Julia were living at the family farm with William Sr. at this time, likely helping out.[40] By the time of his WWI draft record in 1918,[41] William Jr. and Julia were living in Detroit. But by the 1920 census,[42] William Jr. and Julia were back again in Columbus. Then William Jr. was head of household, and his father, at age seventy-three, was living with him. William Sr. was suffering from epilepsy and a broken hip prior to his death in 1922.[4]

Manufacturing was picking up speed in St. Clair as well. By 1920, Luther and Anna had moved from their farm in Columbus to St. Clair City. Even Luther became a wage-earner by then, working as an "engineer" at a mill.[43] By 1930, he was working as a pipe-fitter for the Gas Company.[44]

By 1930, Lucy's husband, Adolph Shirkey, had taken a wage-earning job in St. Clair as a janitor with the Diamond Crystal Salt Company.[45] Adolph was still there in 1940.[46] Diamond Crystal Salt Company was doing well during the Depression with their expansion into table salt products. Their salt was shipped from St. Clair throughout the world.[47]

When the U.S. entered World War II in 1941, Detroit saw tremendous changes once again. The auto manufacturing ceased entirely, and the factories were converted to make tanks, jeeps, and bombers. Using the same production techniques it used for autos, Ford produced B-24 Liberator aircraft at the rate of one per hour or approximately 600 per month.[23] The Briggs Company also became a major supplier to the U.S. army, producing over a million dollars of stamped steel and aluminum products.[34]

At the end of their lives, both Fred and William Jr. returned home to St. Clair County, where their siblings still lived. Luther died first in 1951, at the age of seventy-five, in a fall from a ladder at his home in St. Clair. He and Anna had no children. Luther was described in his obituary as a lake's sailor for several years, like many of St. Clair's men. Following his work as a pipe fitter, later in his 60s, he was a watchman for the thermo plastics division of the Standard Products Company in St. Clair. Later in his adult life, Luther returned to farming.[48] Anna lived on until 1961.[49]

Fred died in 1954 at age seventy-three.[34] Lucy died in 1956 at age seventy-nine,[50] six years after her husband Adolph.[51] Lucy and Adolph had five children together. William Jr. died in 1962 at age seventy-six.[36] William Jr. and Julia had five children. Julia died two years after her husband died in 1964.[52] While Ellis Whittaker died in 1940,[53] Nellie died twenty-four years later in 1964 at age eighty-five.[54] Nellie and Ellis had four children together, in addition to Ellis' other children. Nellie outlived all of her siblings. She lived her whole life on her family's farm, the only sibling to remain in farming.

Throughout all of this time, the family's home in St. Clair County was the anchor, even after some in the family had moved to Detroit. It was where they went when things got tough, when the family needed them, when it was time to retire, or when it was time to die. This was a place central to a family that was all new to me, a place I hadn't known about. We all need a home as an anchor. Yet I would come to learn that my ancestors would experience many pushes and pulls that propelled them to migrate away from their family homes.

4

FAMILIES ON THE MOVE

As I searched back into another generation of Dupees, in the mid-1850s through the turn of the twentieth century, I found they were a part of another period of Michigan's significant growth and expansion.

Huron County, Ontario, shaded here, is on the Eastern shore of Lake Huron, across from Michigan's "thumb.

❖

THE DUPEES ARRIVE
IN MICHIGAN FROM ONTARIO

As noted earlier, Fred's father, my great-grandfather William Dupee, immigrated from Canada in 1862 at age sixteen. William's parents, my second great-grandparents, were John Dupee (1811-1896) and Catherine O'Brien (1813-1899).[1,2] According to the 1861 Canadian census, John Dupee's family of nine at that time were living in a log house in the town of Stanley, in Huron County, Ontario. William was there at age fifteen. They were farmers.[3]

Other records show that John and Catherine Dupee had eleven children. Most of these children eventually arrived in Michigan, although at separate times. Their arrivals illustrate a story about immigration to Michigan during this time-frame.

THE PUSHES AND PULLS FOR IMMIGRATION

John and Catherine's sons were the first to leave Canada. Their oldest son, George, was found in 1860 U.S. Census records as a laborer in St. Clair, Michigan, at age twenty-four.[4] This was a time when St. Clair was a ship-building town, and there were a few remaining sawmills.[5] He showed up on Civil War draft records in 1865,[6] in North Macomb, Michigan (next to St. Clair County where William was living), although it was unclear whether he served in that war. Then, in 1871, George Dupee, with his parents' names listed on the marriage record, married Eliza Currie in Sherbroke, Nova Scotia.[7] George may have changed direction to pursue the Sherbroke NS gold rush that was going on at

40

that time.[8] However, George may have died there because Eliza Dupee remarried in 1889.[9] I was unable to find a death record for George.

John and Catherine's second son, John Dupee Jr., may have left Ontario with his brother George, as neither was living with their family in 1861. Like George, twenty-four-year-old John Dupee appears in 1865 US Civil War records.[10] But by 1870,[11] John Jr. was working in a sawmill in Port Huron, St. Clair County, Michigan; he was living in a residence with other mill workers. In 1880,[12] he was working in another saw mill in East Tawas, further North on Saginaw Bay. By then, he had a wife (Martha Ann Brown) and family. Sadly, John Jr. died in 1886,[13] at age forty-five, in St. Charles, Saginaw, Michigan, another lumber industry town.

Another son, David Dupee, immigrated in 1862,[14] likely with his brother William. David would have been age fourteen then when William was sixteen. David also worked in the lumber industry. In 1870, he was a hoop maker (the hoops were used in making wooden barrels) in Freemont, Saginaw County.[15] In 1900, he was a day laborer in St. Charles, Saginaw County.[14] David died of an injury in 1905, at age fifty-six, in St. Charles.[16] He married twice: Emma Parks, who died in 1878 (sons Alfred and Elmer), and Ellen LaMarsh (sons Woodes, John, and Benjamin).[17-19]

The lumber industry was a big draw for immigrants to Michigan during this time. By 1860, it was second only to agriculture as a livelihood. Because the Eastern states had been mostly clear-cut and the demand for lumber had increased with western settlement, most of the U.S. received their lumber from Michigan. By 1869, Michigan was producing more lumber than any other state. In 1870, there were 400 sawmills and 800 logging camps in the Lower Peninsula, mostly in the Pine region that extended North from the Saginaw valley to the Straits of Mackinac. The stands of trees were so abundant that it was thought the supply was endless; however, the clear-cutting was so extensive that the forests in Michigan were mostly gone by 1910.[20] The landscape was being transformed daily. It was dangerous and deadly work, as

JOHN AND CATHERINE'S CHILDREN

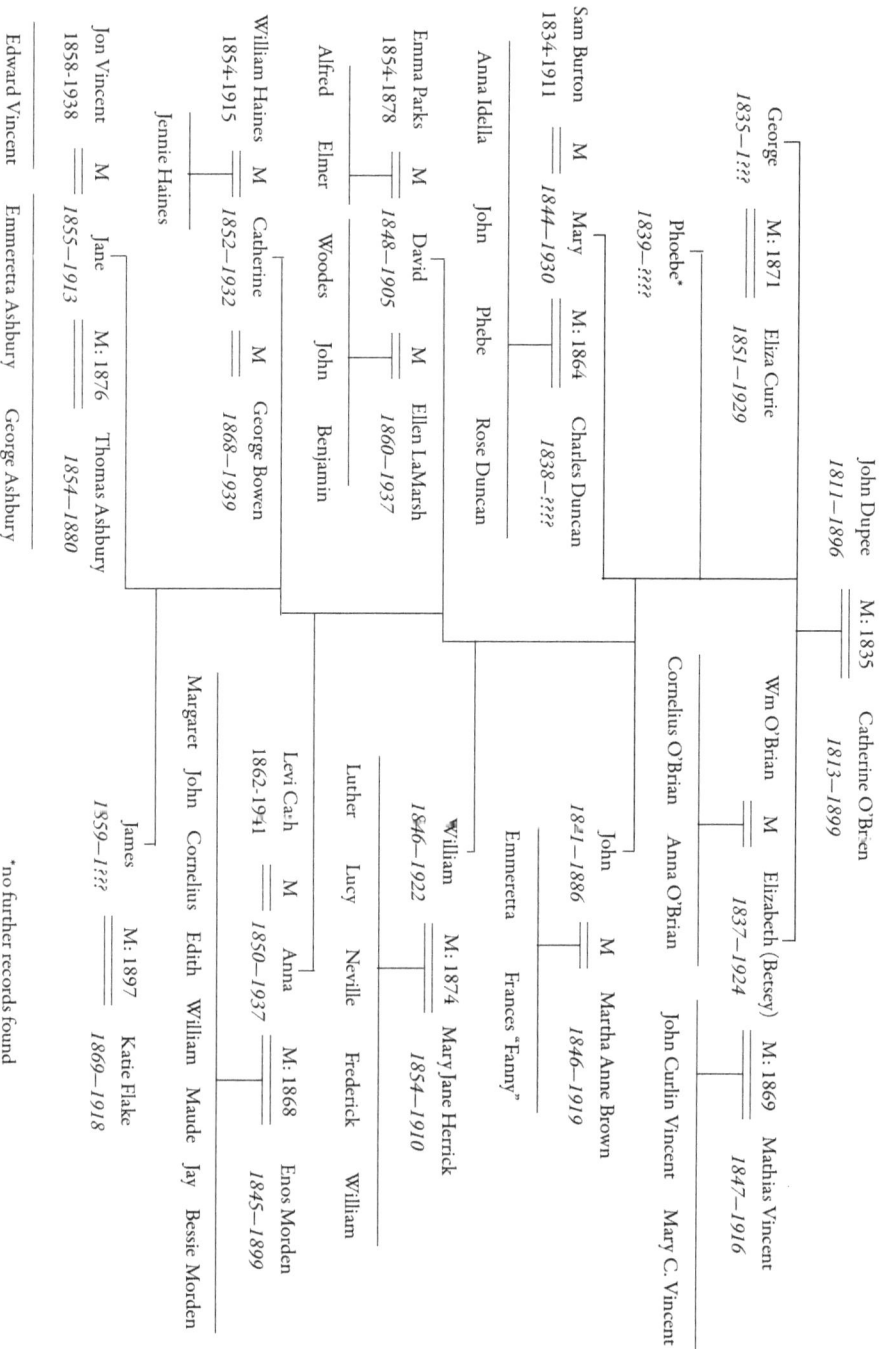

John Dupee
1811–1896

M: 1835

Catherine O'Brien
1813–1899

George
1835–1??? ═ M: 1871 ═ Eliza Curie
1851–1929

Sam Burton
1834–1911 ═ M: 1844–1930 ═ Mary ═ M: 1864 ═ Charles Duncan
1838–????

Phoebe*
1839–????

Anna Idella   John   Phebe   Rose Duncan

Emma Parks
1854–1878 ═ M: 1848–1905 ═ David ═ M: 1860–1937 ═ Ellen LaMarsh

Alfred   Elmer   Woodes   John   Benjamin

William Haines
1854-1915 ═ M: 1852–1932 ═ Catherine ═ M: 1868–1939 ═ George Bowen

Jennie Haines

Jon Vincent
1858-1938 ═ M: 1855–1913 ═ Jane ═ M: 1876 ═ Thomas Ashbury
1854–1880

Edward Vincent   Emmeretta Ashbury   George Ashbury

Wm O'Brian   ═ M ═   Elizabeth (Betsey)
1841–1886   *1837–1924*   ═ M: 1869 ═ Mathias Vincent
1847–1916

Cornelius O'Brian   Anna O'Brian   John Curlin Vincent   Mary C. Vincent

John
1841–1886 ═ M ═ Martha Anne Brown
1846–1919

Emmeretta   Frances "Fanny"

William
1846–1922 ═ M: 1874 ═ Mary Jane Herrick
1854–1910

Luther   Lucy   Neville   Frederick   William

Levi Ca:h
1862–1941 ═ M ═ Anna ═ M: 1868 ═ Enos Morden
1850–1937   *1845–1899*

Margaret John Cornelius   Edith William Maude Jay Bessie Morden

James
1859–1??? ═ M: 1897 ═ Katie Flake
1869–1918

*no further records found

lumberjacks balanced on the rolling logs while maneuvering them into rivers where the logs would float to the sawmills. French-Canadian young men frequently took these dangerous jobs; they needed work, and it was often the only work they could get.

As the land was cleared, farming took over. The 1880 US census was the first where we see John and Catherine living in the US,[21] then ages sixty-nine and sixty-six, respectively, along with their youngest son, James, then age twenty-one. John Sr. and James were both listed as farmers. It may have been soon after John Sr. died in 1896,[22] that their youngest son James moved to Traverse City, as this is where he married Katie Flake in 1897.[23] While Traverse City was also a lumbering center, James' 1900 and 1910 census records show he and his wife Katie were living there on a farm, with James listed as a farmer.[24] They had no children. A 1919 city directory shows them living in the same place. I found no further records on James, although he was listed in his sister Catherine's 1932 obituary as a survivor living in Flint, Michigan.[25]

You might think farming would be in their blood after 200 years in North America as if the hay dust and dirt would seep into their skin by osmosis. Apparently, this was not the case. For families that weren't born into wealth, subsistence farming was almost all they had. Most left farming when other options became available, as we saw in William's and his sons' generations. For this generation, lumbering was a big draw for the boys, as was gold mining for George. Among the brothers, only James and William became farmers, while their brothers died at earlier ages from their more dangerous occupations.

If the boys were the advance team, the rest of the family would follow. Close family ties were common among the French-Canadians, and it was common for families to send a few members out ahead. This pattern was said to minimize the emotional and cultural costs of immigration.[26] Betsey came to Michigan when she married Mathias Vincent, a farmer in Burlington, Lapeer County, on September 12, 1869.[27] Mathias was also born in Canada but moved with his family to Burlington in the 1850s.[28] This was a second marriage for Betsey, as she brought two children from Canada into this marriage (Cornelius O'Brian and Anna O'Brian).[29] Betsey's parents may have arrived in Michigan around the same time, as Jane reported arriving in Michigan around 1870,[30] likely with her parents. Jane would have been age fourteen and James ten at that time. Parents John and Catherine's farm was also in Burlington, Lapeer County, Michigan,[21] the area shaded on the map at right. Thus, this area seemed to be the magnet for others in the family. Lapeer County is just west of St. Clair County, not far from William, John Jr., and David. It looks like William's children would have known their grandparents, aunts and uncles.

Yet, John and Catherine's other daughters didn't come right away. They seemed to prefer to marry in Canada before they immigrated. Maybe they were more confident in finding trusted suitors in their Canadian community. Mary,[31] Anna,[32] Catherine,[33] and Jane all married in Canada and all eventually immigrated to Michigan to live near their parents.[34-35]

Even while Jane had immigrated as a teen with her parents, she returned at age twenty to Ontario to marry Thomas Ashbury. Immediately after the wedding, the couple arrived in Burlington, Lapeer County, Michigan.[36] Thomas was a blacksmith with skills likely useful in his new home state. Unfortunately, Thomas Ashbury died soon after in 1880. Jane then married Betsey's brother-in-law, Jonathan Vincent,[37] a farmer, and they remained in Lapeer County.

Mary's story is a bit different from her sisters. While Mary married Charles Duncan in Ontario in 1864,[31] the family moved to Lockport, New York, near where her husband's family was from. Mary and Charles appeared on the New York State census in 1875.[38] Charles was a painter. But the family seemed to go back and forth, as most of their children were born in Ontario before and after their New York residence. Mary divorced Charles Duncan in October 1904 in Lapeer County, Michigan.[39] The divorce record indicated "extreme cruelty and non-support." Mary then remarried, eight days after her divorce, to Samuel Burton, who was living in Lapeer County, Michigan.[40] She attempted to divorce

Lapeer County Michigan

him in 1907, also for "extreme cruelty," but then withdrew that pursuit.[41] They were still together at the 1910 census,[42] and Samuel died in 1911.[43] Mary remained in Lapeer County until her own death in 1930.[44]

While most French-Canadians were Catholic, the Dupee family had listed their religion as Episcopal for the Ontario 1861 census.[3] In Ontario at the time, with its British majority, the family might well have endured British intolerance of Catholicism, and they would have had few, if any, available Catholic churches. Did this distance from Catholicism free them up to newer ways of thinking about divorce? It is interesting that Mary sought her divorce in Michigan. Divorce was still unusual during these times. Michigan only began recording divorces among vital records in 1897.[45] Yet, back in Ontario, divorce required a private act of Parliament. That process first required the placement of a newspaper petition over a six-month period, stating the names of the petitioners, reasons for the demise of the marriage, and names of co-respondents in the case of adultery. This law didn't change until 1968.[46] Divorce was not easy in Canada. I could see why she would want to move to the United States to pursue her divorce.

Just three years after John Sr. died of "old age" (at age eighty-five),[22] his wife Catherine died of "senile dementia" in 1899, at age eighty-six.[47] Catherine had likely moved in with one of her daughters by then, as several of them were living close by in the final years of Catherine's life.

I can only imagine the challenge of starting over in a new country. They left their community and extended family behind, even though they came from just across Lake Huron. Why did they come? Of course, there was the pull of jobs related to the lumber industry and good farmland that lumbering opened up. Between 1840 and 1930, there were roughly 900,000 French-Canadians emigrating to the United States. Most of these people left Quebec and its poor economic conditions, seeking new industrial jobs in New England. But this exodus also included French-Canadians living in Ontario, who migrated to states adjacent to the Canadian border, thus reducing the financial cost of moving for poor families.[26]

The pull to come to Michigan may also have been influenced by the French-Canadian community already there since the fur trading days. The Dupee family may have been bilingual, as John's family was French-Canadian, and Catherine's family was Irish. Living in English-majority Ontario, they may have felt some discrimination. They would have felt pressure to speak English and to assimilate. And they did assimilate. As with many immigrant families, the second and third generations were more likely to marry outside their cultural group. Not only did John and Catherine do so, but so did all of their children.

There have long been political tensions between French- and English-Canadians that may have been part of the push to emigrate. In the 1860s, The U.S. Civil War brought new tensions. England had sided with the Confederacy, and Canada was, therefore, becoming a safe haven for Confederates. Fearing invasion by the United States, a new militia bill in 1863 required all Canadian men between the ages of eighteen and sixty to serve in defense of Canada.[48] Yet brothers George and John appeared on Michigan's Civil War rosters for the Union side of the conflict. In 1867, the Canadian Federation was formed and brought together all the Canadian provinces (Ontario, Quebec, New Brunswick, Nova Scotia) under one parliament. However, Canada was still not independent of the United Kingdom,[49] in contrast with the United States. There was a brew of cultural, economic, and political tensions. Any or all of these could have been at play for the family and at play differently for various family members.

As I discovered these family stories, I discovered I have a new cultural identity. I am French-Canadian. I also have English ancestry on my mother's side. Therefore, I'm on both sides of this cultural divide. But I knew very little about this cultural group. I wanted to know more.

WHO WERE NORMAN AND JANE DUPEE?

It was not easy to trace this family back further than John and Catherine Dupee. In John Dupee's 1896 Michigan death record,[22] his parents' names were listed as Norman and Jane Dupee. And in John and Catherine's marriage record in 1835,[50] another wedding at the same time was listed for Fanny Dupee and David O'Brien. Apparently, they were John's sister and Catherine's brother. A witness for both weddings was Michael Dupee. These were clues. Other records suggested that Norman and Jane had at least two other sons in Ontario, Michael and Sylvester Dupee.[51] A marriage record for Sylvester clearly stated his parents as Norman and Jane Dupee.[52] Norman Dupee was reportedly born about 1771 in Canada. But where did his family come from?

There are many Dupees in Canada and throughout the United States. The name Dupee was surely Anglicized from the French spelling and pronunciation to make it easier to pronounce by English speakers. The name has many variants: Dupuis, Dupuex, Dupuy, DePuis, dePeu,

Depew, dePue, DePue and many more. The French spelling, Dupuis, is from Latin, meaning "belonging to a well." Therefore, some Anglicized versions of the name might even be "Wells."

Until recently, Norman and Jane were dead-ends in my ancestry research. But now, with the benefit of DNA and a new feature in Ancestry.com, called "ThruLinesTM," I found some unfamiliar names linked to my third great-grandmother "Jane." These people were listed as fourth and fifth great-grandparents, with "Jane" in between! My DNA was linked to cousins from this family! After searching through cousins' public trees, I pieced together that "Jane" was Geneviève Leroux. To confirm I was on the right track, I found that Geneviève married Norbert Dupuis, born in 1771. Their children included Jean Baptiste Dupuis, born in 1811, as was our John Dupee. The French name Jean is usually anglicized as John. Also, in one other public tree, Jean Baptiste Dupuis was shown to have died in Burlington, Michigan, in 1896. Bingo! This opened up my ancestry to many generations beyond John's parents. See more stories on the Dupee and Dupuis families in Chapters 10 through 12.

DUPEE MATERNAL FAMILY LINES

As I traced the Dupee family lines in Michigan, I also explored some of their wives' ancestries. Chapters 5-9 offer more on Leonard's mother, my grandmother Lillian, the Allor family, and their French-Canadian ancestors. First, let's look briefly at what I learned about the heritage of my other great-grandmothers. They were also part of these families on the move.

As described earlier, William Dupee married Mary Jane Herrick, who was born in Michigan in 1854.[53] Mary Jane's parents were Luther Herrick, who came to Michigan from New York state,[54] and Lucy Babcock, who came from Vermont. Lucy's parents, David J. Babcock Jr. and Minerva Randall, migrated to Michigan in 1833 when Lucy was three years old.[55]

In the early 1800s, there were many migrants arriving in Michigan, including New England transplants,[56] like the Herricks and the Babcocks. As the New England population rose, with large Yankee families of ten or more, there was not enough land for all family members to have their own subsistence farm. Therefore, they moved west. When the Erie Canal opened in 1825, connecting the Hudson River with the Great Lakes, many more people came to Michigan. As a result, New England Yankees became a significant part of Michigan's population.[56] When Michigan became a state in 1837, it was still a frontier. Farming was its main economic activity. After the Civil War, Michigan's economy became more diverse and more prosperous. When William and Mary Jane's children were growing up, between 1870 and 1890, the state's population doubled.[57] This must have been an unsettling time for all Michigan residents, even before the auto industry boom of Fred's generation.

Luther Herrick's family can be traced back seven generations to Henry Herrick's arrival in Salem, Massachusetts, from Leicester, England, in 1629.[58] Henry Herrick's wife Edith Laskin arrived in Salem in 1628,[59] also from England. The wives of subsequent Herrick generations can be traced back to England, Germany, and Holland, all seeking new opportunities in the American colonies. The Herricks migrated further West every other generation as the colonies were settled and new areas opened up.

John Dupee's wife, Catherine O'Brien (1813-1899), was reportedly born in Cornwall, Ontario, Canada, which is on the St. Lawrence River, southwest of Montreal. According to Catherine's death record,[47] her parents, James O'Brien and Caroline Smith (birth and death dates unknown), were both born in Ireland. Thus, Catherine has an Irish heritage. So far, our family genealogists have been unable to trace Catherine's family history. I know only that Catherine's older brother David also immigrated to Michigan. In a U.S. 1860 census, I found he was living in St. Clair, St. Clair County,[60] not far from where his sister would live. This is the same brother who married John's sister Fanny Dupee in 1835, but in 1860, he was married to Mary Condon, with whom he had a large family. It's not clear what happened to Fanny.

As I think about all these lives, it seems like we, as a nation—as a continent really, have been on the move from the beginning. Our ancestors came to these shores for a variety of reasons. Then, subsequent generations kept moving westward. They were seeking more land and more opportunity, or they were leaving hardships in their homeland. Most of them were making a choice. It was a choice that came with significant challenges, hard work, and risk. Some lost their lives to it, as did some of John and Catherine's sons. Those who took up the challenge were hardy and resourceful. They had the imagination to start over. They found a new place that became home. I admire them for that.

Still, some of these newcomers encountered anti-immigrant reactions in their new homes. When French-Canadians answered the call for textile mill workers after the Civil War, they came in droves to New England. By 1930, nearly a million had crossed the border looking for work. They lived in "Little Canada" enclaves, housed in crowded tenements set up by the mill owners. They were often criticized for not assimilating as they maintained their culture and language within their small communities. New Englanders, who were particularly anti-Catholic, felt especially threatened by this large influx. By the 1880s, the New York Times and other newspapers ran stories accusing the Catholic Church of a sinister plot to seize control of New England and annex it to Quebec as a new nation-state of New France. This led to burning churches and assaults on priests and Catholic neighborhoods.[61] There were Ku Klux Klan rallies in Massachusetts in 1923 and 1924 as New Englanders resented the influx of Catholic French-Canadians willing to accept lower wages than local workers. Anti-Irish and anti-Italian prejudices were also prevalent throughout this time.[62] In Worcester, Massachusetts, the Klan launched a major recruitment drive. At one rally, speakers inflamed the audience by claiming that Catholics were taking over city government, the police force, and teachers, "When Worcester folks see 20,000 to 30,000

FREDERICK DUPEE'S ANCESTORS

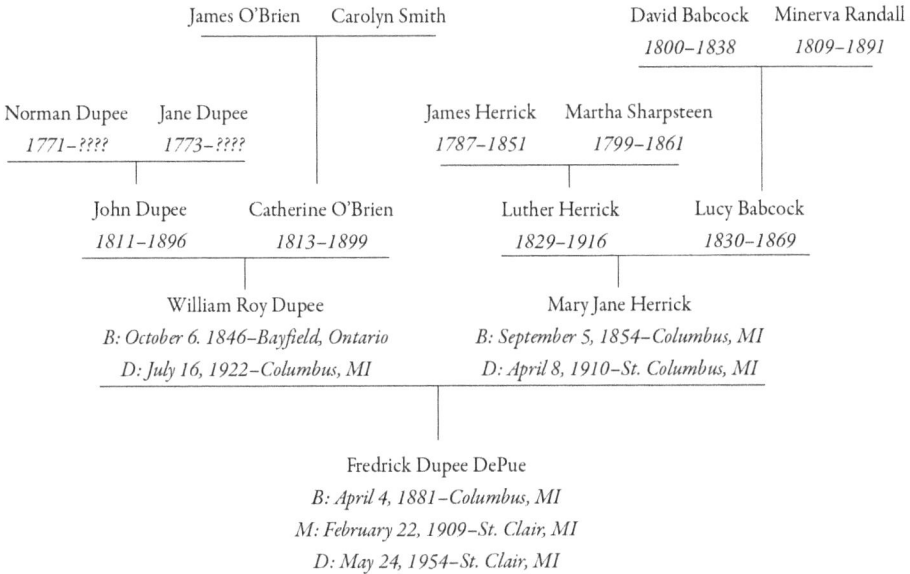

James O'Brien   Carolyn Smith   David Babcock   Minerva Randall
                                                   1800–1838   *1809–1891*

Norman Dupee   Jane Dupee   James Herrick   Martha Sharpsteen
1771–????   *1773–????*   *1787–1851*   *1799–1861*

John Dupee   Catherine O'Brien   Luther Herrick   Lucy Babcock
1811–1896   *1813–1899*   *1829–1916*   *1830–1869*

William Roy Dupee   Mary Jane Herrick
B: October 6. 1846–Bayfield, Ontario   *B: September 5, 1854–Columbus, MI*
D: July 16, 1922–Columbus, MI   *D: April 8, 1910–St. Columbus, MI*

Fredrick Dupee DePue
B: April 4, 1881–Columbus, MI
M: February 22, 1909–St. Clair, MI
D: May 24, 1954–St. Clair, MI

Klansmen in uniform parading the streets of Worcester, and this time is not far off, then we will definitely be ready for action," one speaker predicted.[62] The next year, 15,000 supporters showed up for a mass induction ceremony in the largest Ku Klux Klan gathering ever held in New England. As anti-Klan forces arrived, a riot broke out, raging out of control for the rest of the night. This rally and the reaction to it were part of a national struggle over who could be considered American. They were fearful of what they saw as a decline in the traditional American values rooted in Protestant religion and Anglo-Saxon culture. This fervor continued until the manufacturing base declined and immigration from our Northern border slowed. Then, the fervor shifted to other foreign-seeming immigrants from eastern and southern Europe.[62] This fervor seems to continue today. For the Dupees' immigration into Michigan, hopefully, it was an easier transition with Michigan's long-standing French-Canadian communities. Perhaps this, too, was a "Little Canada." But the French were on this land long before it became Michigan and long before there was a United States.

5

Close Family Ties

Lillian M. Allor

❧

LILLIAN'S FAMILY – THE ALLORS

As I explored my grandmother Lillian's family, the Allors, I saw the same generation as her husband Fred and his siblings (late 1800s through the 1960s), but from a different perspective. Tracing her family back took me deeper into Michigan's history and into my French-Canadian heritage, all the way back to France.

Here, too, I knew nothing about Lillian or her family. The fuzzy photo of Lillian as a teenager, shows a bit of her spark. I have little more to go on. I can see a resemblance to my generation; she reminds me of my sister, Loretta, and maybe myself in my teenage years. Unfortunately, Lillian lived a short life. She married Fred Dupee in 1909 and had three children in three years.[1] Within a month of the birth of her third child, my father Leonard, she died at the age of twenty-five.[2] But who was she beyond these brief milestones? I would get to know her a bit by getting to know her family. As it turned out, my father and his brothers were closer to the Allors than to their father and stepmother.

Lillian's parents were Isadore James Allor (1856-1936) and Mary Frances Furton (1860-1953).[3,4] They were both born in Macomb County, Michigan, and raised in farming families. Macomb County is just north of Wayne County—where Detroit is the county seat and southwest of St. Clair County. Isadore and Mary married in 1882 in Mt. Clemens, Macomb County, when Isadore was age twenty-five and Mary Frances twenty-two.[5] They soon moved to a farm in nearby St. Clair, St. Clair County.[6] This is where their children grew up. This move would put the family near where the Dupees were living and where Lillian met Fred. A neighbor on their 1900 census record was the Hyslop family,[6] whose young daughter Julie would later marry Fred Dupee's brother William

Isadore and Mary Frances Allor

Jr. I got to know Mary Frances and Isadore a bit as well through their record of events.

THE ALLORS DURING
DETROIT'S BOOM AND BUST

Lillian was the fourth of Isadore and Mary's seven children: Elmer,[7] Francis (Frank),[8] Arthur,[9] who died just before his third birthday, Lillian,[2] Edward,[10] Martha,[11] and Viola.[12] The 1900 census shows a family of seven, including eleven-year-old "Lillie," living on their own farm in St. Clair.[6] In 1910,[13] the family was still living at their farm on Marsh Road in St. Clair, but the older children had left home. Edward, then age twenty, was living at home while working as a chauffeur in the auto industry; seventeen-year-old Martha was a dressmaker in a shop, and

Siblings Edward and Lillian Allor

ISADORE AND MARY'S CHILDREN

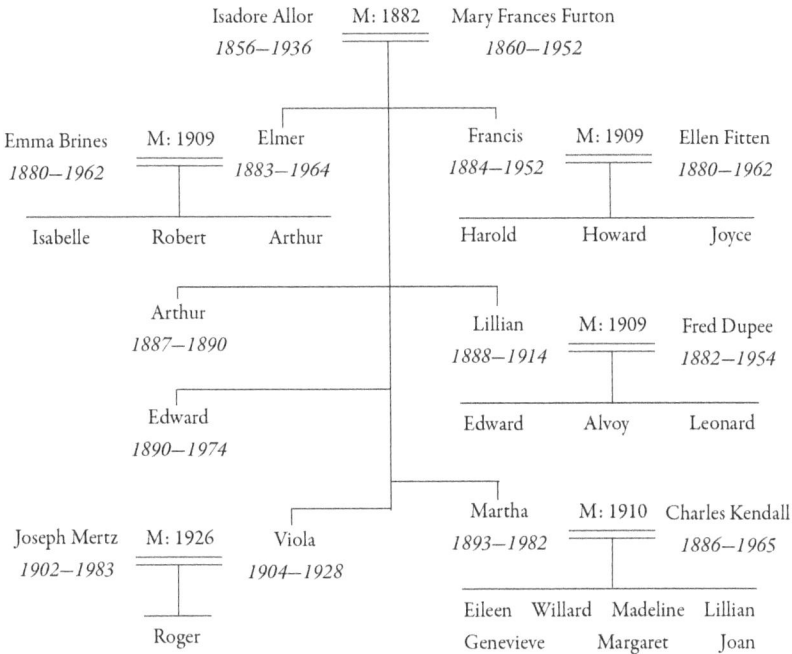

Isadore Allor	M: 1882	Mary Frances Furton
1856–1936		1860–1952

Emma Brines	M: 1909	Elmer		Francis	M: 1909	Ellen Fitten
1880–1962		1883–1964		1884–1952		1880–1962
Isabelle	Robert	Arthur		Harold	Howard	Joyce

	Arthur		Lillian	M: 1909	Fred Dupee
	1887–1890		1888–1914		1882–1954

	Edward		Edward	Alvoy	Leonard
	1890–1974				

			Martha	M: 1910	Charles Kendall
Joseph Mertz	M: 1926	Viola	1893–1982		1886–1965
1902–1983		1904–1928			
	Roger		Eileen Willard Madeline Lillian		
			Genevieve Margaret Joan		

the youngest, Viola, was just six years old. Sometime before the 1920 census,[14] Isadore and Mary had moved to Detroit, to 404 Holden Street, near the Henry Ford Hospital. They likely moved to the city because most of their married children had moved there by this time. It seems they stuck together.

The sheer amount of activity on various genealogy sites also suggests that this was a close family engaged in their family history. Lillian's photos show a happy teenager. With her brother Edward, she has a warm smile and a jaunty hand on her hip. In her wedding photo with Fred, (Chapter 2, p. 13) she is a bit more serious, as wedding photos often were at the time. She is a beautiful twenty-year-old bride, wearing the fashionable hairstyle for women of the early 1900s.

The year 1909 was a big year in the Allor household, with three weddings. Elmer was married on February 20,[15] followed two days later by Lillian's wedding.[1] Frank married on June 1.[16] Then Martha married the following year, in November 1910.[17] Not only were they bustling with the excitement of weddings and marriages, but I discovered much more was at hand.

As with the Dupee men, the Detroit auto industry had clearly beckoned the Allors. Yet, for them, it became a full-fledged family affair. The ball started rolling in early 1909 or before, as Elmer was in Detroit when he married Emma Brines in February of that year. The rest of the family followed. Elmer, Frank, Lillian, and Martha had all chosen their spouses from the St Clair area, but all promptly moved with them to Detroit. This likely accounted for the flurry of weddings in 1909-10.

They all were hustling to take part in Detroit's boom when the automakers called for workers from the countryside and all over. They were in Detroit when Henry Ford created his assembly line in 1910,[18] and most were still there when Ford launched his revolutionary policy to pay $5 per day to reduce turnover.[19] And all found jobs. In 1910, Elmer worked as a machinist at a machine shop,[20] and by 1918, Elmer worked for Ford Motor Company as a toolmaker.[21] He continued in that role in subsequent census reports. But in 1942, he reported on his WWII draft registration that he was working for Chevrolet Gear and Axel.[22] Frank worked as a tinsmith for an auto company in Detroit in 1910,[23] before moving back to St. Clair to become a farmer. Martha's husband, Charles Kendall, worked in a spring factory in 1910,[24] as there was a great demand for steel springs with the growing auto industry. By 1918, Charles was an auto assembler for the Anderson Car Company.[25] He also reported working as an auto assembler in the 1920 and 1930 censuses. Charles reported on his 1942 WWII draft registration that he was working for Fisher Body Service in their repair department.[26] As described in Chapter 3, Fred Dupee worked in an auto factory in 1910,[27] before he moved back to St. Clair following Lillian's death. Then, when he returned to Detroit in 1918, he reported working for Detroit Electric, doing fine assembly.[28] This may have been the same company

Mary Frances Allor as a Red Cross Nurse.

that Charles worked for in 1918, referring to the two names the company had used. Detroit Electric was reorganized as the Anderson Electric Car Company around 1911.[29] Lillian's brother Edward was working as a foreman at the Ford Motor Company before leaving to became a Catholic priest.[30] Even their father Isadore, at age sixty-four, listed himself as an auto industry "helper" for the 1920 census.[14] The auto industry grabbed the attention of all the Allor men, at least initially.

Mary Frances also made herself useful. One photo I found featured Mary Frances Allor as a Red Cross nurse. During World War I, many women volunteered for the Red Cross at home. The Ford Motor Company donated ambulances, trucks, and cars to the war effort. Women of the Red Cross conducted training sessions for women as ambulance drivers outside the Highland Park Plant. Then, during the 1918 Flu epidemic, women transported patients, staff, and supplies using Ford's vehicles to and from the hospitals.[31] The Henry Ford Hospital, near the Allors' home, was also briefly turned over to the U.S. Government in 1918. It became an army hospital to care for wounded soldiers returning from the war. Soon after, the hospital was offered to the City of Detroit to care for the growing number of flu patients. Patients were treated in this hospital regardless of their financial resources.[32] Mary may have served as a volunteer in any of these capacities. This speaks of Mary's spirit of service to her community.

As soon as the newly married couples arrived in Detroit for the auto boom, the babies followed. Lillian had lots of company with her and her siblings' growing families. There were seven babies born between 1909 and 1914, and many more babies were born among her siblings after Lillian's death. Viola, the youngest of Isadore and Mary's children, married in 1926.[33] Sadly, two years later, Viola also died of complications from childbirth at age twenty-four.[12]

They were all in Detroit as the city population doubled, as streets became crowded with the new automobiles and with more and more people. It was certainly a faster pace and higher pitch than was their life in the country. New housing was also booming during this time. It had to be. Detroit needed places to put its exploding population. In 1910 and into the 1920s, housing was a mix of cottages, bungalows, boarding houses, and apartment buildings, all built close together to maximize walkability and access to public transportation out the front door to the street. Horse carriages and the early cars typically accessed homes and their detached garages from an alley in the back. This mode of housing changed by the 1920s, as houses were then built with narrow driveways directly from the street, although the cars were still mostly kept out of sight in garages behind the house. Capitalizing on the influx of auto industry cash, local banks set up mortgage businesses and promoted the new idea that owning a detached single-family home was part of the American Dream. Suddenly, Detroit started building more single-family homes than anyplace else.[34] Remarkably, it was a city of blue-collar home owners. The union-negotiated wage and benefit packages made auto workers more secure and allowed them to become mortgage holders.[18] This all came apart for many with the Great Depression of the 1930s, as foreclosures mounted and banks went bust. After WWII, there would be another building boom, with returning soldiers and GI loans for mortgages. This time, however, the building boom was on the city's edges, in new suburbs.[34]

This pattern seems to fit the Allors. The 1910 censuses showed Charles Kendall and Fred Dupee living in rooming houses when they found their first jobs, before bringing their wives to the city.[24,27] Elmer and Emma were living in a rear apartment rental in 1910.[20] By 1920, Elmer and Emma Allor[35] and Martha and Charles Kendall[36] were living in mortgaged single-family homes in neighborhoods with close-together houses and narrow driveways between. By the 1930 and 1940 census reports, they were living in neighborhoods with more space between houses and plenty of trees. It is hard to say the impact the Depression had on this family. At least all were fully employed at the 1940 census, and they reported the same in 1939. Elmer and Emma raised their three children on Montrose Street in the Dearborn section of Detroit,[37,38] where the large Rouge Ford Plant had opened in 1927. They remained at this address from 1930 through subsequent censuses, and it is where both Elmer and Emma lived until they died in 1964 and 1962,[8,39] respectively. In 1940, Martha and Charles had moved to the LaSalle College Park neighborhood, Detroit, with their seven children.[40] Martha and Charles also remained in Detroit and died there, in 1982 and 1965,[11,41] respectively. They all seem to have adapted to city life.

After Frank and Nellie lived in Detroit in 1910,[23] they moved back to St. Clair before Frank's 1918 WWI Draft registration.[42] Frank and Nellie then lived on a rented farm on Hart Road in the town of China in St. Clair County, where they raised their three children.[43] They alone returned to farming full-time, rejecting the factory-worker lifestyle in the city. This is where Frank and Nellie remained, as in 1930, they were still living on Hart Road and now owned their farm.[44] This is where they were living when they died in 1952 and 1989,[9,45] respectively.

Viola's husband, Joseph Mertz, worked as a Detroit firefighter.[46] While Viola died following childbirth, their newborn son Roger survived. Joseph remarried and had two more children.[47]

FATHER EDWARD ALLOR

Because Edward lived a more public life as a priest, much more was written about him. Still, a less-known and early part of Edward's life was recovered in a trunk purchased from an Assumption Parish garage sale in Windsor, Ontario, in 2001.[30] It contained a 1913 letter addressed to Edward Allor on Ford Motor Company stationary from Harry Hudson, Chief Engineer of the Ford radiator division. Harry Hudson praised Ed for developing the engine part that led to "the great improvement in heat management of the engines being used in the automotive industry." Hudson attributed the patent to Ed, although all patents were the property of Ford Motor Company.[30,48] In the "History of Ford Motor

Father Edward Allor

Company," vice president of Ford, Charles Sorensen, wrote that he would never have sent Harry Hudson to England if he didn't have a "good man" to replace him. That "good man" was Ed Allor.[48] However, at age twenty-four, the year that his sister Lillie died, Ed left his promising career at Ford to become a Catholic priest. Did Lillie's death influence his decision to become a priest? It appears that he brought his many talents to the larger communities he served as a priest.

Ed began his priesthood training by enrolling in Assumption College in Windsor, Ontario, across the Detroit River. After completing four

Basilica Sainte Anne de Détroit

years of High School and one year of college, all in three years, he entered St. Basil's novitiate in Toronto in 1917. He completed his bachelor's degree in 1919 with the University of Western Ontario, clearly on a fast track. Then, he pursued theology training at St. Basil Scholasticate in Toronto and was ordained on December 22, 1923. He served the Assumption Church and parish back in Windsor, before and during the depression, 1924-1937. There, he had a reputation as a "fixer" as "he could fix anything from a clock to a cathedral."[49]

He returned to Detroit, where he served as a pastor in Sainte Anne de Détroit from 1937-1942.[50] St. Anne's is the second oldest continuously operated parish in the United States, founded in 1701 when Cadillac founded Detroit for the French. The current neo-gothic revival cathedral-style church was built in 1886, the eighth church built on this site.[51]

Thereafter, Ed served a number of Canadian parishes, returning to Assumption Church several times, the last time in 1972. In all his parishes, he was known as a capable administrator and for his talent for dealing with people. He was remembered for his pastoral devotion in his home visits with parishioners and his attention to children. Whether in the parish schools or with his nieces and nephews, he was received with joy, as reported in his St. Basil's biography.[50] When back in Detroit, he was very much a part of his original family, and they were very proud of him, judging by the number of family photos in which he appeared.

Another family memory, posted on familysearch.org, described Father Ed's multilingual abilities.[52] The family language was French, although all spoke English as well. He was also in command of both German and Latin, Latin, of course, from his studies as a Catholic priest. His German language skills came from his mother, Mary Frances, who was the second great-grandchild of Jean Baptiste Rivard and Mary Catherine Yax (see more about Mary Catherine in Chapter 8). Mary Catherine Yax was the child of parents born in Germany. Both French and German languages were passed down through the generations. When Father Ed would visit his mother, he would bring a copy of the "Detroiter Abend Post," a German newspaper published by the German community in Detroit. His niece, Joyce Allor Keeley, said that Ed would read the papers to his mother, and then they would discuss the news in German.[52] It appears he had a close relationship with his mother, and their value of community service was shared in common.

Ed suffered from poor eyesight from the time he was ordained, and he required special dispensation because of his difficulty doing readings during the celebration of Mass. Later in life, he suffered from headaches and arterial complications. In 1973, Father Ed returned to Toronto to enter the St. Basil's infirmary. He died a year later on February 12, 1974. He is buried in Holy Cross Catholic Cemetery, in Thornhill, Ontario, Canada.[50]

FAMILY REUNIONS

Mary and Isadore moved down the street to 1348 Holden Street between the 1920 and 1930 censuses.[53] Sharing their household in 1930, as noted in the last chapter, were their grandsons, Edward (age twenty) and Alvoy DePue (age eighteen). By then, Mary and Isadore had lost a son at age three and two daughters at childbirth. They were now holding their grandchildren close. Soon after, grandsons Edward and Alvoy were married and in their own homes. Mary and Isadore lived at their Holden Street home until Isadore died in 1936 of a cerebral hemorrhage at age eighty.[54]

During her later years, Mary lived at St. Joseph's Home for the Aged in Detroit.[55] Her extended family helped Mary celebrate her ninety-second birthday in 1952 at her grandson Edward DePue's home. Since she was a leap-year baby, born on February 29, she said in a newspaper interview that it was actually her twenty-third birthday![56] She joked about being a spry twenty-three-year-old and ready to date. The party was attended by her four living children, seventeen grandchildren, and thirty great-grandchildren. Mary died a year later, in August 1953, at age ninety-three.[57] Isadore, Mary, and Lillian are all buried at Mt. Olivet Cemetery in Detroit. It is interesting that most of the Allors remained in Detroit, unlike the Dupees, who returned to St. Clair County in their later years. It may be because the parents, especially Mary Frances, the heart of the family, had migrated to the city along with their children. The family stuck together.

Family reunions were common in the Allor family. Reunions continued into the 1980s in St. Clair, Michigan. My brother Dave and my sister Loretta attended some of these, as did my father Leonard and his brothers. They were attended by members of both the Dupee and Allor extended families.

But I wonder what it meant for these families to live through this remarkable history as it was happening. I suspect the mystique of the auto boom may have been more exciting than living within it. They traded a farmer's lifestyle for lunch boxes and shift work. They did gain a reliable paycheck, however, along with a house, a yard, and a mortgage in the city that was transforming rapidly. The American Dream before this time was migrating westward for a homestead and a parcel of land of one's own. It was a stake in farming that they hoped to grow. In the nineteenth century, there were millworkers working for wages, but they had little hope of advancement. In Detroit, this first generation of autoworkers had union jobs, greater financial security, and stability unknown to factory workers before. As homeowners, they could hope for modest generational wealth and more opportunities for their children and generations to follow.

The auto boom changed more than their work-life. It changed how they, and all of us since then, travel and what our landscape looks like. Detroit was the first to see expressways and sprawl. As a result, we would spend more of our income on cars than any other consumer product, except our homes. Detroiters and all Americans would spend more and more time in our cars. This car-centric shift, in turn, shaped the landscape—gas stations, drive-ins, strip malls, shopping centers, and all of suburbia.[18] All of this was unfolding for this generation of Dupees and Allors; they witnessed it all. Even those who remained on the farm were impacted greatly by the automatization of farm equipment, the convenience and necessity of car ownership, and the sudden proximity of suburbia and highways. The new car-centric lifestyle has affected everyone.

Yet family life continued amidst all of these developments. The Allors' close family ties come through even with these small bits of information I could gather. These ties surely helped them get through their losses and transitions. I decided to continue my research and explore earlier generations of these French-Canadian families. What will I learn from them?

6

Habitants

Habitant *(h)a-bi-'tä^n:* a settler or descendant of a settler of French origin working as a farmer in Canada

—Merriam-Webster Dictionary[1]

❧

ALLARD-ALLOR FAMILY LINE

THE ALLOR FAMILY HAS HAD MANY DEDICATED FAMILY GENEAL-
ogists, as their family lines are well documented. Of course, it helps that
these ancestors were among the first French to settle in Quebec, and
with their maternal lines, they were first among those to settle in Detroit.
There were indeed pioneers, but more on those stories a bit later. I will
begin with mapping the Allor family line from Lillian's father, Isadore
Allor, whose ancestry goes from Michigan, back to Quebec, and back
to France across eight generations. If you add Lillian, Leonard, and
my own generation, that comes to eleven generations. The Allors and
Allards were mostly farmers; none were famous, but their stories provide
a glimpse of the early French-Canadian settlements and what it meant
for its early inhabitants or *habitants*, as they were called. The name Allor
was Anglicized from Allard by Isadore's grandfather Joseph, sometime
between 1850 and 1860, based on U.S. census reports and consistency
of other records. In French, the last consonant is silent unless there is a
silent 'e' at the end. Therefore, Allard would be pronounced as Allar or
Allor, depending on the dialect or speaker. The name change was closer
to what English speakers would hear phonetically. (see Isadore Allor's
ancestors at the end of this chapter).

JACQUES ALLARD LEAVES QUEBEC FOR DETROIT

Isadore Allor was already the fourth generation of the Allor family
living in Michigan, including before it became Michigan. Isadore's
great-grandfather Jacques Allard arrived in Detroit around 1774,[10] from
Charlesbourg, Quebec (now part of Quebec City). His marriage record

70

Isadore James Allor	M: 1882[2]	Mary Frances Furton
B: August 24, 1846—L'Aanse Creuse, MI		B: February 29, 1860—Chesterfield, MI
D: December 2, 1936—Detroit, MI		D: August 26, 1953—China, MI
James (Jacques) Allor	M: 1854[3]	Marine (Mary) Furton
B: May 3, 1832—L'Aanse Creuse, MI		B: March 15, 1838—L'Anse Creuse, MI
D: June 13, 1920—Mount Clemens, MI		D: December 14, 1876—Erin, MI
Joseph Allard-Allor	M: 1818[4]	Madeleine Tremblay
B: July 29, 1795—Detroit, MI		B: October 31, 1798—Detroit, MI
D: June 19, 1878—Erin, MI		D: August 8, 1881—Erin, MI
Jacques (James) Allard	M: 1780[5]	Geneviéve (Geneva) LaForest
B: October 14, 1746—Charlesbourg, Quebec		B: June 16, 1764—Grosse Pt, MI
D: abt 1800—Detroit, MI		D: May 30, 1797—Essex, Ontario
Pierre Allard	M: 1743[6]	Marie Angelique Bergevin
B: May 1, 1716—Charlesbourg, Quebec		B: October 10, 1722—Charlesbourg, Quebec
D: December 27, 1759—Charlesbourg, Quebec		D: October 29, 1787—Charlesbourg, Quebec
Jean-Baptiste Allard	M: 1705[7]	Anne Elzabeth Pageau
B: February 22, 1676—Old Quebec City		B: January 15, 1686—Charlesbourg, Quebec
D: December 22, 1748—Charlesbourg, Quebec		D: December 23, 1748—Charlesbourg, Quebec
Francois Allard	M: 1671[8]	Jeanne Anguille
B: 1637—Blacqueville, Rouen, France		B: January 3, 1643—Loire, France
D: October 25, 1762—Charlesbourg, Quebec		D: March 11, 1711—Charlesbourg, Quebec
Jacques Allard	M[9]	Jacqueline Frérot
B: 1612—Blacqueville, Rouen, France		B: 1616—Blacqueville, Rouen, France
D: 1696—Blacqueville, Rouen, France		D: May 8, 1658—Auvergne, France

described him as a *voyageur,*[11] indicating he had traveled by canoe for hire between Quebec and Detroit. At that time, what is now Michigan was part of the Canadian Province of Quebec, then under English rule. He had thus migrated from one part of Quebec to another.

The English had taken control of Quebec in 1760, becoming official in 1763 with the Treaty of Paris. Thereby, France ceded all of its colonial lands east of the Mississippi to England. Then, in 1774, with the Quebec Act, Britain expanded Quebec's border south to the Ohio River and west to what is now Wisconsin and Minnesota. While England also controlled the thirteen colonies along the east coast, the Quebec Act irked the American patriots, as it appeared to void their land claims in Ohio. In fact, England hoped to keep this land out of the hands of the thirteen colonies. This and other "Intolerable Acts" led to the American Revolution.[12] Jacques arrived in Detroit just as the American Revolution was getting underway.

But what prompted Jacques Allard's decision to migrate? In 1774, he was twenty-eight years old. He grew up in Charlesbourg when it was an adjacent village to Quebec City, on the highlands above the St. Lawrence River. This area was the capital of New France, and it had been settled and growing for over a hundred years. With the *habitants'* large families, there would have been little available land for younger generations to farm. But more significantly, Jacques grew up during a very turbulent time for his hometown, in the heat of what Americans call the French and Indian War, what English-speaking Canadians or Europeans call the "Seven Years' War," or what people in New France, now Quebec, referred to as the "Guerre de la coquête" or "War of Conquest."[13]

In North America, the war began in 1754 with a skirmish on the Ohio River when the French defeated George Washington for the Virginia colony at Fort Necessity. The Virginia Colony aimed to expand west into this territory, the English wanted to reduce the size of French Canada, and the French wanted to reaffirm their control.[13] In New France, all able-bodied men between the ages of sixteen and sixty were drafted for the militias. Jacques and his brothers were too young to serve, but his father would likely have been drafted. There were many battles with victories on both sides. But by 1759, the capital of New France, Quebec City, became the target.[14]

There was a large English armada with 1,900 cannons on over 200 ships of various sizes on the St. Lawrence River, all aimed at Quebec City. These ships carried 8,500 troops with 13,500 seamen and crew. When all the reinforcements arrived, the English had 30,000 people facing off against 15,000 French, including their Indigenous allies. Most of the local women and children took refuge inland. Quebec's city gates were closed on June 30. The city was protected by its high cliff walls. From July 12 to September 13, the shoreline communities were bombed with cannons, and hundreds of homes and fields were burned every night.[14] Jacques was only twelve years old that summer. Even if Jacques and his family made it further inland, he would have heard the cannon thunder, seen the fiery red skies, and smelled the smokey air. I can barely imagine what it was like living under this terror.

From an upstream village, the English captured prisoners, including some women and children, who had fled the bombing in Quebec. Those women and children were later released near the base of Quebec City's cliffs, and they were observed taking a path where they easily climbed the bank to the city gate. On the morning of September 13, the French militia had expected the English to attack from downstream, and their troops were waiting there. Therefore, they had only one guard posted at the city gate on the cliff. The English troops easily scaled the path up the steep walls and took the city's guard post, arriving at the Plains of Abraham on top of the cliff. It was an hour and a quarter later when the French militia arrived on the scene and when the two armies could face off for battle. The English troops stood in their combat lines waiting for orders to fire while the Canadians and their Indigenous allies started shooting right away. Nonetheless, the French side was greatly outnumbered. The battle was over in a half-hour. Quebec City was seized.[14] Jacques' father, Pierre Allard, died December 27, 1759.[15] Did he die from injuries obtained while protecting his homeland? During the following summer of 1760, the English took Montreal, France capitulated, and the war was over.[14]

Jacques likely observed the tension thereafter as his family and community adjusted to the military regime between 1760 and 1763. The Canadians were required to accommodate English troops in their homes. Catholicism was not tolerated in England, although the local English governors were ordered to prevent soldiers from openly insulting the French inhabitants, now their fellow subjects, about "their inferiority" or the "errors of that mistaken religion." Priests were not allowed to tithe their community, and the men's religious orders were ordered to disband.[16]

Once the Treaty of Paris was signed in 1763, the new Province of Quebec was entitled to a legislative assembly with the rights of English law. However, Catholics were prohibited from holding public administrative positions unless they took a Test Oath forsaking their faith.[16] In 1774, with the Quebec Act, the French Canadians were relieved. They were then given the freedom to profess their Catholic faith, the Test Oath was abolished, and Catholic priests were permitted to tithe their population. They could practice their customary French civil law, and Quebec boundaries were expanded. Still, the English somehow expected the French Canadians to assimilate into their English customs and language when there were about 600 British to about 90,000 French Canadians.[16] However, as noted above, the Quebec Act set in motion the American Revolution.

This turmoil was the backdrop for Jacques Allard's childhood in the Quebec capital area. It is not surprising then that when his mother, Marie Angelique Bergevin, remarried in January 1761, the family moved. (Note that in French custom, women retain their maiden names in official records, while in person, she would be addressed as Madame Allard[17]) The entire family, including her six children from her first marriage and her new husband, Louis Jacques, moved to Bethier, Ile Dupas.[18] Ile Dupas is part of a cluster of islands, with the St. Lawrence River braided between them, about 135 miles upstream from Quebec City, on the way to Montreal. The St. Lawrence River was the main highway for all of New France, between its mouth at the Gulf of St. Lawrence and all the up-river outposts, including those accessed from the major tributaries, the Great Lakes, and beyond. In 1734, the *Chemin du Roi,* or King's Highway, was built between Quebec City and Montreal, which was then the longest road in North America at 155 miles (250 km). It took four to six days on this highway to make the journey between the two cities, but it permitted an alternate mode of travel year-round.[19] Still, the river was the most common route.

Marie Angelique had five more children at their new home, the first of which (Charlotte) was born in October 1761 in Ile Dupas.[18] It must have been a relief to get out of the capital city away from the political tensions. Most of Jacques' siblings later married and settled in this new area around Ile Dupas.[18] From his new home, Jacques would have seen the ship traffic and *voyageurs* as they carried supplies and returned with furs from the outposts. Perhaps this action beckoned the young Jacques. He may have known some of the *voyageurs* or known some of the settlers who had moved further upriver. As his later marriage record described, he took up the occupation of a *voyageur* for one or more trips along the river highway. It was a hundred years earlier when his great-grandfather sailed across the ocean to Quebec from France. That sense of adventure was in his blood, seeking the western horizon, although paddling canoes over hundreds of miles was a difficult livelihood. At age twenty-eight, he decided to settle in Detroit. He arrived just in time to see more war-related tension.

MORE WARTIME EXPERIENCES

During the American Revolutionary War, there were no direct attacks on Detroit, but conditions deteriorated in the region. In 1778, the British built Fort Lernoult, a new stronger fort, to strengthen their position. Land grants were suspended, and even permission to cultivate land was limited.[20]

Jacques married Geneviève Madeleine (Geneva) LaForest in Detroit in February 1780.[21] Jacques was then age thirty-three; Geneva was fifteen. She was born in 1764 to one of the first families to settle in the riverfront area that came to be called Grosse Pointe (see more about these pioneers in Chapter 8). In 1778, Detroit had a population of 2,144.[22] In that small community, it would not have been hard to find eligible young women to wed. But with the wartime land restrictions,

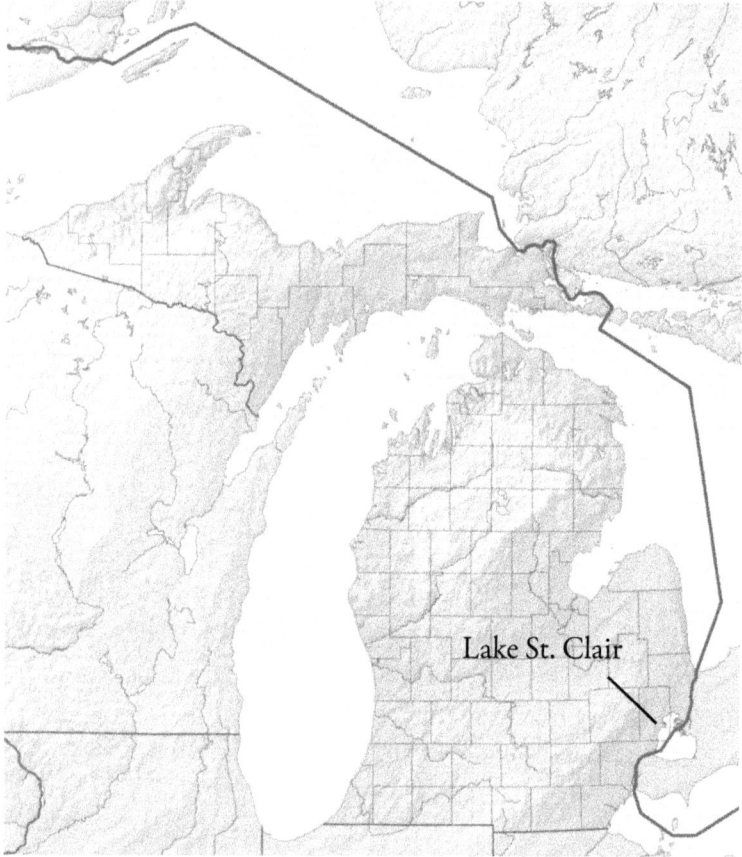

Lake St. Clair is between Lake Erie and Lake Huron

farming and starting a family might have been difficult. They had their first child in 1782.[21]

When the American Revolutionary War ended in 1783, the land that is now Michigan was ceded by England to the new United States. Yet, this land was not officially turned over until 1796, when it became part of the Northwest Territory. In 1800, it became part of Indiana Territory. Then, in 1805, Michigan Territory was established, and in 1837, this area became the state of Michigan.[23] However, even during English rule and during the early years of American rule, this area was mostly inhabited by the French settlers who had been there for generations: *habitants*.

Once the Americans took control in 1783, conditions began to improve. The Americans were initially friendly to the *habitants*.[20] However, over time, cultural conflicts arose with the Americans, as they had with the English, and the Americans attempted to force conformity to their ways. For example, the Americans complained of animal races down the city streets.[23] While the French were devout Catholics, they did like to have fun! It makes me happy to know that.

Jacques and Geneva ultimately had twelve children, all born and baptized in Detroit. Their seventh child, Joseph (b. 1795),[24] was my third great-grandfather. There are no confirmed death dates for Jacques and Geneva.

A large fire in 1805 destroyed most of the wooden buildings in the Detroit settlement,[23] although the fire offered an opportunity to build a larger community without the palisades. Soon, the community extended well beyond where the fort walls had been, with farms all along the Detroit River and onto Lake St. Clair.

The Detroit River connects Lake Erie with Lake St. Clair, and the St. Clair River connects Lake St. Clair to Lake Huron. The *voyageurs* referred to this connection between Lake Erie and Lake St. Clair as the strait, which in French is *le détroit*. As part of the treaty ending the American Revolution, these rivers became the new boundary with British-ruled Canada.[20,23]

At age sixteen, Joseph Allard joined in the War of 1812,[25] as did his brothers Pierre and Louis.[26,27] It was leftover disagreements from the American Revolution and continued British insults that led to the War of 1812. The British built fortifications on their side of the Detroit River. As a result, Michigan became a significant battleground in this new war. Fort Lernoult was renamed Fort Detroit by the Americans.[20,23] Unfortunately, this fort was quickly surrendered to the English in the summer of 1812, in what was considered an embarrassment for the Americans. Joseph and Louis had served as privates in Captain Stephen Mack's artillery company, under the command of Major James Witherell, during that summer's attack on Detroit. The Allard brothers' service was short-lived, from May to August of 1812. Another major defeat in January 1813, at the

River Raisin, just south of Detroit, left the Michigan Territory under a British military regime until the end of the war in 1814.[28] The Michigan militia was deemed to be unprepared and outnumbered.

At least four-fifths of the Michigan militia were French speakers and illiterate. In this brand-new American territory, the French had just recently come from British rule. However, these French militiamen proved to be loyal to their new country. The American forces in Michigan continued to resist their captors.[28] In the summer of 1814, Joseph and Pierre Allard re-enlisted and served in James H. Audrain's Company of Spies.[25,26] In this case, "spy" meant scout or ranger, drawing on their familiarity with the terrain and with the Native American tribes that had sided with the British. Unfortunately, this company went on to have one of the few American defeats during the war.[28]

MACOMB COUNTY SETTLERS

Following the war, Joseph married Madeleine (Mary) Tremblay, his second cousin, on October 6, 1818 in Detroit.[24] They moved to a farm on the shores of Lake St. Clair, where they had seven children together. In 1818, the area bordering this lake had just been established as Macomb County, within Michigan Territory, as highlighted on the map at right. As noted earlier, Macomb County is on the northern border of Wayne County, where Detroit is the major city. Joseph continued to add to his land, and by age seventy-five in the 1870 census,[29] Joseph's farm was valued at $16,000, well above his neighbors on this census. This is equivalent to over $368,655 in 2023 dollars.[30] His closest neighbors in 1870 were his four sons (Joseph Jr., Paul, James, and Andrew), who were all established with their own farms.[29] Joseph had become quite a prosperous landowner.

Joseph and Mary's son, James Allard-Allor, born in 1832, was the sixth of their seven children and my direct ancestor.[31] James married Marine Forton Freton in 1854 when he was twenty-one, and she was fifteen.

Macomb County MI, on shore of Lake St. Clair

[31] The 1860 census listed James' occupation, at age twenty-seven, as a boatman.[32] But later censuses reported his occupation as a farmer,[33] as was the occupation for most residents in this region. The 1860 census reported that neither James nor his father, Joseph were able to read or write. However, later censuses reported that the next generation, including James' son Isadore and his eight siblings, could all read and write.

The Allor family's migration from Detroit to the shores of Lake St. Clair is similar to that of many of Detroit's French-Canadians. While the nineteenth century in Michigan showed significant population growth, with migrants coming from New York and New England and immigrants from Canada and Europe, the Lake St. Clair area remained predominantly French-Canadian. The Allor family continued to choose marriage partners from other *habitant* families. Today, the French-Canadian Heritage Society of Michigan often meets in the library in Mount Clemens,[34] the Macomb County seat, as this area still remains a center of French culture. This society has been very helpful to my research.

So far, I'm learning that French-Canadians are hardworking, fun, loyal, and enterprising. What's not to like?

THE FURTON-FORTON-FRÉTON FAMILY STORY

As I got to know the maternal family names tied to the Allors and Allards, I began to recognize similar names reappearing on different branches of the family tree.

As noted earlier, Isadore Allor married Mary Frances Furton. (see her ancestors at the end of this chapter) I saw Furton, Forton, and Freton. Her marriage record shows her name spelled as Forton, while other records show Furton. Was the handwriting clear? Was the top of the "u" open or closed with the recorder's handwriting? Mary Frances' father's name, Magliore Furton, was spelled differently at various censuses and in marriage and death records, as were his siblings' names. However, the lineage of people in this family appears to be connected. Apparently, these names were misspelled or officially changed over time. Going back in time, Fréton appears to be the original French spelling. I learned that such spelling variations are common among French-Canadian surnames. Most *habitants* were illiterate and, therefore, could not read or write their names. The priests—and even more modern census takers who documented official records—wrote what they heard. This is in addition to the Anglicized spellings that occurred later on.

But there is more to this Furton-Forton-Freton tangle: Isadore Allor's mother was Marine Forton. Marine was the daughter of Genevieve Peltier and Hubert Freton/Forton. Hubert was the son of Julien Fréton Jr. and his first wife, Therese Billeau. Thus, Magliore and Hubert were half-brothers. And therefore, Isadore Allor and Mary Frances Furton were half-cousins.[39] To complicate matters further, Hubert Freton's first wife was Archange Peltier. When she died, he married her cousin, Geneviève Peltier, who was Marine Forton's mother.[39] And, Mary Frances' sister Margaret married Leonard Peltier,[40] a distant cousin. This *is* a tangle!

Mary Frances Furton's grandfather was Julien Fréton Jr. He was a silversmith in the late 1700s in Detroit, according to the US Craftperson files on record at the Henry Ford Museum. However, no objects from his silver trade exist today.[41] Julien Jr. was born in the Grosse Pointe area on July 12, 1760, and he first married Therese Billiau dite Lesperance in Detroit on January 20, 1783, with whom he had ten children, including Hubert.[39] After her death, he married Catherine Thibault, also in Detroit, on May 20, 1811. They had four children, including Magliore,[37,39] leading to the tangle of marriages described above. The family lived in Grosse Pointe until around 1818 before moving to Mt. Clemons in Macomb County.

Julien Sr. was born in 1727 in the diocese of Nantes in Brittany, France. He came directly from France to Detroit in 1758.[37,39] A year later, he married fifteen-year-old Marie-Josephe Gastinon, dit Duchene, on February 12, 1759.[37] She was the daughter of François Gastinon dit Duchene and Marie-Josephe David, who had come to Detroit from Montreal, and were married there in January 1739.[42] They were among the founding families of Detroit.

The Fréton story became more interesting, and these intermarriages made more sense as I began to explore the historical context with these pioneer families in the founding of Detroit.

ISADORE ALLOR'S ANCESTORS

Pierre Allard
1716–aft 1759
&
M Angelique Bergevin
1722–abt 1787

Paul Guillaume LaForest
1725–1782
&
M Marguerite Tremblay
1725–1768

Jacques Allard
1746–aft 1807
&
M "Geneva" LaForest
1764–abt 1807

Francois J. Tremblay
1745–1818
&
Magdeleine Mesny
1754–1796

Jean Bapt Aide-Crequi
1729–1795
&
M Madeleine Gastinon M Gastinon dite Duchene
1747–1824

Julien Freton dit Nance
1728–abt 1767
&
Marie Francoise Mesny
1744–1813

J Biliou dit L'Esperance
1730–1787
&
M Catherine Meloche
1737–1786

Andre Pelletier Peltier
1737–1822
&
Francoise Souchereau
1755–1839

Etienne Godfrey Ballard
1747–1810

Joseph Allard Allor
1795–1878

Antoine Tremblay
1771–1817
&
Mary Louise Crequi
1779–1849

Julien Frérot
1760–1821
&
T Biliou dite L'Esperance
1769–1805

Isaac Peltier
1778–1833
&
Genevieve G. Ballard
1783–1824

James Allor
B: May 3, 1832–L'Anse Creuse, MI
D: June 13, 1920–Mt. Clemens, MI

Madeleine Tremblay
1798–1881

Hubert Fortin
1798–1871
&
Genevieve Peltier
1817–1883

Marine (Mary) Fortin
B: March 15, 1836–L'Anse Creuse, MI
D: December 14, 1876–Erin, MI

Isadore James Allor
B: August 24, 1856–L'Anse Creuse, MI
M: May 30, 1882–Mt. Clemens, MI
D: December 2, 1936–Detroit, MI

MARY FRANCES FURTON'S ANCESTORS

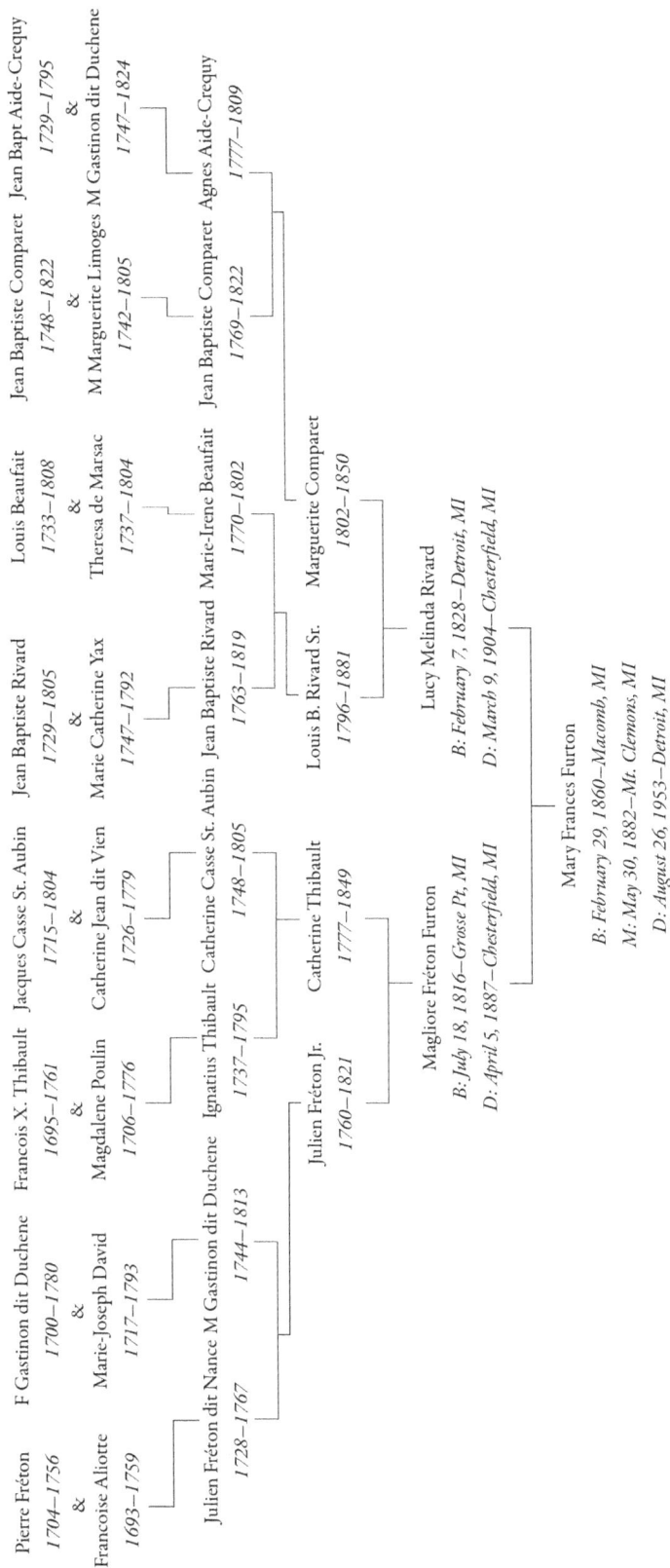

Jean Baptiste Comparet 1748–1822
Jean Bapt Aide-Crequy 1729–1795
&
M Marguerite Limoges 1742–1805
M Gastinon dit Duchene 1747–1824

Louis Beaufait 1733–1808
&
Theresa de Marsac 1737–1804

Jean Baptiste Comparet 1769–1822
Agnes Aide-Crequy 1777–1809

Jean Baptiste Rivard 1729–1805
Marie Catherine Yax 1747–1792

Marie-Irene Beaufait 1770–1802

Marguerite Comparet 1802–1850

Jacques Casse St. Aubin 1715–1804
&
Catherine Jean dit Vien 1726–1779

Jean Baptiste Rivard 1763–1819

Louis B. Rivard Sr. 1796–1881

Lucy Melinda Rivard
B: February 7, 1828–Detroit, MI
D: March 9, 1904–Chesterfield, MI

Francois X. Thibault 1695–1761
&
Magdalene Poulin 1706–1776

Ignatius Thibault 1737–1795
Catherine Casse St. Aubin 1748–1805

Catherine Thibault 1777–1849

Magliore Fréton Furton
B: July 18, 1816–Grosse Pt, MI
D: April 5, 1887–Chesterfield, MI

Pierre Fréton 1704–1756
&
Francoise Aliotte 1693–1759

F Gastinon dit Duchene 1700–1780
&
Marie-Joseph David 1717–1793

Julien Fréton dit Nance 1728–1767
M Gastinon dit Duchene 1744–1813

Julien Fréton Jr. 1760–1821

Mary Frances Furton
B: February 29, 1860–Macomb, MI
M: May 30, 1882–Mt. Clemons, MI
D: August 26, 1953–Detroit, MI

Le Détroit: The Strait

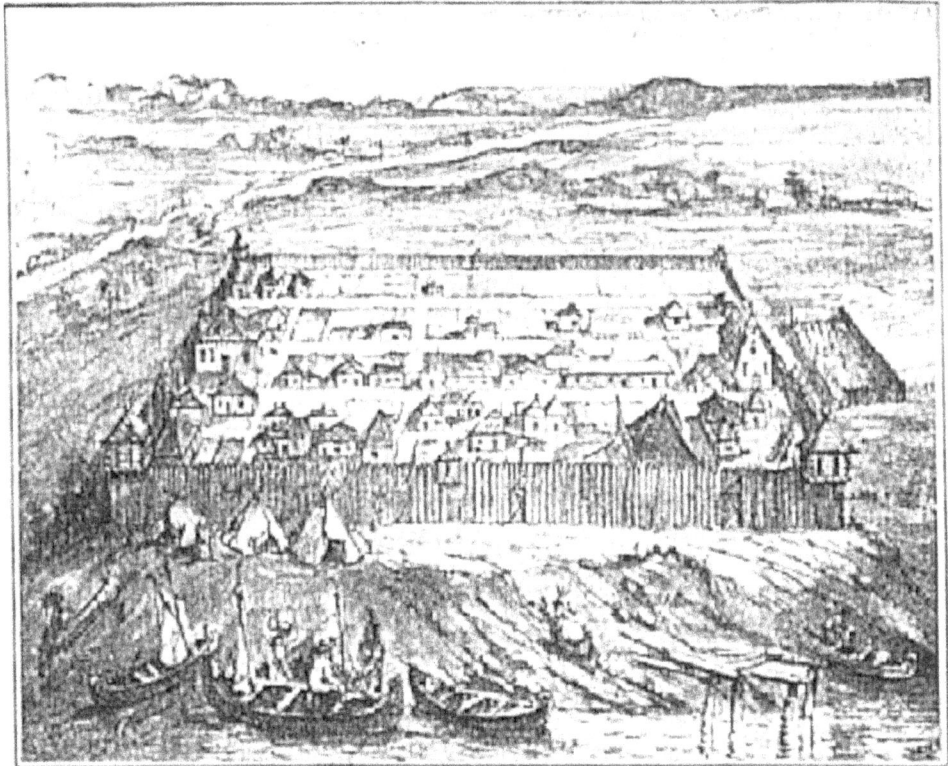

Fort Pontchartrain du Détroit

✤

THE FOUNDING OF *LE DÉTROIT*

As early as the 1600s, France had been establishing forts and settlements in North America to keep the British from moving west out of New England and to maintain a monopoly on the fur trade. Antoine de la Mothe Cadillac lobbied with French King Louis XIV that *le détroit*, or the straits, as it was called, would be a good place for such a fort. It was halfway between the French settlements on the Mississippi River and Quebec City.[1] The area was said to be uninhabited at the time, as the Iroquois had driven out the local tribes a few years before.[2]

On May 5, 1701, Cadillac received word from the king about funding and that he would be the commandant of the new fort. On June 4, 1701, Cadillac set sail for Detroit from Montreal with twenty-five canoes, fifty soldiers, and fifty-two *voyageurs* or hired men. The fort would be called *Fort Pontchartrain du Détroit*, named after the Comte de Pontchartrain, Minister of Marine under King Louis XIV.[3]

Cadillac's initiative would not have been possible without the Great Peace of Montreal treaty with the Indigenous nations. In the summer of 1701, 1300 representatives of around forty Indigenous nations, from as far away as the Mississippi, came by canoe to Montreal to reach a lasting peace with France.[2,4]

But the bold and impatient Cadillac left with his convoy while the peace negotiations were still underway. The Iroquois tribes lived along the southern shores of the St. Lawrence River, Lake Ontario, and Lake Erie, and they were unfriendly to the French. Therefore, Cadillac took the Northern route, away from any Iroquois threat along the Great Lakes, in case the agreement did not come about. The northern route went from the St. Lawrence, up the Ottawa River, connecting to the French River, to the French mission at Sault Ste Marie, and down Lake Huron. This route required thirty portages around rapids and waterfalls and between water routes, carrying the canoes and supplies on their backs over rough terrain at each juncture. The somewhat easier southern route followed the St. Lawrence River, Lake Ontario, and Lake Erie. After peace was secure, this shorter route would be used for both directions. These routes had been used by fur traders for many years, but no travel could be made during the long winters.[5]

Cadillac's convoy arrived at *le détroit* on July 24, 1701. Construction of the fort was completed about a month later. The men huddled in hastily assembled shelters while building the fifteen-foot-high fort walls with oak stakes that were sunk three feet into the ground. Bastions were constructed at each corner. This palisade surrounded an area of about one acre. The men then built the *magasin* or warehouse, which stored all the supplies, before constructing their dwellings. It was only men at first. In the Fall of 1701, a few women arrived, including the wives of Cadillac and his lieutenant, Alphonse de Tonty.[6] Other wives would not come for a few more years.

The fort had to be independent of the outside world for most things. The *voyageurs* and some of the soldiers returned to Montreal before that winter. But there would be many canoe trips, back and forth to Montreal, in the years to come. They carried supplies and merchandise for trading in the new settlement, and they would carry back furs for the European market.

I recognized several names of my ancestors within this history. Jacques Campeau (born 1677 in Montreal), one of my seventh great-grandfathers, first arrived at the fort in 1703. He was a blacksmith, edge toolmaker, and gunsmith. He was hired to provide the garrison with metalwork, such as hinges and gun parts. He and his brothers Etienne, Michel, and Jean were hired as *voyageurs* to carry the people and merchandise to and from the Fort. Jacques and Michel eventually brought their wives and settled there.[7,8]

Another of my seventh great-grandfathers, Jacob de Marsac (son of a medical doctor and baptized as protestant in 1675 in Poitou, France), was a sergeant in the Marines. He joined Cadillac's soldiers in 1706 and brought his wife with the 1706 convoy.[9,10]

Jean Casse dit St. Aubin, one of my sixth great-grandfathers, was a corporal (born around 1659, son of a merchant, in the diocese of St. Aubin-de-Blaye, in Gironde, France). He arrived in New France by 1700. He went to Détroit in 1706 and brought his wife the following year.[11] While Jean Casse dit St. Aubin's dit name refers to his hometown in France, his fellow soldiers referred to him simply as St. Aubin, and this is how his descendants came to be known.[12]

Living conditions in the fort were not good. Imagine the one-acre community inside the palisade walls: The early houses were made of vertical logs driven into the ground and sealed with grass and mud in the traditional French construction style called *poteaux-en-terre*. These houses had no windows, as glass was scarce and costly. Shutters would have been used instead. Roofs were made of straw or bark and sometimes covered with skins. Doors were propped up against the houses, as hinges were rare at the time.[14] It must have been cold inside during Winter. Eventually, with more supplies and with Jacques Campeau's blacksmithing skills, hinges would be added. Floors were hard-packed earth. Houses were barely tall enough to stand inside. Cadillac and his family had a larger house, although his house was built in the same traditional style.[13] There was a separate bakehouse and icehouse. The church was one of only two buildings built of logs, the other being the warehouse. The church would be called Sainte Anne's, and it has appeared in marriage and baptism records for generations (including in Father Ed Allor's time, as described in Chapter 5). Two priests, one Jesuit and one Recollet, accompanied the first party. Outside the fort walls, no less than half a gunshot away, as a measure, was a stable and barn for storing crops. There were some garden plots outside as well. Later, in 1706, a mill was built nearby.[14]

In October of 1703, a fire broke out inside the fort. It destroyed the church, along with Cadillac's and Tonty's houses. Initially, Jacques

Campeau attributed the fire to one of the Indians. Later, he testified that the fire had been caused by one of the soldiers. Ultimately, it came out that Madame Tonty had instigated the fire, and Jacques Campeau lied to protect the soldier and Madame Tonty, who had been ill at the time. The other soldier admitted to setting the fire. Jacques was fined to atone for having lied. He was never accused of setting the fire, although some early Detroit histories laid the blame on him. Later, after both Tonty and Cadillac had died, in 1734, King Louis XV exonerated Campeau completely due to his "impeccable reputation since the condemnation he was subjected to."[15]

Cadillac invited several Native groups to establish villages in the area, including the Huron, Ottawas, Miamis, and others, as these were his trading partners. Their proximity would facilitate this trade and hedge against their trade with the English. The Native people caught beaver and other animals, prepared the pelts, and then traded these for European supplies they learned to enjoy, including cooking pots, fabrics, axes, knives, guns, and alcohol. In 1703, there were about forty cabins of different Native Nations living in Detroit. By 1708, there were about 150 cabins of Native Americans living near the fort.[16]

The 1701 peace treaty didn't mean there were no longer any disputes between the tribes. In June 1706, while Cadillac was away, there were quarrels among several of the tribes at Detroit. The Ottawa attacked and killed seven of the Huron chiefs. Other Huron and Miami took refuge inside the fort. The French ordered the gates shut and fired on the Ottawa, who fired back in return. Meanwhile, some of the Miami tribe, now inside the fort, broke into the warehouse and stole the weapons intended for trade. During the battle, a few Miami, thirty Ottawa, and three Frenchmen, including a priest, were killed. Fearing retaliation from the French, the Ottawa left the area, and their Detroit village was burned.[17] Following the Ottawa's departure, Cadillac would grant this land to his settlers.[18]

There was longstanding disagreement about selling alcohol to the Native Americans. The priests argued this was immoral, as the Native people would trade a great part of their furs for brandy, not leaving enough for other products they needed. The King prohibited the sale of alcohol to the Natives, but Cadillac openly sold brandy from his office to his soldiers and the Natives for a profit. He claimed that he would not sell enough at a time to intoxicate the Native people. Cadillac also argued that if the French didn't sell the brandy, the Native people would buy it from the English.[19]

The success of the fur trade and the long reach of the French into North America would not have been possible without a strong working relationship with the Native population. French communities were always open to Native Americans. They joined one another for foot races, lacrosse, and hunting parties and sat side-by-side in saunas. They learned one another's languages and entertained each other with songs and stories on the long winter nights. The Native people taught the French how to make birch-bark canoes, moccasins, and snowshoes as the French learned how to adapt to the harsh Northern climate. They exchanged cultural practices on diet, clothing, diplomacy, and war. The Natives would not consider a military alliance without establishing social relationships. The English and Anglo-Americans looked down on this familiarity as they maintained their traditional European dress and practices, regardless of the climate and conditions. Native Americans became allies in the many French wars against the English, who in turn had their own relationships with different tribes, especially the Iroquois.[20]

A MORE PERMANENT SETTLEMENT BEGINS

During the first years at Fort Ponchartrain, there was only a small cadre of men supporting the post. Cadillac himself was absent between 1704 and 1706 while he was in Montreal and Quebec, answering charges for illegal fur and alcohol trading. Although Cadillac was the Commandant of Fort Ponchartrain, he was responsible to the private company that managed the fur trade, the Governor of the Colony, and ultimately the King. But he had a free-wheeling and autocratic style, which brought on a lot of dissent. By 1705, he was exonerated of the charges. By then, however, the private fur trading company was in financial trouble; therefore, the King gave Cadillac total responsibility for the Fort and its fur trade. Permission was also granted to invite wives and families to settle in and around the fort.[21]

A flurry of marriages ensued as Cadillac hired the *voyageurs* and soldiers for the 1706 convoy to return to Detroit. This flurry included Jacob de Marsac. Soldiers were not permitted to marry without the commandant's permission. Sometimes, a marriage contract was used one to two years before the church wedding because the soldier's permission to marry had not yet been granted.[22] This was the case with Jacob, who undertook a marriage contract in 1704 with Therese David before he was sent off on a military campaign to fight the English.[23]

The marriage contract, in the Custom of Paris, was a legal agreement in anticipation of marriage, and these records provide a window into relationships and circumstances of the times. The contract is signed by key witnesses and is often accompanied by a celebration more elaborate than the wedding itself. It identifies commonly held marital property, as well as separate property, such as for second marriages, especially where there were children from the earlier marriage. Inheritance laws are also part of this contract.[23] In Jacob's case, it could serve as a will, leaving all his possessions to his intended bride in case he didn't return from combat. Sometimes, one or more children were born before the church wedding. In fact, Jacob and Therese had a son in 1704 in Montreal. This son died before they departed for Detroit. Jacob's bride, Thérèse David, was the forty-year-old widow of Massé Martin. She had six children from her prior marriage, including Claude Martin, who was himself a *voyageur* to Detroit.[24] Their formal wedding occurred on June 12, 1706,[10] just before the convoy's departure on June 20.[24]

The 1706 convoy, with Jacob de Marsac and his pregnant wife, included 270 people (twenty-five families, 150 soldiers, and hired men).

Sixteen of the twenty-five families included new brides. The convoy arrived on August 8, 1706.[21,24] Jacob and Thérèse had a son, Francois de Marsac, my direct ancestor, born on October 22 that year; another son (Jacques) was born the following November 1708.[25] Cadillac granted Jacob de Marsac two lots inside the fort that bordered Cadillac's own village lot, along with a garden plot and a larger farm.[10] The Marsacs were clearly industrious and lived a relatively prosperous life for the time. The elder Marsacs, Jacob and Thérèse, died in Detroit in 1747 and 1727, respectively.[10,25]

Cadillac made 150 land grants to heads of families, soldiers, and *voyageurs*. This included sixty-eight lots inside the fort, thirteen garden plots outside the fort, and thirty-one larger farms along the river. Individual lots inside the fort were roughly twenty-five by twenty-five feet.[26] Land grants didn't mean the recipient owned the land. In the custom adapted from French common law, the land belonged to the Crown, and grantees paid annual usage fees. Cadillac also brought some cattle, and he sold the milk for a significant profit.[27] The cattle multiplied and eventually became a foundation for expanded farming. A brewery was built in 1706, as Cadillac had sent for a master brewer from Montreal to join the community.[28]

Jean Casse St. Aubin made his way back to Quebec City, where he married Marie-Louisa Gauthier on February 2, 1707. He was then in his mid-forties, and she was twenty-eight, unusually old for a bride. They had two children in Quebec City. Then, in March 1708, Jean was granted a lot inside the fort, which he later exchanged for other property. In September 1708, Jean and Marie Louise borrowed funds for merchandise needed for a voyage to Detroit. They departed that Fall for Detroit with their two young sons.[12] They had eight more children there, including my direct ancestor Jacques Casse St. Aubin (b. 1718).[29] Jacques Casse St. Aubin's descendants led into Mary Frances Furton's family tree. The elder Jean Casse dit St. Aubin died in Detroit in 1759 in his nineties, although some records show he was a hundred years old. Marie-Louisa lived another ten years when she died at age eighty-nine.[12]

They were a hearty couple, especially considering the rugged conditions in which they lived.

VOYAGEURS

Jacques Campeau already had a wife back in Montreal, as he had married Cécile Catin there in 1699 when he was age twenty-two and she was eighteen. They started their family between Jacques' trips back and forth, traveling with his *voyageur* brothers. Three of their children were born in Montreal between 1702 and 1707.[8]

Voyageurs were like the truck drivers of their day, carrying goods and people on the watery highways. Only it was considerably more arduous! They always traveled in convoys for safety, teamwork, and protection from the English or Iroquois during times of war.

Voyageurs were hired to paddle the canoes. Most were prohibited from trading, although Cadillac permitted his Detroit settlers who had fulfilled their obligations (i.e., they paid their annual rent) to bring as much merchandise as they wanted from Montreal and sell it to the Indians and other French settlers for a profit. Therefore, not only did families make the difficult journey to move to this distant outpost, far from any conveniences in the home colony, but many husbands and some wives went back and forth frequently. The *voyageurs* were required to register in Montreal and carry their trading license or permission with them.[30,31]

Canoes during that period were about thirteen to sixteen feet long with two paddlers or eighteen to twenty-four feet with three or four paddlers. Clothing was also carefully selected. Men wore loose clothing, with leggings or bare legs and moccasins. Native-style clothing was much more practical than trousers and leather shoes. Women also wore practical clothing, such as moccasins and shorter skirts than would be worn in Montreal.[31]

Records show that both Jacques and Cécille borrowed funds to purchase supplies for their 1708 voyage. On their behalf, funds were also borrowed by Cécille's father, Henri Catin, a merchant butcher in Montreal, and Jacques' widowed mother, Catherine Paulo. Cécille herself signed another obligation for merchandise, as she apparently had power of attorney to sign for her husband.[8] These records document the entrepreneurial spirit and financial risks these families made to create a livelihood in the distant outposts. They clearly had their extended family's support.

Yet, it was much more than a financial risk for the family. In September 1708, Jacques and Cécille departed for Detroit with their three children, ages fourteen months to six years old. The journey of more than 650 miles would take five to six weeks, including the eight-mile portage around Niagara Falls. Canoes were packed with as much merchandise for trade as possible, leaving little room for people or food. The Women and children were squeezed in the middle, with paddlers in front and behind them. They spent fourteen to sixteen hours each day in the canoes between camps.[31]

Leaving from Montreal, the convoy's route went upstream, against the current, on the St. Lawrence River. Before reaching Lake Ontario, there was a long stretch of rapids that required one or more portages. Each canoe had to be completely emptied before it was carried upside-down on a man's shoulders to the next point of the voyage. Other men carried two ninety-pound packets of supplies on their backs. Women carried the small children to keep them close over the rough terrain. It did not get any easier once they reached the Great Lakes. The large lakes brought winds and choppy waters. It was safest to paddle close to shore, but it was always tempting to save time by crossing a bay. That could be dangerous if winds came up quickly out on the open water. Canoes could capsize, people could drown, and supplies would be lost. It was critical to keep an eye on the weather.[31]

During the six-week journey, they certainly experienced some rain and wind, and they got wet from rain or splashing waves. The children surely got restless or afraid. It was no better on sunny days, as the sun would bear down relentlessly on the open water. Mosquitos and black flies would hover over them like clouds, and the travelers would pray for wind or waves. But there would also be the soothing rhythm of paddling, hypnotic strokes in synchrony with one another. The paddlers would sing old French folk songs to keep them going on the long days.

At night, the canoes were rested on their sides, with a tarp over for shelter. Evergreen boughs or animal robes were used as bedding. The soft cargo was used as pillows. The men would hunt and fish to supplement the convoy's dried provisions. All would have to share in camp duties, including watching the young children to make sure they didn't wander off into the wilderness or drown in the river or lake.[31]

In July 1710, Jacques and Cécille returned to Montreal together, this time with four children, ages eighteen months to eight years. Only, this time, during the eight-mile Niagara Falls portage, on her way down the long descent from the falls to the river, Cécille gave birth to a son. A *voyageur*, Nicolas Rose, provided an emergency baptism rite with the application of holy oils and the renunciation of Satan. Once they arrived in Montreal, a proper church baptism was conducted. Nicolas Rose was named the newborn's godfather, and the boy was named Nicolas in his honor. Later, Nicolas Campeau became known as Niagara Campeau.[8] Cécille had another son, Jean Baptiste Campeau, in Montreal the following summer of 1711. Then, in 1713, Jacques Campeau was granted a license to work again as a tool-maker back in Detroit. The family returned to Detroit in September of 1713, this time with six children on board.[8,9] The couple had another daughter, my direct ancestor Thérèse Cécille Campeau, in the summer of 1714 in Detroit.[32] The family made yet another voyage back to Montreal in late 1714 or early 1715. Cécille died at age thirty-four in Montreal, following the birth of their eighth child on August 25, 1715.[7,8]

Jacques Campeau returned to Detroit with his children. He didn't remarry. In 1734, he was awarded forty arpents (approximately thirty-four acres) outside of the fort. That same year, Jacques' daughter, Thérèse Cécille Campeau, married Jacob de Marsac's son, François de Marsac.[32] Thérèse and François had a daughter, Thérèse de Marsac, who in turn married Louis Beaufait, whose descendants lead into Mary

Frances Furton's family tree. By the 1740s, in addition to blacksmithing, Jacques had developed one of the best all-purpose merchant houses, buying and selling furs, wheat, corn, and bread. By 1750, he became too ill to work and died the next year at age seventy-three.[9] This is what it took to be an entrepreneur in early Detroit. This is grit!

RIBBON FARMS

Over time, living conditions improved. The early rough houses were clapboarded over and whitewashed. Second floors or lofts were sometimes added. Yards were enclosed with picket fences. As the population grew, the fort walls were pushed out.[13]

The larger farm lots outside the fort were later referred to as "ribbon farms." These were long, narrow lots, giving each family river frontage of 400 to 900 feet and a depth of two to three miles. Ribbon farms were also common along the St. Lawrence River in Quebec, and evidence of them is still observable today. The river was the highway, allowing the farmers to transport their goods to the marketplace. It was also the source of drinking water and fishing. Farmhouses were all close to the river, permitting easier communication between lots and increased safety in this proximity. During times of conflict, the farm families would move inside the fort for further safety. The long lots also permitted more variation of soil and drainage. Over time, orchards were planted, along with wheat and barley.[33]

Cadillac was not popular. Many called him a tyrant. There were frequent complaints as he charged his soldiers for food and supplies when they should have received room and board in exchange for their service. He was often accused of mismanagement of funds. He frequently quarreled with the priests. A report to the French minister Pontchartrain in 1708 stated he was hated by the French and the Indians for his tyranny, and his behavior threatened the loss of French control over the Great Lakes.[34] By 1710, he was pushed out. He was reassigned as the governor of the Louisiana colony.[35]

Remnants of ribbon farms as seen today in Quebec

The first census in Detroit in 1710 totaled thirty-four settlers. This number included farmers with wives, married men whose wives didn't come with them to Detroit, and soldiers who had houses.[36,37] This small cadre had to be close-knit in order to manage this isolated outpost.

CHIEF PONTIAC AND FRIENDS

The decades after Cadillac's departure were difficult for the settlers. Despite Cadillac's and other Detroit commandants' urging, the French government saw the fort as primarily a trading post and not as a settlement. The government provided minimal support. Settlers continued to come nonetheless. One of these new settlers included my sixth great-grandfather, Pierre Meloche. Pierre was born in Montreal in 1701.[38] In 1729, he entered into an agreement to lead a canoe expedition to Detroit as an agent for his father, Francois.[38] Five of Pierre's six brothers were *voyageurs,* and his father was a merchant. But Pierre was also a carpenter, having skills that would be valuable in the Detroit settlement. Pierre departed from Lachine, near Montreal, in August 1729, one week after he married Jeanne Caron.[39] The family settled on land near Parent Creek, which joins the Detroit River near Belle Isle. He and Jeanne had thirteen children together at this farm. Their daughter Marie Catherine Meloche married André Pelletier, whose descendants married into the Allor family.[38]

Pierre's home was opposite his workshop. He also had a sawmill on the opposite side of the river. Pierre Meloche had a close friendship with Chief Pontiac and the Ottawa tribe, as did most of the French families in the region.[40] While Pierre died in 1760, the land stayed with the family. The family friendship with the Ottawa tribe would become historically important a few years later.

After the British conquest of the French colony in 1760, the new British Commandant of Fort Pontchartrain rigidly tightened the fur trade, which angered both the French *habitants* and the Indians and sparked what became known as Pontiac's Rebellion in 1763. The Ottawa Chief Pontiac rallied other tribes and captured the fort, holding siege for several months. During this siege, Pontiac camped on the Meloche family farm. When the British attempted to break Pontiac's siege, this land was the site of the Battle of Bloody Run, where Chief Pontiac and other Indians defeated the British on July 31, 1763. Parent Creek was renamed Bloody Run after this battle.[40] The siege ended in a stalemate in October. Pontiac lifted the siege when he realized the French were not coming to his aid and some of his followers had waned.[41]

This rebellion became much bigger than Detroit, however. Indian tribes throughout the Great Lakes were unhappy with the new British policies. The British treated them more as conquered people than as allies, as they had been with the French. The British no longer provided the Indians with supplies for their fur trade. The British were distrustful of the Indians and would not sell them gunpowder, which they used to hunt for food for their families. In turn, the Indians thought the British were withholding ammunition with plans for war against them.[41] The Indians were not wrong about that.

Pontiac may not have orchestrated other rebellions, but various tribes overtook several former French forts in Pennsylvania, Ohio, Illinois, and elsewhere in Michigan. There were heavy casualties, including white settlers attempting to flee those areas where Native people had been living a generation earlier. In turn, these events led to raids on Indians who had been living peacefully among white settlers in western Pennsylvania.[41] News traveled fast, even in the mid-eighteenth century. Things got ugly. Fort Pitt in Ohio country had been taken siege by Delaware Indians, with 330 soldiers and 200 women and children inside. The British commander gave out smallpox-infected blankets to representatives of the Delaware Indians, a crude biological warfare. However, the war continued with many more costly battles on several fronts.

By 1765, the British decided the Indian occupation of the former French forts could be better resolved with diplomacy than military force. They sought a treaty with Pontiac, mistakenly believing he had power over all the other tribes. A rather symbolic treaty was signed in July 1766 at Fort Ontario. No land was ceded, and no prisoners were exchanged. The British did proclaim a boundary between the British colonies and the Indian lands West of the Appalachians. However, this became another factor contributing to the American Revolution, as many of the colonists sought westward expansion.[41] With the British conquest of New France, suddenly, all the rules changed for the Native people. They were no longer treated with respect, as allies and friends. We also know that relations between the Americans and the Indians went further downhill from there.

I had covered some of these historical events in school in my American history classes, albeit briefly. But they didn't stick in my memory, at least not beyond the final exam. And I'm sure we didn't learn that Cadillac was a scoundrel and a tyrant. We didn't learn about *voyageurs* that I remember. But that was more likely covered in Canadian history, which I didn't cover at all, certainly not from a French-Canadian perspective. With my own family members as players in these stories, suddenly, history is interesting again!

8

THE KING'S RATIONS

1750

United Kingdom
France
Spain

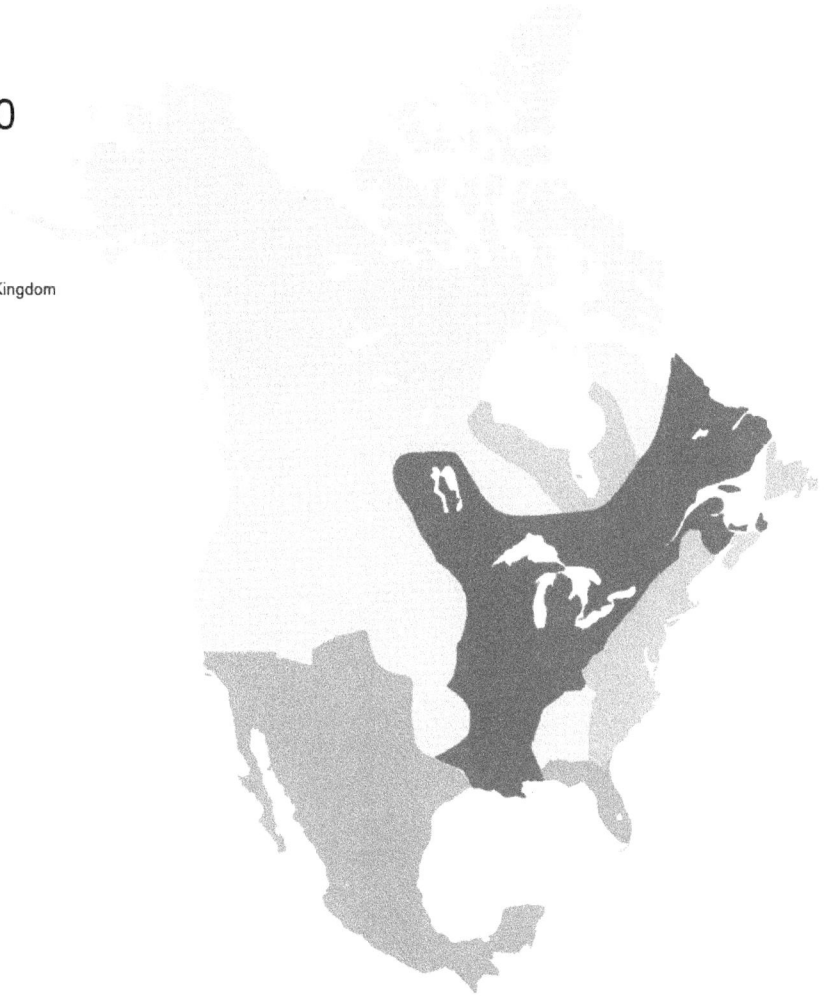

French colonization in 1750, shaded dark

❧

DETROIT 1749-1763

To understand the larger context of French settlement in North America, the territory that was colonized by France as of 1750 extended from near Hudson's Bay and the Labrador Sea in the north to the Great Lakes region and Canadian prairies in the west and to the Gulf of Mexico in the south. The English had settled colonies along the east coast, and Spain held Florida and the southwest. There was serious competition for the North American resources and the interests of the Indigenous people who already lived in these regions. This brought several significant military conflicts. Therefore, the map of territories would change multiple times over the next few years.

By 1749, the French King Louis XV became more concerned about English incursions into the Great Lakes region and thought he needed more incentives to bring French settlers into this frontier.[1] Therefore, in May 1749, the following proclamation from the King was posted in villages along Quebec's St. Lawrence River:

> *Every man who will settle in Detroit will receive gratuitously one spade, one axe, one ploughshare, one large and one small wagon. He will make an advance of other tools to be paid for in two years only. He will be given a cow of which he will return the increase, also a sow; seed will be advanced the first year to be returned at the third harvest. The women and children will be supported the one year. Those will be deprived of the liberality of the King who shall give themselves up to trade in place of agriculture.*[2]

102

Along with these "King's Rations," the settlers would be given land on which to farm. As was the case with Cadillac's land grants, the land belonged to the Crown, and the settlers would be required to pay annual usage fees.

Among the first to accept the King's "invitation" in 1750 were the brothers Pierre, Augustin, and Ambroise Tremblay, along with Paul Guillaume LaForest, who was married to their niece, Marguerite Tremblay. Ambroise was married to Marguerite Simard, while her sister Magdalene Simard was married to Pierre Tremblay. Augustin Tremblay was married to LaForest's older sister, Marie Judith. Thus, it was an extended family of Tremblays and LaForests that paddled Westward with their eleven children.[1] It was truly a family affair. In 1751, they became the first permanent settlers of Grosse Pointe, near the junction of the Detroit River and Lake St. Clair. They all came from the rural village of Baie-Saint-Paul on the north shore of the St. Lawrence River,[1] halfway between Quebec City and the river's outlet on the Atlantic Ocean. Three of these families are my ancestors. It was Mary Geneva LaForest, daughter of Marguerite Tremblay and Paul Guillaume LaForest, who married Jacques Allard after he arrived from Quebec (as described in Chapter 6). Then, Jacques and Geneva's son Joseph Allard married Madeleine Tremblay, a great-granddaughter of Ambroise Tremblay and Marguerite Simard.[3]

The King's Rations incentive seems akin to the Homestead Act a century later, which spurred many American settlers to head west on wagon trains. These were the subject of many television westerns in my childhood. This was a French-Canadian version, where the wagon trains were convoys of canoes. I imagine the challenges en route were similar to those wagon trains, although Hollywood may not have imagined all that these families encountered.

THE YAX FAMILY—FIRST GERMANS IN DETROIT

Michael Yax and Catherine Herbinne have a remarkable pioneer story of their own. Both were born in Germany, and their story is recounted in books that acclaim them as the first Germans in Detroit. Their families frowned upon their relationship because one was upper-class and the other was from a lower-class family. Furthermore, Michael was Catholic, and Catherine was Lutheran. Therefore, due to family and society's disapproval, they left Germany to start a new life together. Their ship "Lydia" docked in Philadelphia in 1740. Michael changed his name from Jacks to Yax upon arrival. The couple married in Philadelphia and settled briefly in the Germantown colony in Pennsylvania. Then, around 1747, they decided to walk to the Mississippi River. There were no roads or maps, only Indian footpaths at the time. They aimed to join a German colony at Point Coupée, Louisiana (near present-day Baton Rouge). The couple walked across Pennsylvania, across what was then wilderness. In the area that is now Kentucky, the family was captured by a band of Ottawa Indians. This tribe was from near Detroit, and they made forays into the area of Kentucky from time to time. The Ottawas apparently thought one or more of the family would be valuable for ransom, so they took their prisoners to the fort of Detroit and ransomed them to the Commandant, M. De Longuiel. The Ottawa capturers were rewarded, and the Yax family was freed.[4] Another version of the story states that the Ottawas took Catherine, intending to sell her to the French as a slave. Michael was spared death because of his ability to cut new trails in the wilderness and perform other tasks due to his training as an engineer and surveyor.[5] In both versions, they arrived in Detroit, where the French released Catherine to her husband, Michael Yax. The couple had a daughter named Marie Catherine, born February 2, 1747. They were far from their original destination, but they decided to stay. Fortunately, with the benefit of the King's Rations, the family was given three arpents (2.53 acres) of land in 1751 at Grosse Pointe, along with supplies, and they settled down to farming.[4]

Catherine Herbinne has her own distinction. While she was raised Lutheran and remained so after her marriage to Michael Yax, she became the first convert from Protestantism to be received into the Catholic Church in Detroit in 1755. This became a major event in the small French community, presided over by Father Bouquet and representatives of the King; it became the longest baptismal entry devoted to an individual in the pages of St. Anne's register.[4,6]

The Yaxes had eleven children, the oldest of whom was Marie Catherine, my direct ancestor, who was born possibly on the route from Pennsylvania or in Detroit in 1747.[7] It was Marie Catherine Yax who passed her German language down to her great-great-granddaughter Mary Frances Furton Allor and in turn to Mary Frances' son, Father Edward Allor, as described in Chapter 5.

A NOTEWORTHY WOMAN

It seems that for women to be noteworthy in history during these times, they had to be either extraordinary or scandalous. It is unclear which descriptor applies to my fifth great-grandmother, Marie-Francoise (Mary) Mesny (sometimes spelled Mini or Meny). Much of women's history comes from church records, so these are the recorded milestones from which her history is known. Mary had a long string of church records. She was born in Detroit on June 17, 1744, and she married Jean-Baptiste Billiau dit Lesperance in Detroit on May 8, 1758, when she was not quite fourteen years old.[8] It was not uncommon for girls that age to get married, usually to older men, although you might wonder about her maturity to start a family. Jean Baptiste was then age twenty-seven. According to the marriage record, Jean Baptiste was a French soldier, and he may also have been a *voyageur* and merchant to the Miami tribe in Indian country,[8] suggesting he traveled quite a bit in what is present-day Illinois, Indiana, and southern Michigan. The couple settled on the south side of the Detroit River in what is now Windsor, Canada.

The couple had six children between 1760 and 1770 (Jean-Baptiste, Mary Jane, Louis, Francois Xavier, Therese, and Catherine).[9] Their daughter and my ancestor, Therese Billieau dit Lesperance, was the first wife of Julien Fréton Jr., as mentioned in Chapter 6, and the second great-grandparent of Mary Frances Furton.

Sometime after 1771, Mary met Charles Morand dit Grimard, whose wife Marguerite Simard died at childbirth on May 9, 1771.[10] Charles and Marguerite's infant son died three months later. In fact, before Marguerite and Charles married, Charles, then at age forty-one, had been a long-term bachelor. Marguerite Simard was the widow of Ambroise Tremblay, one of the founding families of Grosse Pointe described in Chapter 8,[1] and she was my ancestor as well, as noted above. To make matters even more complicated, Marie's sister, Magdeleine Mesny, was married to François Tremblay, who was Ambroise Tremblay and Marguerite Simard's son. Thus, the Mesny sisters are both fifth grandmothers to me through the Allor family tree. This story is so entangled!

Charles and Mary Mesny went on to develop a relationship and had three boys together (Antoine, Charles, and Pierre) between 1773 and 1776, while Mary was still married to Jean-Baptiste Billiau dit Lesperance. All of these boys took Mary's husband's surname.[9] Was Jean-Baptiste away a lot during these years so that he didn't notice? Maybe she thought he would not return or he was dead. Charles lived in Grosse Pointe; therefore, he was across the river and a canoe trip away from the Lesperance household. He was not a close neighbor. Where did they meet up? At that time, families lived in one-room houses with kitchen, living, and sleeping space all in that one room. There was no privacy for a tryst. With her husband away, Mary would have been responsible for managing her household and farm, along with feeding and caring for her many children.

In the baptism record for their son Antoine in 1773, Charles admitted he was the father from an adulterous relationship.[12] At that point, Mary was twenty-nine, and Charles was forty-four. The church excommunicated both Charles and Mary on January 23, 1774,[11] but they had two more children after that. Those baptism records also indicated that each child was *fils adulterin,* the adulterous son of (Mary) Francoise.[12] Throughout this time, Mary was still married to Jean-Baptiste. Divorce was very rare at the time. After two attempts at ex-communication from the Catholic church that went as far as the authorities in Quebec, it was obvious the church was not influencing what was going on in the lives of Charles and Mary.[11]

Mary Mesny's story didn't end there. Mary had another child, Monique, in 1784, who was said to be the child of her husband, Jean-Baptiste. Monique lived just two months.[9] Charles Morand dit Grimard died in 1785.[13] There is no record of Mary's husband Jean-Baptiste's death; he may indeed have disappeared during his travels and was declared dead before 1788. In February 1788, Mary remarried to Michel Houde.[14] She and Michel Houde had a child together in November of that year (Geneviève Houde) when Mary was forty-four. Michel Houde died in 1793.[15] Mary remarried yet again in 1804 to Simon Drouillard,[16] but he died the following year.[17]

It is unclear whether Mary was really excommunicated, given that all these marriages and her children's baptisms were performed in the Catholic church. Her later husbands apparently were not put off by her earlier history. Mary was also documented as participating in the Catholic Day of Adoration in 1805.[18] In fact, in 1805, Father Gabriel Richard, who was reported to be a "no-nonsense priest," called Mary "a flower of the flock"![11] Mary died in March of 1812 at age sixty-seven,[19] after four marriages, including her unofficial marriage. She outlived all of her husbands! She also raised eleven children, mostly on her own. She apparently reconciled with her church. Did she find redemption between these few recorded milestones? Mercy is a Christian tenet, after all. It would be too easy for us to judge this woman from a distance of 200 years. If she were in our family today, would we disown her? Or, would we see the sinner/woman, with all the messy flaws of all humans, still deserving of mercy and redemption? Was she extraordinary, or was she scandalous? She may have been both. I think she was at least a very resilient woman.

THE BRIDES' LEGACIES

Once the French and Indian War broke out in 1754, Fort Pontchartrain became a major supply post for the war. After the British conquest in 1760, Detroit was under a military regime as elsewhere in Quebec (noted earlier and in Chapter 6). The *habitants* were allowed to occupy and cultivate lands that had been assigned under the French regime. Now, the fees for this privilege would go to support the British garrison at Fort Pontchartrain.[1] Yet even these disruptions did not stop settlers from arriving. Many new arrivals during this period seemed to be bachelor young men who married daughters of families that had arrived earlier. These brides were often very young, aged fourteen or fifteen. They produced many children who could share in the farm work.

Julien Fréton Sr. arrived directly from Nantes, France, in 1758 and settled in Grosse Pointe. A year after he arrived, he married fourteen-year-old Marie-Joseph Gastinon dit Duchene,[20] who became my fifth great-grandmother. A few years later, Marie-Joseph's sister, Marie Madeleine, married Jean Baptiste Aide dit Crequy IV, who arrived around 1762.[21] Marie Madeleine was then age fourteen herself, and she became another of my fifth great-grandmothers. These sisters' parents, François Gastinon dit Duchene and Marie-Josephe David, were married in Detroit in 1739 and had already established a farm at Grosse Pointe.[1]

Another arrival directly from France was Louis Beaufait in 1761; he married another fifth great-grandmother of mine: Therese de Marsac,[22] daughter of Francois de Marsac and Thérèse Campeau, from among the early Detroit settlers' families. Louis Beaufait played an important role in Detroit's history after it came under American rule. He became a justice of the peace and an associate justice of the Court of Common Pleas. He also held offices in the militia.[23]

By 1762, there were ten new land grants along the lake in Grosse Pointe.[1] These included two more of my ancestor families. Jean Baptiste Rivard obtained a farm next to the Yaxes, and he married their fifteen-year-old daughter, my fifth great-grandmother, Marie Catherine Yax.[24]

Ignatius Thibault arrived in 1768. That same year, he married my fourth great-grandmother, Marie-Catherine St. Aubin,[25] who was then a mature age of twenty! They also settled on a ribbon farm at Grosse Pointe. Catherine St. Aubin was the granddaughter of Jean Casse St. Aubin and Marie Louise Gauthier, described earlier among the Detroit pioneers.

This is a lot of names—too many to remember. None of them carries a particular story that survives. But from these names and the stories that have survived, I confirmed I am part of the first eighty years' history of French settlement in Detroit. Interestingly, it was by following the maternal lines of Isadore Allor's and Mary Frances Furton's family trees that led me back to these many great-grandparents in Michigan. There, I found the Campeaus, St. Aubins, de Marsacs, and many others (see the family trees at the end of Chapter 6).

While it is the men's names that more often show up in history, the women were pioneers in their own right. They braved the elements on the voyages, along with their husbands and children. They created a working household and farm from scratch with minimal supplies. They cared for the children, tended the fields, and managed the farm while their husbands were away for many months trading and trapping.[1] They clearly shaped the destinies of their families and the region. The King's Rations brought many of the bachelors, but it was the available brides that ensured they would leave a legacy.

Of course, these families came from the earlier generations of intrepid pioneers who arrived in North America and settled in Quebec.

QUÉBÉCOIS—INHABITANT OF QUEBEC

Statue of Samuel de Champlain in modern Quebec City[6]

❧

FRANÇOIS ALLARD WAS THE FIRST OF THE ALLARD FAMILY TO arrive in Quebec from France in 1666.[1] François was the great-great-grandfather of Jacques Allard, whom we met in Chapter 6 when he migrated from Quebec to Detroit in 1774. We'll come back to François' story shortly. But there are connecting family lines that take us back all the way to the very first French settlers of Quebec.

WHO WAS HÉLÈNE DESPORTES?

HÉLÈNE WAS THE FIRST WHITE CHILD BORN IN THE SAINT LAWrence area. She was born in the second half of the year 1620 in Quebec.[2] This was around the same time as when the Pilgrims landed in Plymouth, Massachusetts.

Hélène was named after her godmother, Hélène Bouille,[3] the wife of Samuel de Champlain, who had founded the Quebec settlement in 1608.[4] Samuel de Champlain is considered the father of Quebec. Hélène Bouille had traveled with her husband to the colony in 1620, and she was present at Hélène's birth. Hélène Desportes' parents were Françoise Langlois and Pierre-Phillipe Desportes, who was a lawyer in the Paris Parliament and an investor in Champlain's colony.[3]

Champlain had explored the St. Lawrence River and Great Lakes as early as 1603,[4] but exploration of this area began long before. The first to claim the territory for France was Jacques Cartier, who spent the winter of 1535 in the vicinity of Quebec. He explored other nearby areas as well but abandoned them all around 1543 and returned to France.[5] Decades before these explorers, there were French, Portuguese, Dutch, Basque, Spanish, and English who fished on the Grand Banks off Newfoundland and off the North American mainland.[5] By the end of the sixteenth century, the French had a well-established fur trade along the St. Lawrence River.

Champlain was the first to establish a permanent settlement here in 1608, choosing a narrow stretch of the river below a great promontory at the water's edge. He judged this site could be controlled by a few choke points on the river, and it was close to the fur trade. The Algonquin tribes called this area "kebec," meaning "the narrows." Champlain borrowed this term to name his settlement and to recognize the Native peoples' history there.[7]

It was still a very primitive settlement in 1620. During that Winter, there were just sixty individuals, with just six women and one other child who had been born in Paris. They all huddled in Champlain's "Habitation" on the riverbank, with the cliff behind them. On top of that cliff, a fort was built, along with a stone farmhouse belonging to Louis Hébert, Quebec's first farmer who would later become Hélène's father-in-law. Rising beyond that was the blue-green silhouette of the Laurentian Mountain range. The Habitation was built over a two-year period, from 1608 to 1610. It held lodging for Champlain, the governor, and for all others, including the newborn Hélène. It also included a kitchen, a dovecote, a munitions warehouse, a blacksmith shop, and a cellar. A second-story gallery encircled the structure, surrounded by a wooden stockade, outside of which was a ten-foot-wide promenade extending to the border of a moat. A drawbridge over the moat could be raised as necessary. Canons were mounted on platforms inside the stockade.[8,9]

The settlement included a small posting of soldiers, missionaries, clerks, workmen, stonemasons, carpenters, a butcher, needlemakers, and farm laborers. Not everyone chose to stay in this wilderness over the winter, instead sailing back to France at the end of summer. It was a long winter, with ice forming on the river at the end of October and staying until May. Initially, all supplies were brought in from France, and ships sailed only between May and early Fall.[9]

Champlain's Habitation in Quebec[8]

While there was a small kitchen garden, it took several years before the settlement could grow enough food during the short growing season to carry them over the winter. Hunger was common in winter. Soup was the typical diet of the French on both sides of the Atlantic, along with the large round loaf of bread. Peas were the base of the soup, garden vegetables were added, along with some mushrooms and edible roots from the woods, and sometimes salt pork, meat, or fish would be added, if available. In winter, the soup was much thinner. A piece of bread would go in the bottom of the soup bowl, and soup would be ladled on top of it from the hearth.[10] Pea soup would become a staple in the diet of the *Quebecois* for generations to come. Now, whenever I eat pea soup, I feel a connection with my French ancestors. I'm choosing it more often.

In 1629, the tiny Quebec settlement was captured by the British. Hélène and most other settlers were sent back to France. When France reclaimed the colony in 1633, Hélène returned to Quebec, where she spent the rest of her life. She married twice, first to Guillaume Hébert (son of that first farmer Louis Hébert) and second to Noel Morin (my ancestor). She had fifteen children from the two marriages and earned the profession of midwife. Her name frequently appeared on birth records, suggesting she was literate or at least she could sign her name. During her married life, she lived in what became known as the Upper Town, which was built on top of the cliff above the St. Lawrence. The Upper Town became the seat of religious and administrative institutions, including the seminary, convent, Hôtel-Dieu (hospital), fort, and governor's residence, while the Lower Town and its port remained the marketplace. Hélène died at age fifty-five in 1675. Despite her humble background, she was a leading citizen of the small colony, as she and her husband mingled with the most prominent figures. She was a respected midwife and a responsible community member. There were many times during her lifetime when the continued existence of the colony was uncertain. But by the time of her death, the permanent settlement could be considered a success.[11]

Hélène is a ninth great-grandmother for my generation. Her daughter Agnes Morin was my eighth great-grandmother, followed by Marie-Françoise Gaudry, Marie Anne Pilote, Marguerite Tremblay, and Genevieve (Geneva) LaForest, respectively. Thus, Hélène was the fourth great-grandmother of Geneva LaForest, wife of Jacques Allard, following Geneva's maternal lines.

INTERACTING WITH INDIGENOUS PEOPLE

Champlain's vision for a colony was quite different from that of the Spanish and English in the New World. As a young man, he traveled with a Spanish squadron as a crew member as they voyaged to parts of their empire in Central America and the Caribbean. He was horrified to see the cruelty of the Spanish conquerors, as they often enslaved the Indigenous people and plundered their riches and natural resources. He found the Native people in Central America to be very intelligent, and he marveled at their superbly built temples and houses.[12] He dreamed of harmony with the Native people in a New France then yet to be established. On his initial visits to St. Lawrence, he made it a point to engage the Indigenous leaders; he approached them without weapons, learned their customs and languages, and began building alliances.

The Indigenous people who occupied what is now Canada before European arrival are now called First Nations in Canada, including their present-day descendants. As noted earlier, the Indigenous people already had relationships with the French and other European fur traders many years before Champlain's settlement. Several First Nations tribes used the river system, canoeing down the many tributaries to various trading posts along the St. Lawrence River. They traded beavers and other furs for metal tools, utensils, clothing, and weapons. Because of this beneficial trade to both sides, neither the French nor the Native people were interested in destroying or displacing the other.

The tribe that most often used the area surrounding the Quebec settlement was called Montagnais (mountain people in French), although they called themselves the Innu, which means "people" in the Innu language.[13] They were a semi-nomadic people who came to the river to fish in summer. They moved inland in winter, where they would hunt for larger prey using snowshoes. They did not grow any crops, instead living as hunter-gatherers, using what was available during the season and traveling to where food could be found.[13] They frequently visited the settlement, and Champlain encouraged interaction. Sometimes, they could not find enough wildlife to get them through the winter. Some individuals or families would come into the settlement looking for food. The French had minimal supplies, but they shared what they had. The Montagnais also shared their food, providing a gift of game or fish when it was plentiful. All participated in religious festivals and banquets.[14] The food was likely more of a draw to the settlement than were the religious teachings.

While Champlain dreamed of harmony with the native people, he also hoped they would eventually behave more like the French and adopt the Catholic religion.[14] The Jesuit and Récollet missionaries also shared that vision, as they came from monasteries in France with a zeal to save the souls of the Native people. They wanted others to know the wonders of their faith as they did, but they saw only their worldview and only their faith as valid.

In 1632, the Jesuits established a school for the children of the natives.[15] In time, a settlement of cottages was built specifically for the native people who had converted, with the hope they would give up their semi-nomadic life. Some natives lived in the cottages, and some camped nearby. However, in winter, most moved to their inland hunting grounds.[16]

In 1639, Ursuline and Augustinian nuns arrived in Quebec to set up schools and hospitals. As with the priests, their aim was primarily to serve the Indigenous people. The Ursulines aimed to establish a convent and educate the Native girls in the French religion, language, and culture, hoping they, in turn, would educate their families in the faith. They also expected the Native girls to make good wives for the Frenchmen.

At the same time, the Augustinian Hospitaller nuns aimed to establish a hospital or Hôtel-Dieu.[17] The Native people were somewhat suspicious of the hospital care, as they believed the French may have brought diseases. They were not wrong about that. The French settlers' families also benefitted from these schools and hospitals, but they were secondary to the aim of religious conversion for the local tribes. Hélène Desporte's children received their early religious education alongside the Native children.

The fur trade brought the settlers into contact with other Indigenous tribes. The Huron tribe, also called Wendat, were the richest and most powerful Natives in the Great Lakes area and controlled most of the fur trade.[18] They were agricultural, growing corn, beans, and squash and storing supplies to help them get through the long winters. Both the Huron and Montagnais were subtribes of the Algonquins, sharing similar languages. The Algonquin people were all long-time enemies of the Iroquois, which included the Mohawk, Oneida, Cayuga, Seneca, and Onondaga. The Iroquois people lived south of the St. Lawrence River and south of Lake Ontario and Lake Erie, mostly in what is present-day New York.

The Algonquin people negotiated with Champlain to help protect them against the Iroquois, and Champlain agreed. He led two successful campaigns against the Mohawk in 1609-1610, which held peace until the 1630s. The leaders that followed Champlain were unable to keep it going.[19] Thus, as the French were allies to the enemies of the Iroquois, that made the French enemies of the Iroquois also. Between 1608 and 1665, about 200 French had been killed by the Iroquois.[20] Those killings rarely occurred near Quebec City. However, Hélène Desportes' son, Joseph Hébert, was one of those captured, tortured and murdered by the Iroquois in 1661.[21]

The Iroquois attacks more often came upon the tiny mission settlement in Montreal that began in 1642. Hélène Desportes' daughter Marie Morin entered the convent at Hôtel-Dieu in Montreal in 1662. Marie described these attacks in her written reports. At the first sign of attack, one of the nuns would ring an alarm bell to call all able-bodied men to battle. Some of the braver nuns also grabbed weapons and joined in. Others tended to the fallen and the priests, while other men and women—who were less brave—went to the chapel to prepare for their death. The residents of the convent learned to live with the constant threat. Sister Morin noted that Iroquois warriors frequently hid in the bushes near the Hôtel-Dieu, waiting for some unsuspecting person to come out after dark.[20,22] Fear of Iroquois attacks kept most homesteads close to the forts all along the St Lawrence River from the 1640s into 1660s, and this threat inhibited other French immigrants from arriving.[20]

While some native people converted to Catholicism and many of their children achieved their first communions, most never fully adopted Christianity or let go of their Native lifestyle. A much bigger impact on the Indigenous people came from the series of epidemics brought by the Europeans. Some epidemics migrated from the New England colonies, while others came on French ships. In 1615, Champlain had estimated a population of about 30,000 Hurons alone, but this tribe was reduced by more than half over the next twenty-five years. A smallpox epidemic arrived in 1639 on the same ships with the nuns, lasting through the following winter. The Jesuits estimated about 12,000 natives were living near their missions in the vicinity of Quebec in the Spring of 1639, with higher numbers in previous years; however, after the "extraordinary diseases," few remained.[23] (Note, there were still only about forty French families living in Quebec between 1639-42.[24] Thus, the native people far outnumbered the settlers at the time.) But by the end of 1675, most of the Indigenous people had been wiped out by diseases. The French tried to integrate more with the Native people than other European colonialists, albeit aiming to assimilate them into French ways. However, it was the European diseases that displaced most of the Native people from their homelands in this region. In time, as more Europeans arrived and new leaders emerged with their own visions, the remaining Native people were pushed back as they were in other colonies. Either way, the Europeans' impact on the First Nations' people was devastating. Thereafter, it was mostly the settlers' families attending the missionaries' schools and hospitals.

MÉTIS ANCESTRY

Métis means people with both Indigenous and European blood. Many of the early French pioneers, and especially the fur trading *voyageurs,* married local Native women. Early on, there were few, if any, European women available and fewer yet who would wish to live in the rugged conditions that the early pioneers found. There are many claims of *Métis* ancestors in French-Canadian family trees. Not all are easily confirmed.

A confirmed Indigenous ancestor of mine, one of my seventh great-grandmothers, is Marie-Suzanne "Jeanne" (Capciouékoué or Capie8suec8e) Richard (there are many spellings that try to capture the Indigenous pronunciation). She was born of the Kaskaskia tribe, once part of the Illinois Confederacy and one of many Algonquin-speaking tribes in North America.[25] Her birthdate and parents' names are unknown. In about 1701, in Kaskaskia, Illinois, Jeanne married French *voyageur* Jean Gauthier, who was born in 1669 in Montreal, Quebec.[26] Jean Gauthier and two of his brothers were *voyageurs* between 1690 and 1709. At least two of five documented contracts show that Jean was hired to collect furs in Illinois territory and bring them back to Quebec.[27] Apparently, he liked the Indian life, as he chose to marry and make this his home. The French established a mission in Kaskaskia. This became the capital of Upper Louisiana, in the Mississippi River Valley, as all this area was part of New France at the time. The community consisted of a few French men and numerous Kaskaskian and other Illinois Indians.[25] The couple had four children there between 1702 and 1713, including their daughter Marie (Suzanne) Gauthier, my direct ancestor, who was baptized in Kaskaskia on January 6, 1702.[26]

Jean Gauthier's backstory is also interesting. His father, Pierre Gauthier dit Saguingoira, arrived in Montreal from France in 1668, and he married Charlotte Roussel, a *fille du roi,* that same year.[28] (you'll read more about these imported brides below). The family moved to the nearby village of Lachine in 1676.[29] On August 5, 1689, in the middle of the night, the village of Lachine, with its 375 inhabitants, was attacked in a raid by 15,000 Iroquois. The warriors destroyed most of the village by fire, killed twenty-four residents, and captured 60 others.[29] Jean, with his five brothers and two sisters, was able to escape into the woods; however, his parents were both captured. Pierre and Charlotte lived with the Iroquois for the next ten years. Charlotte Roussel is believed to have died in captivity prior to January 22, 1698, the date that Pierre Gauthier returned to Lachine. Pierre lived the remainder of his life in Lachine; he died there on December 5, 1703.[27,28]

The terror felt in the 1689 raid on Lachine is an extension of the terror felt among the *Quebecois* during Hélène Desportes' lifetime. But such events didn't happen in isolation. These events were part of the Beaver Wars over the economic dominance of the fur trade that was heightened as beaver supplies were becoming more scarce.[30] The

Iroquois were also taking revenge against incursions on their people and territory. It was an Indigenous cultural practice that if a native person felt wronged, they would seek retaliation against the wrong-doer's family or tribe. Similarly, if a Native felt wronged by a Frenchman, he would seek revenge on the next Frenchman he met.[31] Therefore, Lachine was an easy and unwitting target.

It is interesting that Jean Gauthier married a native woman after his parents were taken captive during the 1689 Iroquois raid in Lachine. Jean signed his contract as a *voyager* in September of 1690, at age twenty-one, just a year after his parents had been captured. But Jean's fur trade was with the Algonquin people, and he married an Algonquin woman. These tribes were allies with the French settlers. The Iroquois tribes were longtime enemies of the Algonquins.

Jean and Jeanne's daughter, Suzanne Gauthier, married Frenchman Jacques Souchereau dit Langoumois in 1732,[32,33] and they raised their nine children in the Montreal area. Three of their daughters migrated with their husbands to Detroit, including my ancestor Françoise Souchereau dit Langoumois, who married Etienne (Stephen) Godfroy Ballard dit Latour.[27,34] Thus, Françoise is a fifth great-grandmother for my generation, and she is a second great-grandmother of Isadore Allor via maternal lines of his mother, Marine Furton.

A ROYAL COLONY

A turning point for Quebec came when King Louis XIV took a personal interest in his colony, which was on the verge of economic collapse. From its beginning, the affairs of the colony had been run by the managers of the fur trading business. The population of the English colonies to the South vastly outnumbered that of New France, which was a concern as it threatened their foothold in North America. In 1663, King Louis took direct control. Two problems required attention for the colony's survival—pacification of the Iroquois and population growth.[35]

The King first ordered war on the Iroquois by sending regular French troops to New France. He sent the Carignan-Salières Regiment of 1200 soldiers in twenty-four companies. They arrived in September 1665. The total Quebec population at that time was only 3,215. Therefore, 1200 soldiers made quite an impression. Many were lodged with private families. Others were sent to build a series of forts along the St. Lawrence River and Great Lakes. These forts helped to make their imposing military force known, and soon, three of the five Iroquois nations signed a peace agreement without a fight. Then, in the winter of 1665-66, an attempt to pacify the other two Iroquois nations, the Oneidas and Mohawk, failed. But another attempt, in the summer of 1666, convinced these two nations that the French militarily could overpower them. They signed a peace agreement.[35] These peace treaties held for a number of years, although the Lachine massacre, referred to above, indicates there were still some outbreaks. The 1665-66 peace treaties, however, brought enough stability to encourage more immigration of settlers, along with the King's incentives.

The soldiers were encouraged to settle in the colony. The officers were promised land grants in the form of *seigneuries*. The *seigneurial* system along the St. Lawrence River was an adaptation of the French feudal system.[36] Both the *seigneur* or land manager and *censitaires* or grantees had rights and duties. The *seigneur* was responsible for clearing the land, building roads, recruiting grantees, building houses, and ensuring each grant had enough land to support each settler and his family.[36] He had to live on the *seigneury* and build a communal mill and oven. The *censitaires,* in turn, would give every fourteenth bushel to the *seigneur* in addition to rent or *"cens."* The land grants specified the number of days of work detail to which the *censitaires* were bound. The *seigneurs* were also required to work for the colonial administration as needed.[37] This system was in place early on in the colony, as early as 1622, with Louis Hébert, who was Hélènes Desportes' first father-in-law and Quebec's first farmer.[38] Hélènes' second husband, Noël Morin, held more than one *seigneury* during his lifetime. The prospect of obtaining land in New

France was much better than in the mother country, inspiring many settlers to immigrate. Still, only about a third of immigrants who came to the colony before 1663 decided to stay. Their reports back to the mother country of the wild landscape, poor soils, short growing season, and scarcity of supplies gave New France a poor reputation.[39] Still, in 1666, with the new incentives, 403 of the 1,200 soldiers decided to stay.[35]

Other incentives encouraged early marriage and large families. Grooms were given a gift of twenty *livres* from the King on their wedding day. Parents could be charged fines or lose hunting, fishing, or trading privileges if they didn't marry off their children early. Marriage was encouraged for male children by age twenty and female children by age sixteen. Annual allowances also were given for large families—300 *livres* for ten living legitimate children or 400 *livres* for twelve or more children.[35]

These incentives would not have been successful, however, without enough women to marry. In 1663, for every woman in the colony, there were six unmarried men.[35]

FILLES DU ROI—DAUGHTERS OF THE KING

King Louis XIV reasoned it would be easier to populate the colony by recruiting marriageable women and promoting births than by sending large numbers of new settlers. The King made a significant investment in this plan. Recruiters were paid ten *livres* for each girl. The young women were paid thirty *livres* for clothing and household items and sixty *livres* for transportation expenses, along with a dowry of fifty *livres*. Military officers' brides received a dowry of a hundred *livres* or more. Between 1663 and 1673, 850 women were sent from France. About ten percent died at sea during the six-to-nine-week voyage, bringing about 770 brides to New France.[40, 41]

Besides the financial incentives, what motivated these women to make the dangerous trip across the Atlantic and brave the wild conditions

The Arrival of the French Girls at Quebec, 1667

in the new world? Most came from humble backgrounds—daughters of minor artisans, servants, or laborers. Most could not read or write. About one-third came from the Hôpital Général (General Hospital) in Paris, which took homeless people off the streets, most of whom were orphans. These women had limited opportunities to marry, have a home, and raise a family.[40] Some women (about twelve percent) were from the upper classes or minor nobility who had lost a father or a fortune, making it difficult to marry well in France. These women were important in providing suitable matches for the officers and other men of rank in the colony. Some were not from France. The brides' ages ranged from early teens to middle age, with twenty percent widows.[41]

The brides-to-be were chosen for their hardiness as it was made clear they would be helping to set up new farms in the wild lands of the new colony. Recruiters frequently sought women from reputable institutions or with the local priest's recommendation. They were closely supervised on their journey until they found a husband. All but thirty-two of the 770 married, many within a month of arrival and most within six months.[40, 41]

They had a healthier life in the New World, with clean air and access to fresh grain, fruit, meat, and fish, compared with the malnutrition common among the poor in the mother country. Fewer women died in childbirth, and life expectancy was longer, with an average age of sixty-two at death. It would be another 200 years before this longevity was found in France.[40]

I found seven *filles du roi* ancestors related to the Allard-Allor family lines:

Catherine Paulo married in 1663 to Etienne Campeau
(Parents of Jacques Campeau)

Charlotte Roussel married in 1668 to Pierre Gauthier dit Saguingoira
(Parents of Jean Gauthier)

Marie Piton married in 1668 to Jean Bergevin
(Grandparents of Marie Angelique Bergevin)

Jeanne Petit married in 1672 to François Séguin dit Laderoute
(Great-grandparents of Marie Françoise Mesny and Magdeleine Mesny)

Marguerite Raison married in 1671 to Bernard Deniger dit Sancoucy
(Other great-grandparents of Marie Françoise Mesny and Magdeleine Mesny)

Catherine Gateau married in 1671 to Jean dit Vien
(Great-grandparents of Catherine St. Aubin)

Jeanne Anguille married François Allard in 1671

FRANÇOIS ALLARD AND JEANNE ANGUILLE ARRIVE IN QUEBEC

Against this backdrop, François Allard arrived in Quebec in 1666 at age twenty-nine. [1,42] He came from the farming community of Blacqueville on the River Seine, about sixteen miles (twenty-six km)

Northwest of Rouen in Normandy, France. His parents were Jacques Allard and Jacqueline Frérot.[42] By 1666, the colony's population had already increased to about 4,200.[35] Like other *habitants* in New France, he was recruited to live on and work the land in a *seigneury* for a period of three years. *Habitants* had more freedom than *paysans* (peasants) in France. If they decided to stay in the colony, they could eventually own land, they would have rights to hunt and fish, and they would pay less taxes than their counterparts in France.[43]

Thus, François started out working as a laborer for Anne Ardouin, the widow of Jacques Badeau (women could own property if widowed, but when married, all property was owned by her husband), on the *Seigneury* of Notre-Dame-des-Anges, near the mouth of the Beauport River.[1] After her husband's death, she struggled with the farm and needed help. François would travel by canoe to reach this property, as there were no roads at the time. The widow kept a farm of thirty arpents (about twenty-five acres) fronted on the St. Lawrence River. François learned how to cultivate the land and raise animals in these harsh conditions and developed good relationships with his neighbors. This apparently earned him his employer's respect, as she later sent a representative to attend François' wedding on her behalf. While the majority of *seigneurial* recruits returned to France after their three years, François decided to stay. In 1669, he was granted a thirteen-arpent farm (about eleven acres) in Bourg Royal (later renamed Charlesbourg). Soon, he had cleared enough land and built a house,[1] making him a good catch for one of the *filles du roi* arriving each summer.

That wife would be Jeanne L'Anguille, *a fille du roi*, who arrived in 1671 from the farming village of Artannes on the Indre River,[44] in the Loire Valley of central France. Her parents were Michel L'Anguille and Etiennette Toucheraine. Jeanne's father reportedly died earlier in 1771,[45] leaving his wife and four daughters. Jeanne was the eldest of their living children, and she was unmarried at age twenty-eight. Among her three sisters, two were already married (Etionnette and Marie), and the youngest (Michelle) was just twelve years old at the time.[46] With her father's death, a guardian would likely have been appointed, and his approval would be needed for Jeanne's marriage. But at age twenty-eight, her marriage prospects would be limited. The only respectable roles for women in the seventeenth century were a wife, mother, or being in a religious community. Women had little opportunity to make their own decisions. As a *fille du roi*, however, finding a husband was a near certainty; she could make her own choice, and no parent or guardian's approval was needed.[40] The family reportedly had better than average means, and Jeanne brought a dowry of 300 livres, in addition to the promised King's dowry of fifty livres, to her marriage.[1]

Even if we could understand her motivation, Jeanne was still remarkably brave to take on this cross-Atlantic adventure. The voyage itself was daunting. Ships were about 80 to 110 feet long and twenty-five to thirty feet wide at the time. This space held about 200 passengers, including 115 *filles du roi* in Jeanne's year,[41] along with live animals that would be cooked en route or carried to the colony. The hold was accessed from the deck by a spiral staircase, where the single women would bunk tightly side-by-side on narrow straw-filled mattresses at one end, followed by families with children, and then by the single men traveling to the colony. The tight quarters were also infested with fleas, lice, and mice. Meals onboard consisted of dried fish, dried meat, soup, and hardtack biscuits, supplemented by any animals killed during the voyage. As the six- to eight-week voyage went on, the food supplies would be diminished, or they'd become infested with maggots. The water supply would become polluted. The water could be replaced with hard cider or diluted wine, but the food was consumed in any condition. This contributed to some of the onboard illnesses. On good days, the passengers could walk on the decks, but in stormy weather and after dark, all would be crammed below deck where it was completely dark. Candles and other lighting were forbidden, except for one light on deck, because a fire on board the ship could be disastrous.[47]

There were no toilet facilities for passengers, except for buckets to be emptied overboard. There was little air circulation in the hold below deck. Therefore, everyone endured the smells of human and animal waste and the effects of rancid food and seasickness. The sounds of waves and creaking of the ship as it rocked would be mixed with the animals' sounds and the passengers' moans, groans, cries, and prayers. Anxieties beyond these traveling conditions and stormy weather included pirates, icebergs, and death from disease outbreaks. If only one or two died en route, it was considered a successful voyage![47] Would I have taken on this adventure? Maybe.

Upon her arrival in late summer, Jeanne would have been escorted to the Ursuline convent and its dormitories. There, the arrivals would receive instruction on how to care for a home under the conditions in New France. They were also coached to ask suitors if they had a house to live in and had already stored up supplies for the upcoming winter. The brides' selection process resembled speed dating. The girls stood around the sides of the room while their suitors walked around, stopping briefly to talk as they went by.[40] Jeanne and François must have clicked on that first go-around. After an initial verbal agreement to marry, Jeanne and François signed a marriage contract on Sunday, October 18, 1671, in Quebec City.[48] Then, on the first Sunday in November, the couple married at the chapel in Beauport where the missionary Jesuit priest, Guillaume Mathieu, would be passing through.[1,49]

François and Jeanne lived on and raised their eight children on that farm in Charlesbourg. The census of 1681 shows them living modestly with fourteen arpents of cleared land and two livestock. By 1685, François added forty arpents which he bought (44.8 acres total) from his neighbor.[1] Jeanne died at age sixty-eight in 1711.[50] While the cause of her death is unknown, there was a yellow fever epidemic documented in 1711.[41] In 1720, François ceded his property to his daughter and her husband, Jean Rénauld. In return, they took care of François for the remainder of his life.[1] François died at age eighty-nine in 1726 in Charlesbourg.[51] Both François and Jeanne are interred in Charlesbourg in Saint-Charles Borromée Cemetery, along with many of their children and their families.

THE VILLAGE OF CHARLESBOURG

As the village of Charlesbourg became the hometown of the Allard family, it also became a character in their story. The village was built in the 1660s by the Jesuits, although there had been settlers in the area since 1626. Called *Trait-Carré*, the village was built with triangular land parcels that radiated out (see photo) from a central square where the church was located. The farmhouses were situated close to the square, making it easier for everyone to help out with community tasks and festivities while also being in a position to defend the village from Indian attacks. Farmland and pastures extended out further on the parcels.[52]

Charlesbourg and neighboring Beauport were the only two settlements arranged in this way. More common were the ribbon farms—long, narrow properties where each fronted the river, which was the primary means of transportation. Charlesbourg is located northeast of Quebec City, although, since 2002, it has been incorporated as a borough of Quebec City.[52]

Part of the Charlesbourg story and the settling of Quebec is told through the Allard family marriages. Initially, the Allards all married into other Charlesbourg families. François and Jeanne's son and my direct ancestor, Jean-Baptiste Allard, married Anne-Élisabeth Pageau in 1705.[53] Anne-Elizabeth's father, Thomas Pageau, had arrived in Quebec from France in 1659 at the age of twenty-one and he worked for the Jesuits as a tailor. By 1667, he obtained land in Charlesbourg and built a house there. By 1675, Thomas married Catherine Roy, daughter of Mathurin Roy and Marguerite Bire, who had arrived in Quebec together in 1646.[54] Mathurin Roy was a master mason.[55] Settlers with trade skills were especially sought for immigration to the colony. The Roys settled in Charlesbourg when masonry was surely needed.

The marriage story is more interesting in the next generation. Jean-Baptiste Allard and Anne-Elizabeth Pageau had seven living children, *four* of whom married children of Ignace Bergevin and Genevieve Tessier. This includes my direct ancestor, Pierre Allard, who married

Charlesbourg in 1937

Marie Angelique Bergevin in 1743.[56] Furthermore, two of Ignace and Genevieve's other children married Jean-Baptiste's brother Thomas Allard's children, making six of the eight living Bergevin children who married Allard siblings or cousins! All were living in Charlesbourg. Even more amazing is that Ignace and Geneviève Bergevin had two sons named Pierre (born in 1716 and 1727); the two Pierre Bergevins married cousins with the same name, Marie Charlotte Allard, both of whom were born in 1726 and both died in 1811, but on different dates in those years. This is very confusing for genealogists! But others have confirmed these events as well.[57] This likely illustrates how close village life in early Quebec led to marriage partners from nearby. Everyone became related. I wonder if the *Trait-Carré* arrangement made intermarriage more likely than the more common ribbon farms, where at least one could move around by canoe. Nonetheless, it is not unusual to find the same name among cousins, but naming two living sons with the same name is beyond my understanding!

It was Pierre Allard and Marie Angelique's son Jacques Allard, from the third generation of Allards born in Charlesbourg, Quebec, who traveled to Detroit around 1774, as described in Chapter 6. This is after Pierre Allard died in 1759 during the English conquest.[58] His wife Marie Angelique remarried in 1761,[59] and the entire family moved out of Charlesbourg. By then, there would have been limited, if any, land available for their descendants in the village. They moved upriver, between Trois Rivières and Montreal, and settled in the area around Ile Dupas and St. Cuthbert, which was just inland from Ile Dupas. Jacques Allard went furthest away to what would become Michigan, which loops us around to Chapter 6. Thus, the story of *les Quebecois* is one of migration. But after the English conquest, I learned that such moves could take on new challenges, further pushing cultural and language boundaries.

FRANCO-ONTARIANS: MIGRATION FROM DUPUIS TO DUPEE

❧

MY THIRD GREAT-GRANDPARENTS' STORY ON THE DUPEE SIDE was largely a mystery. It was like an archeological dig, unearthing small clues, like shards of pottery, one at a time. But slowly, I was able to piece these clues together to reveal some of how this family may have lived. As noted in Chapter 4, I discovered that my great-great-grandparents, John and Catherine Dupee, and most of their children immigrated to Michigan from Ontario in the early 1860s. John's marriage and death records listed his parents as Norman and Jane Dupee. Through my Ancestry.com DNA, I was linked to distant cousins from descendants of three of Norman's other children (Michael, Genevieve, Marguerite), in addition to cousins from descendants of John and Catherine's children (David, Anna, John, Mary). I found DNA cousins from descendants of some of Norman's siblings (Augustin, Joseph, Anastasie). I also found DNA cousins from descendants of Jane's siblings (Marie Catherine Leroux, Augustin Couillerier). This led me to the French spellings of Norman's and Jane's names: Norbert Dupuis and Geneviève Leroux.

Solid clues came from baptism records. I found these exciting because they revealed dates, places, and key relationships. Norbert Dupuis was born and baptized (at Basilique Notre-Dame) on June 5, 1771, in Montreal, Quebec; his parents were Sylvain Dupuis and Françoise Leblanc.[1] Geneviève Leroux was born and baptized on May 3, 1773 (St-Joseph-de-Soulanges) in Les Cèdres, Quebec. Her parents were Michel Leroux dit Rousson and Catherine Poirier dite Desloges.[2] Geneviève's family apparently lived for some time in Les Cèdres, Quebec, based on baptism records of her siblings.[3] Les Cèdres is on the north shore of the St. Lawrence River, about twenty-seven miles (forty-four km) southwest or upstream of Montreal. I found no record of Norbert and Geneviève's marriage. However, a closer look at their children's baptism records shed light on where they lived during their early married life.

A FARMER AT *LAC SAINT-FRANÇOIS*

Church records were found for only four of Norbert and Geneviève's nine children. These records came from two different places, St. Regis Mission and Les Cèdres. But thanks to a kind Ancestry.com member, who translated one of these records, and a closer look at the others (in their blurry handwritten French), I could see the same phrase in all four of these children's records. Norbert Dupuis was *un cultivateur du sud du Lac Saint François*: a farmer from the south of Lake Saint Francis. Lake Saint Francis is a large freshwater lake that is part of the St. Lawrence River. It borders southeastern Ontario and southwestern Quebec and is near northern New York on the south side of the St. Lawrence River. This lake is another thirty miles southwest and upstream from Les Cèdres.

These records included the burial of an unnamed son in 1796 at the parish of St-Joseph-de-Soulanges in Les Cèdres; this son was reportedly born in 1795, died on January 15, 1796, and was buried on February 3, 1796.[4] Then Norbert (Jr.) was born July 20 and baptized on October 6, 1797, also at St. Joseph's in Les Cèdres.[5] Later baptism records for Marguerite (1809) and Jean Baptiste (1811) report these events were performed at St. Regis Mission,[6,7] which was on the tip of a peninsula in the St. Lawrence River, near the New York border. At the time, the mission at St. Regis served the Native American population, as well as Scottish and French-Canadian Catholics who sought them out. These clues, from their first born to their last, suggest the family may have lived in the same general area during the years when all their nine children were born.

These records also suggest the family's farm may have been far from a parish church, and they utilized nearby Catholic churches when

NORBERT AND GENEVIÈVE'S CHILDREN

Sylvain (Sylvester)
B: ~1793 or 1799—Glengarry, Ontario
D: 1878—Bayfield, Ontario

Unnamed son
B: 1795
D: 1769, burial recorded in Les Cèdres, Quebec

Norbert (Wells)
B: 1797, baptised at Les Cèdres, Quebec
D: unknown

Michel (Michael)
B: ~1798 or 1804
D: 1893—Enniskillen, Ontario

Geneviève (Mary)
B: 1807
D: 1867—St. Anicet, Huntingdon. Quebec

Marguerite
B: 1808—baptised at St. Regis, Quebec
D: 1891—Prescott, Ontario

Françoise (Fanny)
B: 1810
D: unknown

Jean Baptiste (John)
B: 1811—baptised at St. Regis, Quebec
D: 1896—Burlington, Michigan

it was convenient to travel, often a few months after the vital event. Marguerite's baptism record, on January 25, 1809, stated this was four months after her birth. It may have been easier to travel to the mission church by crossing the river during the winter, after the harvest season, and when the river was frozen. The priest who performed Marguerite's baptism also stated that this service was a concession to the parish of St. Joseph in Les Cèdres, which had been the home parish for Geneviève Leroux's family.

I also discovered a book on the early history of what became Huntingdon County, Quebec,[8] that borders Lake St. Francis and the southern shore of the St. Lawrence River. Norbert's older brother, (Augustin) Eustache Dupuis, was reported to be one of the first white settlers on the south of Lake St. Francis. He arrived in 1795 with his young family. This was a time when much of this area was still Indian lands with the Mohawk-Akwesasne people. He was described as a lumberman who made a living harvesting tall pines used for ship's masts. While Augustin was twenty years older, he may have attracted his younger brother, Norbert, to this area. Augustin also named one of his own sons Norbert. (This Norbert Dupuis was born in 1792,[9] and his records are easily confused with his uncle and my direct ancestor, Norbert Dupuis, who was born in 1771.) Another of Norbert's brothers, Joseph, was also nearby. Joseph's son, Roache Joachim Dupuis, was baptized at St. Regis in September 1796,[10] and a daughter, Angelique, was born in January 1806 and was baptized at St. Regis in November 1806. These records list the parents, Joseph Dupuis and Marianne Parrot, as "a farmer living on the side called Indian lands in the Seigneury of St. Regis."[11] Thus, it appears that at least three brothers came to this area and had children there.

For Norbert and Geneviève's son Sylvain/Sylvester, I found no baptism record, but Sylvester self-reported in his 1870 marriage record that he was born in Glengarry, Ontario,[12] a part of Ontario that borders the north side of Lake Saint Francis on the St. Lawrence River. It is another piece of evidence, this time suggesting an Ontario residence, or Upper Canada, as it was known at the time. Glengarry County, Ontario, was founded in 1784 as a home to Scottish loyalists, mainly from the clan McDonald, who had emigrated from the Mohawk Valley in New York during the American Revolutionary War. The British crown granted them land to compensate for their losses in New York.[13] Even though Glengarry County was across the border from Quebec (called Lower Canada at the time), Norbert's later service in the Upper Canada militia suggests he may have resided here at some point before the war.

NORBERT IN THE WAR OF 1812

The birth of their youngest child in 1811 brought the family to the eve of the War of 1812. I knew for sure only that Norbert was a private in the ninth company for the Incorporated Militia of Upper Canada, serving under Captain John McDonnell, that he was discharged in 1814 at York (modern-day Toronto) and was later awarded a land grant for his service.[14] In his wonderful book, *Redcoated Ploughboys, the Volunteer Battalion of Incorporated Militia for Upper Canada, 1813-1815*, Richard

Feltoe brings color to these farmer soldiers' experiences.[14] With Feltoe's help, I could begin to imagine some of Norbert's experiences.

The prelude to this North American war occurred in the shadow of the Napoleonic Wars between Great Britain and France in Europe. That war seriously constrained trade options for the new United States, whose ships were caught up in embargos and military advances between the European rivals. Many Americans also resented any British presence in North America following their revolutionary victory. They wanted to see Canada as part of the United States. As war talk grew, Canadian leaders in Upper Canada became nervous about the limited number of regular British troops in the colony in the event of an American invasion. As the British government was preoccupied and financially drained from its European war, it was unresponsive to Canada's calls for help.

Canada's response was the Militia Act of 1808, which sought to supplement the regular British army troops with a part-time militia: "Every male between the age of sixteen and sixty and capable of bearing arms" was to enroll in periodic training and subsequent militia duty. This militia used a new county-based regimental system that would see individual companies or regiments called out or "embodied" for varying periods as circumstances required. These corps would be referred to according to their county name and collectively as regiments of "embodied militia." Those persons not enrolling would be fined ten shillings.[15] Norbert may have enrolled in his county rather than face a fine.

After war was declared in June of 1812 by U.S. President James Madison, there were small-scale raids, including along the St. Lawrence River. It is unknown whether Norbert was active in the embodied militia service at that time. But it soon became clear that a full-time, better-trained militia was needed for the duration of the war. Therefore, the New Militia Act of 1813 created the "Incorporated Militia of Upper Canada." This act enlisted officers from the earlier embodied militia to recruit a quota of men who would serve under their command. Incentives included a promise of a future land grant, uniforms, pay, and allowances on par with regular troops. Each company would consist of one captain, one lieutenant, one ensign, three sergeants, three corporals, one drummer, and fifty privates—being "men between sixteen to forty-five years of age, if strong and healthy."[16] In 1813, Norbert was forty-two years old. (Norbert Jr. would have been age fifteen at the start of the war, so it seems likely that the records refer to Norbert, the father). We know that Norbert served as a private under Captain John McDonnell. It makes sense that if Norbert was living in Glengarry, the area of the MacDonald clan, he was recruited by one of his neighbors. This new system of recruitment created a bond between officers and rank and file, unlike the rigid social structure of the regular British forces.[16] Wives and children of recruits could follow the militia and stay at the base if chosen by lot. It is unknown whether Norbert's family was chosen to follow him or if they stayed home.

There is no record that his older teenage sons served in this war; however, a later amendment of the Militia Act stated that "every male inhabitant of Upper Canada between the age of sixteen and sixty and physically able to bear arms was automatically deemed a militiaman and was required to enlist for prospective service."[17] All had three-month periods of active duty by means of a ballot system, while the remainder were on reserve for subsequent call-ups. This newly embodied militia would be engaged with the full-time Incorporated Militia (IM).

During the rest of 1813, the Eastern regiment was assigned to a base in Prescott on the St. Lawrence River. To get into fighting shape, they practiced drills for twelve-hour days.[16] Two other regiments were based at York and Niagara. By early 1814, all these regiments were consolidated into a single battalion with a company structure that would be based in York. John McDonnell was then assigned to captain Company No. 9. Private "Norbin Dupee" was listed as part of this company.[14]

The entire Prescott regiment was transferred to York (modern-day Toronto) in mid-February of 1814. Norbert/Norbin would have been part of this transition. With mid-winter storms, boat travel would be treacherous; therefore, the entire regiment walked the 225 miles to York. A lucky few got to ride on a sleigh. They marched sixteen miles per day on average, and the march included not only columns of men and officers but also their wives, children, baggage, tents, furniture, and all the military accounts and equipment deemed essential. They trudged through snow and mud on rutted tracks that were the roads of the time.[17]

When they arrived at York during the first two weeks of March, they found only a partially rebuilt fort after it had been sacked twice in 1813. The town of York had also been burned by the Americans. Incoming troops and families were lodged in the partially rebuilt barracks, barns, stables, or whatever space was available. Some stayed in York residences.[18] After a harsh winter and war damage to Upper Canada's farms, the troops also found a shortage of food. This shortage forced a General Order to evacuate most of the women and children who had just marched almost 225 miles to get to York. After protests, the leadership allowed families to stay, but they were not permitted to draw on military rations for food. Families would need to fend for themselves either by returning home on their own or in the hardscrabble of the war-damaged town.[18]

Over the next few months, the consolidated militia was drilled up to a standard where they could fight alongside the regular troops. Before long, their drills would be put to use. In early July 1814, after British losses on the Niagara frontier, the York troops were ordered to provide reinforcements, leaving behind only a small detachment to protect the fort. They huddled on ships to cross the lake and marched all night in the rain and into the next day until they met the army in retreat. They halted for a few days to plan their next offensive.[19]

The Incorporated Militia was formed into a "Light Brigade" with the regular British Army in Canada, the Glengarry Light Dragoons. The Light Brigade was assigned rear guard as they marched up to the hilltop of Lundy's Lane, near Niagara Falls, during the night of July 24. Other units joined them. As the Americans probed northward, the British and Canadian army fanned out in a solid line on the hilltop, with the IM and Glengarries on the left and right flanks. The enemy attacked from the woods, and Captain John McDonell received a musket ball through his sash but was unhurt. Soon, more American troops came through the woods, and a firefight ensued where both sides suffered casualties. Captain McDonell was able to extricate his men. While the American's main thrust was to the center of the line, one probe was directed to the left at McDonell's company, where they were caught between two sets of fire. This line of fire served as a distraction that allowed the Americans to capture the British guns. The British attempted to retrieve the guns but were twice driven back by enemy fire as the lines clashed. The battle continued into the evening of July 25, and it ended in a stalemate as both sides withdrew in the dark. Captain McDonnell was hit in the left arm, and later, his left arm was amputated. This ended his direct role in the war. The Battle of Lundy's Lane was one of the bloodiest battles of the war and one of the deadliest in Canadian history.[20]

As an American myself, it was strange reading about the Americans in this war as "the enemies" with my family on the other side. But then, the French-Canadians were fighting against the British not long before, during the Conquest of Quebec in 1760-63 (Chapter 6); here they are fighting *with* the British. Soon after the Revolutionary War, when the British ceded Michigan to the United States, my ancestors there switched sides again to fight *against* the British on that front of the 1812 War (also in Chapter 6). In any case, war is never a romantic adventure. It involved long marches in all kinds of weather and states of exhaustion. The Canadian militia wore threadbare hand-me-down uniforms with little protection against the weather or the enemy. They were short on equipment and ammunition. Food shortages continued, and rations were frequently cut as they fought on. Incidents of sickness were common.

It is unclear whether Norbert saw this action with his company. I know for sure only that he was discharged in 1814 while at York, sometime between April and October of that year. He was listed as "unfit for Service."[14] I also know that he survived this service. Examples of this designation included dysentery, pneumonia, or debility. This list did not include soldiers who had been injured in battle. However, the debility could have occurred en route to or from the battle, from trudging through and sleeping in the wet-to-the-core conditions, from hunger-induced weaknesses. In 1814, any of these debilities could be quite serious, as there was no adequate medical care, and soldiers were expected to be fit for long marches and hand-to-hand battles.

During their retreat along the North shore of the Niagara River, the IM troops could see that American soldiers had pillaged and burned the villages and farms. The farmers were struggling to harvest the crops that remained. The IM troops, who were farmers themselves, slipped away from their march to lend a hand. The soldiers were also hungry as their rations had been cut again due to American blockades of supplies. The soldiers could have been punished, but General Drummond saw an opportunity. The general stopped and negotiated with the farmers for part of the harvest in exchange for help bringing it in.[21] The troops were fed for a short time.

This war had more bloody battles, but Norbert was no longer involved. The war ended in a draw in 1815. The IM had successfully and continuously fought alongside the regular army. The IM service was widely heralded, and the farmer-soldiers were lauded as heroes for decades to come.

LAND GRANT IN WEST NISSOURI, ONTARIO

Feltoe's book went on to describe the land grant process as an abyss of delays and procrastination that lasted decades. The best tracts often went to political cronies, leaving plots for others that were often unsuitable for agriculture. The delays left some veterans too old for the backbreaking work of clearing the virgin forest according to the timetable to secure permanent ownership.[22] From this perspective, Norbert did not do too badly as his land grant came through on March 10, 1820, and the transfer occurred two years later on July 29, 1822, with the hundred acres given to privates. The land was in West Nissouri, Ontario. He was then age fifty-one.

Norbert's Military land grant was identified on 10 Mar 1820:
Surname Christian Name Concession Lot Twp Date of Patent Acres
Dupie Norbin 4 E part 8 West Nissouri 29/07/1822 100[23]

The Land Grant Register indicates that Norbert/Norbin was then
working as a laborer for York Township. It appears that Norbert and
Geneviève were living in York while waiting for their land grant to
come through. Daughter Geneviève married at St. Regis Mission on
February 12, 1821,[24] and Marguerite married at St. Anicet, Quebec
on February 3, 1823.[25] Both marriage records indicated their parents,
Norbert Dupuis and Geneviève Leroux, were living in York at the time.
Geneviève, the daughter, referred to as "Mary," married Louis Saucier
at about age fourteen. Louis and Mary's family continued to live in St.
Anicet until Geneviève-Mary's death in 1867 at age sixty.[26] Marguerite
married Joachim Chatel a year later when she was fourteen. They raised
their family in St. Anicet and later moved to Prescott, Ontario, where
Marguerite died in 1891 at age eighty-two.[27]

The village of St. Anicet is in Huntingdon County, Quebec, near
the south shore of Lake St. Francis and across the lake/river from
Glengarry, Ontario. In addition to their daughters, several cousins
lived in St. Anicet, Quebec, including nephew Norbert Dupuis (son of
brother Augustin Dupuis, as described earlier), who married Josephte
Chatel.[28] It was Josephte's uncle Joachim Chatel who married Norbert
and Geneviève's daughter Marguerite. Thus, the families were close.
Now, their daughters would be living in Quebec, among relatives and
other French-Canadian families. I expect this offered some comfort to
the parents. They were also able to see two of their daughters married
before they moved further away.

West Nissouri is in the northeast corner of Middlesex County, near
London, Ontario, which is between Lake Erie and Lake Huron. (In
2001, West Nissouri merged with its neighbor to form the new township
of Thames Centre.) This move took the remaining family to the frontier
of western Ontario, further from their Quebec homelands. However,

the pre-confederation land map of West Nissouri shows three other French surnames on properties bordering Norbert.[29] Likely, all had been awarded this land for their military service.

I can imagine the trek to this new home. I imagine they would have set off in the Spring of 1823, sometime after Marguerite's February wedding, after the winter's edge had worn off. It is about 400 miles (644 km) between St. Anicet and West Nissouri, but the bigger portion of that was the 300 miles from St. Anicet to York. That part of the route would have been more familiar, at least. From York on, the next hundred miles would have been less traveled. The land grants would bring a few settlers, perhaps traveling around the same time on this route. Did they travel in a caravan with the other war veterans who would be their neighbors? Did they even have a horse and wagon at the time? They might still see snow flurries on route in early spring at these latitudes, even into May. There would also be cold rainy days, with sticky, sucking mud in the rutted tracks. But in time, the trees would blossom out, and meadows would become green. They were surely accompanied by the return of migrating birds, serenading the migration of settlers.

In the Spring of 1823, Norbert would turn fifty-two, and Geneviève would turn fifty. Their youngest child, John, was then twelve, and Norbert Jr. was twenty-five. They would have time to reflect on their long days' journey. They had been pioneers since they had set out as a young family from Les Cèdres. They cleared land to build a home, grew their own food, and dealt with whatever came along. During the war years, they were often on the move, essentially homeless for ten years. Growing food in York would have been difficult if it was possible at all. Military provisions were scant if they were lucky to have them. On Norbert's discharge in 1814, he was ill and would have to recover. As this was before the war's end, there were likely few, if any, of the provisions (cash, clothing) given to discharged soldiers at war's end. Even then, the cash-strapped government could offer little to their soldiers. More likely, what cash they had would come from itinerant labor that anyone in the family could muster. They would all compete with many other hungry families for work. The trek to Nissouri would have required supplies and cash to carry them several months before they could bring in their own harvest and live in their own cabin. But as the warm air brightened their surroundings along their way, they might have recognized that as they started from scratch before, they could do it again. This time, they would have their own land. The crowded towns in the east provided limited land and opportunities for new generations of growing families. While Norbert and Geneviève were growing older, they had to think about opportunities for their sons and their remaining daughter. This is what drove many families to move west.

After the land 1822 transfer and their daughters' weddings, I was unable to find further records for either Norbert/Norman/Norbin Dupee or for Geneviève/Jane. Only a later record registered the transfer for the West Nissouri land from son "Wells Dupie," his "heir at law," to David Young on November 30, 1846.[30] Thus, the family held this land for twenty-four years. The family apparently succeeded in meeting the grant requirements of clearing and building on the land in order to keep their property. It also appears that Norbert Jr. referred to himself as "Wells," which is an English translation of the French term du puits: from the well. Perhaps he also used this name to distinguish himself from his father. Apparently, Norbert, the father, died in 1846 or earlier. If so, he would have been seventy-five years old.

The Dupee brothers' militia service was documented for their residence in Upper Canada in April 1829, as they were required to enroll in the local regiment of the provincial militia and attend the annual muster.[31] The roster shows four Dupee men with their ages: Dupe Wells, thirty-one; Dupee Sylvester, twenty-nine; Dupee Michael, twenty-four; and Dupee John, nineteen. These ages fit our Dupee brothers. In addition to annual musters, these militias were used if there was political unrest, when residents were unhappy about government actions, or when their representative did not appear to have listened to their wishes.

Once census records began in this area, it was clear that all names had been anglicized. The Dupee children's reported religion also varied:

Baptist, Episcopal, or "English Church," on various records. It is possible there were no Catholic churches in these reaches of British Canada. Most of the Dupee children were married in Nissouri in the Baptist Church of Christ by Rev. Salmon Vining. As noted in Chapter 4, John Dupee married Catherine O'Brien on January 1, 1835, and John's sister, Fanny Dupee, married Catherine's brother, David O'Brien, at the same time. Michael Dupee was a witness for both.[32] All reported living in Nissouri at the time. On March 18, 1838, Reverend Vining officiated at the marriage of Sylvester Dupee and Susannah Stanton, both of Nissouri.[33] Sylvester's brothers, Michael and John Dupee, were witnesses. Finally, Rev. Vining officiated at the marriage of "Norbear Dupre" and Dorothy Marsh, both of Nissouri, on March 8, 1840.[34] Was this "Norbear" Norbert the son or Norbert the father with a second marriage? No record was found of Michael's marriage to Susanna Sturtevant, reportedly in 1828. There were also no further records found for Frances (Fanny) Dupee. Census records show the brothers (Sylvester, Michael, and John) were all farmers. Only an 1851 census report shows Wells Dupe, age fifty-eight, was a laborer then living in East Nissouri.[35] He was listed alone at that time.

Both Sylvester and John appear in 1861 Canadian census records in Stanley, Huron County, Ontario, just before John and his family moved to Michigan. This is where Sylvester remained. After his wife Susannah died, he remarried Mary Donahue in 1870.[10] His gravestone in Stanley, Ontario, states he was eighty-four when he died in 1878,[36] no birth date was given. Sylvester's birth year varies on various records. His gravestone age suggests he was born in 1793 or 1794, while his 1829 military record suggests he was born around 1799 or 1800.

It appears from census records and directories that Michael Dupee stayed in West Nissouri until at least 1890. After his wife Susanna died, he married Caroline Congdon, and according to census records, he later lived with Harriet "Hattie" Young. Michael died in 1893 and was buried in Enniskillen, Lambton County, Ontario,[37] near Lake Huron, where his first wife Susannah was buried. According to his gravestone photo on Ancestry.com, Michael was age ninety-five when he died. Based on his gravestone, he was born in 1798, while his 1829 military records would put it in 1804. I have seen birthdates all in between these dates in various records.

I have been fortunate to be in touch with two of Michael's descendants through Ancestry.com contacts, Jerry Jasper and Rosalie Duffin. Both have been very helpful collaborators in my research. Rose is a fourth great-granddaughter who, by coincidence, lives on a farm very near the lot awarded in 1822 to Norbert/Norbin from his land grant. She said there is nothing left of the original cabin, but it is still an operating farm.

As I write this, I find that I dreamt of visiting my third great-uncle, Michael, in his later years. I suppose in a way that I have. These relatives are seeping into my subconsciousness.

GENEVIÈVE LEROUX'S FAMILY

My third great-grandmother's branch of the family tree brings a myriad of other stories, some sad, some colorful, and even an intersection with another tree branch. Geneviève's immediate family story was quite sad. As noted earlier, Geneviève grew up in Les Cédres, near Montreal. Her parents, Michel Leroux and Catherine Poirier, married there in 1769,[38] when Catherine was seventeen and Michel was nineteen. During the next five years, the couple had four children. However, Michel died in July 1775,[39] leaving his pregnant wife and four young children. Catherine had another son in December of that year. But in September of 1776, she lost that son and her youngest daughter.[40] It can't have been easy for Catherine. She lost her mother at age fifteen, and her mother had lost several children before her own death.[41] Such losses were common, but still very difficult, I'm sure. Catherine Poirier soon remarried to her cousin Michel Couillier.[42] They had four more children together and raised Catherine's other three as well.[43]

This was also a tumultuous time in Les Cédres and Montreal. The spring and summer of 1775 was the start of the American Revolutionary War. One of the American's first military initiatives was to attack British-controlled Quebec and try to convince those residents to side with them in overthrowing the British. After all, the British took control of Quebec only fifteen years earlier. Under General Richard Montgomery, the American Continental Army took Fort St. John, just south of Les Cédres, in September 1775. They moved on to take Montreal in November and went on to Quebec City to join General Benedict Arnold's troops in December of 1775. The Americans failed in their conquest of Quebec City during a brutal snowstorm. Montgomery was killed. By then, the American army was significantly reduced from expired enlistments, hunger, smallpox, and battle casualties. Still, both Montreal and Quebec City remained under a months-long siege by the Americans. Les Cédres itself saw skirmishes with the Americans in May of 1776. By this point, the British had received reinforcements of several thousand troops, including Hessian allies, and they pushed the beleaguered American army back to Fort Ticonderoga in New York.[44]

While Michel Leroux died before this action, anyone living in the Montreal area would have been impacted. There were American sympathizers in Montreal. But this sympathy was misjudged. The Continental Army's invasion and siege left a bitter taste among the local people. Support for the Crown was strong among clergy and landowners. American sympathizers were driven to the countryside. Even the merchants, who had disliked paying taxes to Britain, now took the side of Loyalists. Most of the *habitants* preferred to stay neutral and not take up arms against either the British or the Americans.[44]

Geneviève Leroux's family also intersects with another relative and earlier story from Chapter 9. There, I focused on my ancestor, Jean Gauthier dit Sanguinoira, a *voyageur,* and his Indigenous wife. Here it is Jean's sister, Marie Josephte Marguerite Gauthier dite Sanguinoira, who would become Geneviève Leroux's great-grandmother. Both Jean and Marie were children of Pierre Gauthier dit Sanguinoira and Charlotte Roussel, who were taken captive in the Lachine massacre in August 1689.

THE POIRIER LINE

Michael Leroux dit Rousseau *1750—1775*	M: 1769	Catherine Marguerite Poirier dite Deslonges *1751—1842*
Jean-Baptiste dit Desloges *1719—1795*	M:1742	Marie Geneviève Hunault dit Deschamps *1724—1766*
Joseph Poirier dit Desloges *1685—unkown*	M: 1709	Marie J M Gauthier dite Sanguinoira *1684—1728*

While the children hid in the woods, their parents were taken away by the Iroquois, and the whole town was burned. The minor children, including seven-year-old Marie, were cared for by a guardian, as they assumed their parents had been killed. Marie's father returned from captivity nine years later, although his wife had died. In 1702, at age eighteen, Marie married Alexander Turpin, a sixty-year-old widower; Marie's father served as a witness. A year later, her father, Pierre, died. And three years after that, Marie's husband died. Marie then remarried Joseph Poirier dit Desloges in 1709. Joseph was twenty-four and a soldier. Marie's life became a bit more settled after this. She and Joseph had eight children together, including Jean Baptiste Poirier dit Desloges, who was Catherine Poirier's father and Geneviève Leroux's grandfather. Marie died in 1728 in Montreal at age forty-four, when her son, Jean Baptiste, was just eight years old. For women during these times, it must have seemed that so much of their life was outside of their control.

However, I found one woman who tried to take control of her life. You'll see where it got her.

A MONTREAL FOUNDING FAMILY

The Leroux and Poirier families had lived mostly in the Montreal area, and their ancestors were among the first Montreal settlers. Geneviève's second great-grandfather was Sir Hubert Leroux (1639-1681), the son of Sir Hubert Leroux, a Royal Notary in Vitry-le-Francois, a section in Marne, France. Hubert, the son, arrived in Montreal in 1672-73 to set up a fur trade business.[45] This is when the original street layout was still underway (just ten streets at the time). When the first Montreal census was conducted in 1666, there were 659 French (mostly men) and 1000 Natives. By 1716, the French population in Montreal had grown to 4,409, and the Natives were 1,177.[46]

Hubert would soon marry a young woman, Anne-Marie Van Zeigt (1655-1722). Her German name was given many spellings in the records, such as Vansegue, Fannenche, or Phansèque.[45, 47] Her story is perhaps the more interesting one, more colorful as you'll see, than that of her husband. Anne-Marie was the daughter of a nobleman, Captain Christien Van Zeigt, of the Imperial troops in Hamburg, Germany. Hamburg was then a free state and a big commercial center. Hamburg families had close relationships with French high-society families. But Anne-Marie's father was deceased, leaving her without a dowry. She thus became part of the last group of the *Filles du Roi* (King's Daughters project), which provided travel funds and a dowry for the girls. Upon arrival in Montreal, she was received by the nuns under the direction of Blessed Marguerite Bourgeois at St. Gabriel's farm. The nuns were assigned to monitor the girls' interaction with the bachelors of the colony in order to ensure good morality in the process. Girls of Anne Marie's background were selected for the higher-ranking bachelors. Anne Marie Van Zeigt signed a marriage contract before a notary (barrister/solicitor) with Sir Hubert Le Roux on November 7, 1673; they were married in January. She was sixteen at the time, and Hubert was thirty-four. Several noblemen in the colony witnessed the wedding as evidence of the couple's noble status.[45] They had three children together (the middle child, Jean-Baptist Leroux, was my direct ancestor). But shortly after their youngest was born, Hubert died on October 7, 1681, at age forty-two.[47] Anne-Marie remarried nine months later to Gabriel Cardinal and had one son with him.[48]

Up to this point, Anne-Marie's life is not so different from other *Filles du Roi* brought to the colony, a noblewoman at that. In later

THE LEROUX LINE

Michael Leroux dit Rousseau *1750—1775*	M: 1769	Catherine Marguerite Poirier dite Deslonges *1751—1842*
Jean-Baptiste Leroux III *1705—1750*	M:1731	Marie-Angelique-Elizabeth Libersan *1711—1806*
Jean-Baptiste Leroux I *1678—1759*	M: 1702	Louise Chaussé *1682—1756*
Hubert Leroux *1639—1681*	M: 1673	Anne-Marie Van Zeigt *1657—1722*

years, however, her name showed up frequently in public records.[49] As it happened, her first husband left her with debts, and her second husband was prone to fights and was absent a lot as a *voyageur* of sorts. This left Anne-Marie mostly on her own with her four children and no money.[49,50] She had to find a way to feed her children.

Around 1788, she opened a public house or cabaret in her home on St. Jacques Street in Montreal. It was not unusual at the time to open one's home as a cabaret, even though it wasn't legal. It was there she was accused of running a "house of debauchery," of selling alcohol (wine), and that "all sorts of people frequent(ed) her house, where many disorders and drunkenness are committed during the day and almost every night." Anne-Marie was also accused of selling the favors of her fourteen-year-old daughter, Anne Charlotte, who had married thirty-eight-year-old Michel Claude Leblond a year earlier. Anne-Charlotte reportedly had returned to her mother's home for protection because she was afraid of her husband. When Leblond tried to get his wife out of her mother's house, Anne-Marie threatened her son-in-law to the point that authorities came to protect him from her.[49, 50] A mother's fury may know no bounds when protecting her children!

In 1692, Anne-Marie's husband, Gabriel Cardinal, had apparently disapproved of his wife's lifestyle. He initiated a formal separation of properties and debts that was approved in January of that year. At the same time, Anne-Marie's younger children were taken from her and put into guardianship. Sometime later, Gabriel left for a voyage to Hudson Bay and never returned. Anne-Marie would not learn of his death until 1696.[50]

Still, Anne-Marie pursued her business enterprise to support herself. In March 1693, Anne-Marie was visited by Indians to whom she had sold a dog for food. She invited them into her home. An all-night drunken spree ensued, and one man ended up dead. Anne-Marie was charged with the serious offense of selling alcohol to Indians; she was forced to kneel before the court and was publicly berated. Daughter Anne Charlotte was also berated for behaving seductively. Anne-Marie was fined and imprisoned for her crimes. She was still in jail in 1698. Daughter Anne Charlotte was warned that she, too, would go to prison if she was convicted of an offense again. In 1695, Anne Charlotte was convicted of adultery, but she ran away before she was to appear in court; her husband asked for clemency, and the search for her was dropped.[49,50]

Anne-Marie nonetheless lived a long life. She no longer lived in Montreal, although she was located when needed to endorse a variety of legal documents; she apparently learned to sign her name at some point after her first marriage. She missed her son Jean-Baptiste's 1702 wedding. She was found to sign a document when living in a shelter for the poor in the General Hospital in Quebec in 1703. In 1704, she returned to Montreal to confirm a transfer of land, which had been owned by her first husband, to her son Jean Baptiste. In 1705, she gave power of attorney to an agent to rent her home on St. Jacques Street, Montreal. In 1719, she returned to sell her St. Jacques Street house, which was then falling apart. She received payment partly in cash and partly in clothes and shoes. She was barefoot at the time. She died on Ile Jesus, a river island north of Montreal, in 1722, at age sixty-five.[50,51]

The 5th of December 1722, I undersigned priest doing the parish functions in St-Joseph de la Rivière des prairies, buried in the cemetery of the parish of St-François de Sales on Île Jésus the body of an old woman aged around 70, Irish, in origin, of whom I was unable to

*Saint Jacques Street in modern-day Montreal
is in the banking district*

*learn either the given name nor family name, other than she was
known on the coast as la bonne femme Cardinal (old lady Cardinal),
deceased suddenly last evening at the home of Kenoche La jeunesse,
without having received any sacraments, but after having asked for
a priest, said her rosary, asked forgiveness of God, witnesses Kenoche
La jeuness.[50,51]*

It appears that Anne Marie did not die alone, at least. Apparently,
she was in the home of a friend. But the last twenty years of her life
were a mystery. She seemed to have been a nomad in those years. In
any case, she had little contact with her family. She made some hard
decisions and lived with the consequences. While her priest forgave her
on her deathbed, it seems her society and her children never did. It was

a sad life. What would I have done in her circumstances? I admire her enterprise as a single mom needing to support her family. Only I hope I could have avoided the scandals when there were few legal options for women to earn money. She couldn't go back to her parents' home as my mother did to escape an errant husband. Once again, if it weren't for her scandals, I wouldn't know about her and the plight of women of her time. Her plight is a meaningful part of this history.

There was a silver lining for her son Jean Baptist Leroux, my sixth great-grandfather. He did okay despite the scandals surrounding his mother and sister. Jean Baptiste was fortunate to have lived in the home of his guardian and tutor, Mr. Lory, as he learned how to read and write. This was a rarity at the time. He married Marie Louise Chaussé, and they had thirteen children together, of whom eight lived to adulthood. They lived in Lachine, where Jean Baptiste was a carpenter and where he tended the land that his father had owned. Jean Baptist Leroux lived to be eighty years old.[52]

NORBERT DUPUIS' ANCESTORS

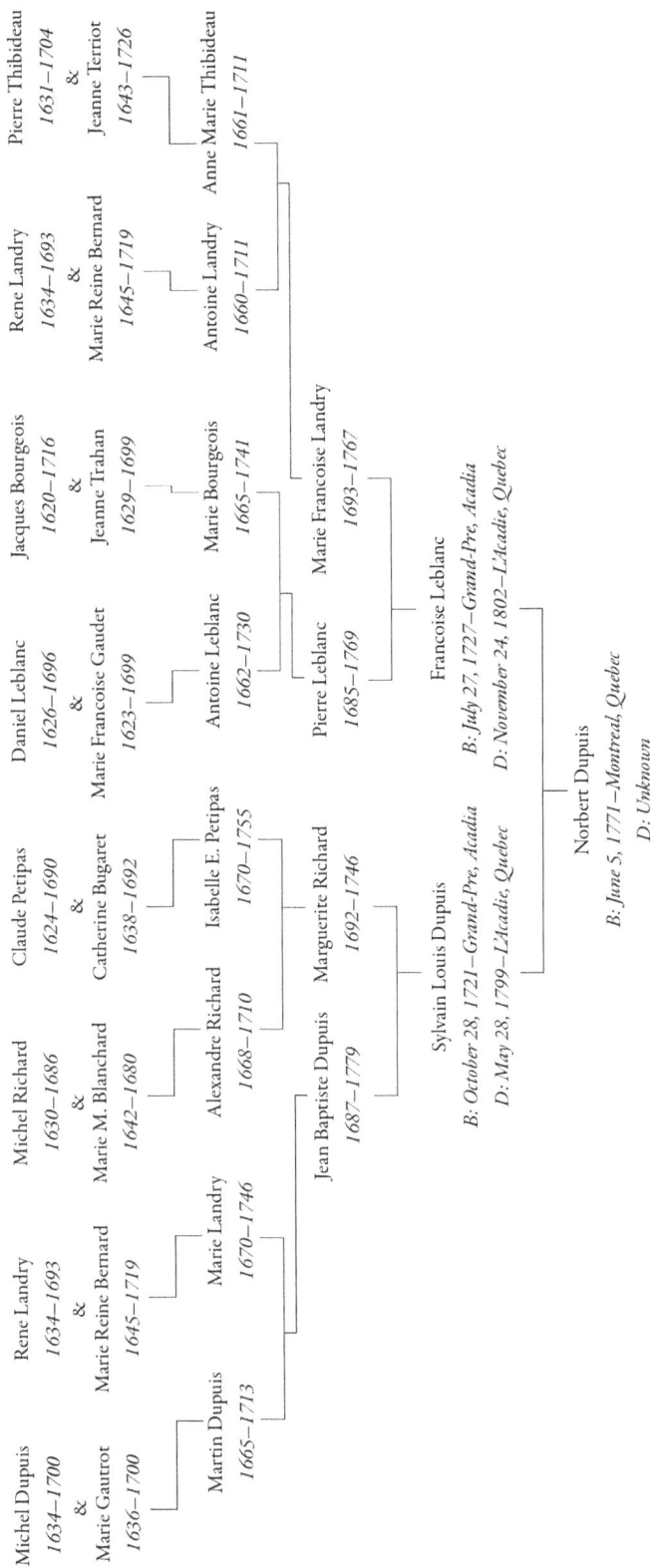

Michel Dupuis
1634–1700
&
Marie Gautrot
1636–1700

Rene Landry
1634–1693
&
Marie Reine Bernard
1645–1719

Michel Richard
1630–1686
&
Marie M. Blanchard
1642–1680

Claude Petipas
1624–1690
&
Catherine Bugaret
1638–1692

Daniel Leblanc
1626–1696
&
Marie Francoise Gaudet
1623–1699

Jacques Bourgeois
1620–1716
&
Jeanne Trahan
1629–1699

Rene Landry
1634–1693
&
Marie Reine Bernard
1645–1719

Pierre Thibideau
1631–1704
&
Jeanne Terriot
1643–1726

Martin Dupuis
1665–1713

Marie Landry
1670–1746

Alexandre Richard
1668–1710

Isabelle E. Petipas
1670–1755

Antoine Leblanc
1662–1730

Marie Bourgeois
1665–1741

Antoine Landry
1660–1711

Anne Marie Thibideau
1661–1711

Jean Baptiste Dupuis
1687–1779

Marguerite Richard
1692–1746

Pierre Leblanc
1685–1769

Marie Francoise Landry
1693–1767

Sylvain Louis Dupuis
B: October 28, 1721–Grand-Pre, Acadia
D: May 28, 1799–L'Acadie, Quebec

Francoise Leblanc
B: July 27, 1727–Grand-Pre, Acadia
D: November 24, 1802–L'Acadie, Quebec

Norbert Dupuis
B: June 5, 1771–Montreal, Quebec
D: Unknown

Les Acadiennes—The Acadians

THE DUPUIS ANCESTORS BACK TO FRANCE

WITH THE HELP OF MANY PREVIOUS FAMILY GENEALOGISTS, THE Dupuis family line is clearly documented from Norbert back five more generations to their arrival in Acadia (modern-day Nova Scotia (NS)) from France in the mid-1600s. I did not know the Acadian story before discovering this family line. It's an amazing story! The Dupuis family was among the first families to settle in this area. In Quebec, settlers had arrived over a long period of more than a hundred years. The numbers surged with the influx of the *Filles du Roi* (King's Daughters project). In Acadia, however, most of the early settlers arrived between 1632 and 1654. Marriages occurred among neighbors, and they produced large families. As a result, most of the pioneer Acadian families soon became related to one another, and all of the Dupuis family marriages in Acadia were traced back to those first families. There were six colonial wars between 1613 and 1713, with numerous attacks in between. The colony changed hands between French and English rulers several times. Therefore, the Acadian story for these families is turbulent and ultimately heartbreaking.

THE SETTLING OF *L'ACADIE*, A NEW FRANCE COLONY

L'Acadie (Acadia), as the colony was called, was claimed by French explorers in 1604. This was before the settlement in Jamestown, Virginia, before the pilgrims landed in Massachusetts, and even before Quebec was established. Of course, fishermen from France and other nations had been fishing and fur trading along the coast for a hundred years earlier.

Norbert Dupuis	M: 1796[1]	Geneviève Leroux
B: June 5, 1771—Montreal, Quebec		B: May 3, 1773—Les Cèdres, Quebec
D: Likely in W Nissouri, Ontario		D: Likely in W. Nissouri, Ontario
Sylvain Dupuis	M: 1747[2]	Francoise LeBlanc
B: October 28, 1721—Port Royal, Acadia		B: July 27, 1727—Grand-Pré, Acadia
D: May 28, 1799—Acadia, New France		D: November 24, 1802—Acadia, N. France
Jean Dupuis	M: 1713[3]	Marguerite Richard
B: 1687—Grand-Pré, Acadia, N. France		B: 1692—Grand-Pré, Acadia, N. France
D: 1779—St. Philippe, Quebec		D: Unknown
Martin Dupuis	M: 1686[4]	Marie Landry
B: 1665—Port Royal, Acadia, N. France		B: 1670—Port Royal, Acadia, N. France
D: August 8, 1713—Grand-Pré, Acadia		D: September 20, 1746—Grand-Pré, Acadia
Michel Dupuis	M: 1664[5]	Marie Gautrot
B: 1634—Poitou-Charentes, France		B: 1636—Port Royal, Acadia, N. France
D: aft. 1700—Port Royal, Acadia		D: aft 1700—Port Royal, Acadia
Martin Dupuis	M: 1632[6]	Perrine Theriault
B: 1612—Poitou-Charentes, France		B: 1610—Champagne-Ardenne, France
D: bef. 1671—Port Royal, Acadia		D: Bef. 1671—Port Royal, Acadia

L'Acadie included all of what today is known as the Maritime Provinces of Canada—Nova Scotia, Prince Edward Island, New Brunswick, the Gaspé peninsula of Quebec, and eastern Maine. In 1604, an exploratory expedition included navigator Samuel de Champlain, along with leaders Jean de Biencourt, sieur de Poutrincourt, who was eager to establish the first French agricultural colony on the North American Coast, and Pierre Dugua, sieur de Mons, the viceroy and captain general of New France, who was eager to monopolize the fur trade. A group of eighty colonists, all men, attempted to spend the winter on an island in the middle of the St. Croix River, the present-day border of Maine and New Brunswick. It proved disastrous, as thirty-six men died of scurvy.[7,8]

The next summer, in 1605, the explorers found a better site. They called it "Port Royal" on *Baie Francaise*, the large body of water separating the Acadian peninsula from the mainland (it is now called Annapolis Royal, Nova Scotia, on the Bay of Fundy). This appeared to be an excellent base for a colony. The mountains to the north and rolling hills to the south surrounded an expansive river valley. It offered beautiful meadows suitable for grazing livestock and a large harbor that could hold numerous ships. Champlain's party at Port Royal included Louis Hébert, the apothecary who would later settle with Champlain in Quebec and become father-in-law to my ancestor Hélène Desportes, the first child born in Quebec (see Chapter 9). Hébert would conduct experiments in the cultivation of wheat, rye, and hemp--crops that could support a growing colony.[7,9] They built a small fort and "habitation," using materials they had moved from the earlier St. Croix site. This fort was a forty-eight- by sixty-foot rectangle to protect them from European attackers. The settlement was like a fortified farming hamlet in France. The local indigenous people, the Mikmaq, were friendly. As he did later in Quebec, Champlain encouraged the settlers to live in harmony with the Indigenous people and learn their ways. They shared their tables as equals. Champlain sent off young French gentlemen of the highest rank to live with the Mikmaq and learn their language. Unlike any other leader in New France, Champlain sought out the Native leaders in their own territory, with only one or two companions. He built enduring friendships with many Native leaders throughout the area. As it did later in Quebec, this alliance was critical. The native people taught the settlers their methods of hunting, fishing, and foraging, which would prove essential for surviving in this region. In turn, the Mikmaq benefitted from access to European trade. Forty-five settlers stayed for this winter, including Champlain, a Catholic priest, and a Protestant pastor. Only twelve died of scurvy this time due to a milder winter and the Mikmaq provision of fresh meat. Still, food was scarce, and they eagerly awaited a supply ship from France in the Spring.[10,11]

It was July 1606 when Poutrincourt returned from France with fifty new colonists and brought plenty of supplies, along with some swine and poultry. De Mons had remained in France to shore up investors. Poutrincourt's vision for Acadia was to establish a feudal utopia where he would be a benevolent ruler for the good of the whole.[12] He was granted the *seigneury* of Port Royal and was given two years to establish a colony. The fifty new colonists included gentlemen, artisans, journeymen, skilled and unskilled laborers, and servants. Again, it was men only. Poutrincourt and Champlain encouraged the colonists to work for the colony and themselves, devoting a small part of each day, two to three hours, to collective tasks and the rest of the day on their own gardens. They also developed a barter economy, trading artisan, mason, and carpentry skills for food, game, and fish. This combination of feudal and entrepreneurial systems worked well for the colony. There was still a social order, like that in France, that belied equality or democracy. The gentlemen were more likely to recognize the humanity in Native people than in their servants and laborers.[12]

This first attempt at a colony was short-lived, however. De Mons was challenged on his commercial monopoly, and his company failed. By 1614, most of the French were chased out by the English. Acadia was renamed Nova Scotia (NS) in 1621 when it briefly became a colony of Scots.[7,9]

L'Acadie was returned to France with a 1632 treaty. This prompted the arrival of permanent settlers in the area. The earliest arrivals, once again, were craftsmen, soldiers, and fishermen, many of whom were hired to build forts and other infrastructure necessary to support a colony. Some of these men came to Le Hève (present-day LaHave, NS) on the east coast for its access to fishing and Atlantic trade. But Port Royal offered better farmland, so the capital was moved there, and it soon became the largest settlement. Most of those men returned to France after their contracts, but a few stayed. The first French families with women and children arrived in 1636 on the ship Saint-Jehan. Importantly, farmers started arriving, as they would establish the necessary agriculture. These settlers developed a system of dikes in the swampland to create larger, more fertile fields, drawing on centuries of silt deposited from the tides. The marsh grass produced healthy livestock. Trading in furs, timber, and fish for profit also improved the colony's sustainability.[9]

These first settlers included a number of my ancestors, my seventh and eighth grandparents, whom I will feature here to illustrate the Acadian story out of their stories. As I learned these French names during my research, I now see the names everywhere among their ancestors in modern times. They are my cousins!

Guilliaume Trahan was an officer in the cavalry, a toolmaker, and an armorer. He arrived on the ship Saint-Jehan in 1636 with his wife, Françoise Corbineau, and two children from Bourgueil, France.[13,14] Also arriving on the Saint-Jehan in 1636 was Bernard Bugaret, a Basque carpenter. Bugaret traveled several times between New Rochelle, France, and Acadia.[14] It's unclear whether he permanently settled in Acadia, but he and his wife (her name is unknown) had a daughter, Catherine Bugaret, who was born in Acadia in 1638 and who would later become a maternal ancestor of mine.[15]

Jean Blanchard was among the first five settlers to receive land grants in Port Royal. He may have arrived earlier on his own and sent for his wife and family afterward. Jean married Radegonde Lambert in 1642, most likely in France. They owned a lot adjoining the old fort, which was later expropriated to enlarge the fort. Jean and Radegonde's first child, daughter Madeleine Blanchard, was born in 1643 in Port Royal. They had six children by 1656.[13,16]

François Gautrot, a farmer, was also among the first arrivals in Port Royal. He married his first wife, named Marie, around 1635 (location unknown). They had two children, likely in France, including daughter Marie Gautrot in 1636, before the elder Marie died. There is speculation that François's first wife, Marie's mother, was Indigenous, Mikmaq, but this is unconfirmed, based on the DNA of her descendants.[17] In 1644, François married a second wife, Edmée Lejeune, in Port Royal, and they had ten children together. François owned a lot near the old fort, which, like Jean Blanchard's lot, was expropriated when the fort was enlarged.[17]

Jacques Bourgeois arrived in Port Royal in 1641. His father, also named Jacques, was an army officer at Port Royal. Jacques Jr. was trained as a surgeon in France, and he intended to set up a practice in the new colony. In 1643, he married Jeanne Trahan, who was one of the two children arriving in 1636 with Guilliaume Trahan.[13,14] In 1646, Jacques and Jeanne were granted an island in the middle of the Dauphin River, upstream from Port Royal. In addition to being a surgeon, Bourgeois became a fur trader and merchant. He built flour and lumber mills in Port Royal and traded with the Mikmaq and the Bostonians. He learned English and eventually became an interpreter between the English and French. In 1671, the family had twenty arpents of cultivated land in two locations. Jacques and Jeanne had ten children together: three sons and seven daughters.[18,19]

Daniel Leblanc, a farmer, arrived around 1645. In 1650, he married a young widow, Françoise Gaudet, in Port Royal.[20] Françoise's father, Jean Gaudet, is often considered the "Abraham of Acadia" because his descendants are so numerous. Jean Gaudet may have arrived as early as 1634 or perhaps even with Champlain's expedition, although his family would have arrived later. Jean Gaudet was the oldest person during the Port Royal census in 1671, at the age of ninety-six.[21,22] Apparently, even rugged pioneers could live long lives. Daniel and Françoise made their home and farm on the North bank, about nine miles up the river from the fort. Their family of seven children included one daughter and six sons. All their descendants had large families with many sons, making the Leblancs the largest of Acadian ancestral families,[20] including part of my ancestry.

Pierre Thibodeau arrived in Port Royal in 1654. He married Jeanne Theriault around 1660; she was the daughter of Jehan Theriault and Perrine Breau, who had arrived in Port Royal earlier. Over time, Pierre developed a gristmill and a sawmill on Stream Loup Marin, near his brookside farm in Prée Ronde (present-day Round Hill, NS) outside of Port Royal. Pierre and Jeanne had sixteen children: seven sons and nine daughters.[23,24]

My seventh great-grandfather and direct ancestor, Michel Dupuis, was born about 1634 in the area of LaChaussée, Vienne, in Western France.[5] He arrived in Port Royal sometime before 1650 with his parents, Martin Dupuis and Perrine Theriault. Martin and Perrine apparently died before the first census in 1671; therefore, their story and the pedigree before Michel are unconfirmed in Acadian history.[13] However, Martin and Perrine were reportedly buried in the Port Royal cemetery.[6]

Why did they come? Most were hand-picked by the first Lieutenant Governors, Isaac de Razilly, and his successor in 1635, Charles de Menou d'Aulnay. D'Aulnay remained in charge of Port Royal until his death in 1650, and he continued to recruit colonists during that time, mostly from his own family *seigneuries* in the French villages of Poitou, Martaizé, and LaChaussée. Land grants at that time were based on the semi-feudal *seigneurial* system. In Acadia, d'Aulnay was the governor and the *seigneur,* and he granted land to individuals as his tenants. As in Quebec, tenants in Acadia would have a better chance to own their own land than back in France, where it was highly unlikely or impossible for peasants to do so. That hope was certainly an incentive to cross the Atlantic. Some also came because their region in France was devastated by epidemics in the 1630s. Some were protestants pushed out by the religious wars in France. But all wanted a better life. Most were peasants who were unable to read or write. Less than one in ten of the initial recruits decided to stay.[25] I can only imagine their bravery and determination.

They cleared land to build their individual homesteads and kitchen gardens. They joined forces to build dikes and common fields for larger crops. Some contributed other skills to make tools, mill lumber, and flour, and tend to basic surgical needs of the time, such as tooth extraction and broken limbs. Working together, men and women, they formed a fledgling settlement. By 1650, there were fifty families living and farming in the Port Royal area.[25] However, there would soon be new challenges to contend with.

In addition to the settlers, the French troops numbered around 130 to protect the small settlement. These included Michel Richards, a young soldier who arrived around 1652.[13,26] It was mostly a quiet duty. However, in 1654, Major Richard Sedgwick from Massachusetts arrived with 300 British soldiers. This was not part of a declared war. Sedgwick sought to control trade along the entire coast on behalf of England. The French troops attempted an assault on the attackers, but they were quickly overpowered. Sedgwick sent most of the French soldiers back to France, including officer Jacques Bourgeois senior. Michel Richards stayed. The French settlers were offered a choice to return to France or stay in Port Royal. If they chose to stay, they could keep their land and practice their religion, but they had to sign an oath of loyalty that they would not bear arms against the English nation. Most settlers chose to stay.[27,28]

A PEACEFUL PERIOD

For the next sixteen years, Acadia was under English rule. When under French rule, local governance was the responsibility of the local governor or the *seigneur*. Under English rule, Sedgwick established an "inhabitants council," appointed to manage day-to-day affairs based on the New England governance system. It was presided over by resident Guillaume Trahan. They were watched over by the Massachusetts governor, who remained in Boston. Therefore, the Acadians were mostly left to themselves. Even the priests had been sent away. The English had long distrusted Catholics, and the New England Puritans distrusted them even more. They assumed the priests were instigators of treachery. Only an occasional missionary passed through during these years. Village elders led liturgical chants and prayers. The community included Catholics and Protestants, and they lived comfortably together.[27,28]

Over time, they developed their own egalitarian form of self-rule. While it started with the Inhabitants' Council, it drew on their own communal system of managing the dikes together and on the Mikmaq example of consensus building. With the same philosophy applied in Champlain's initial settlement, they used a combination of community property management and entrepreneurial tasks as individual families tended to their own gardens and fields. Only now, there were no French gentlemen to maintain a hierarchy. Community values were held strongly. Such values would be important to their survival during hardships in these early years and hardships yet to come.[27]

Without the French hierarchy in charge, the feudal *seigneurial* land system soon faded, and many settlers moved up the *Riviere Dauphin* (now the Annapolis River) to claim new land plots and accommodate their growing population. Several hamlets of eight to ten interrelated families grew up along the river. They enjoyed a life of abundance. They raised ample crops of grains, peas, flax, and fruit, along with their cattle, sheep, and hogs. They ate well and were much healthier than if they had returned to France. The life of French peasants was one of scarcity, as most of their produce went to the landowner for his own profit. While they no longer traded with France, they enjoyed a prosperous trade with New England, trading produce and furs for goods they couldn't produce themselves. A drawback, however, was that the marriage pool had shrunk without a stream of French immigrants coming in. A few sailors and fishermen passing through were persuaded to marry local women, but intermarriages among cousins were common.[27]

The next generation of marriages began to occur. The single men who arrived earlier married daughters of other settlers. In 1656, Michel Richards married Madeleine Blanchard in Port Royal. I understand why he chose to stay when other soldiers returned to France if he had his eye on young Madeleine. The Richard's family homestead was on the south side of the river, about ten to fifteen miles east of the fort. By 1671, Michel and Madeleine had fourteen arpents (about twelve acres) of cultivated land, along with fifteen cattle and fourteen sheep. They eventually had ten children together.[13,22,26]

Catherine Bugaret, daughter of Bernard Bugaret, married Claude Petitpas around 1658. They would have thirteen children. Claude was a laborer who later became a royal notary and clerk of the court or *syndic* (chief civil officer) in Port Royal.[29] By the 1671 census, they had developed a homestead with thirty arpents (about twenty-five acres) under cultivation, with twenty-six cattle and eleven sheep.[22] Of the fifty-six households reporting cultivated land in 1671, only twelve had ten or more arpents, suggesting they were somewhat more prosperous.[29] Their daughter Isabelle Petitpas would marry Alexander Richards, son of Michel and Madeleine, around 1690 to become my sixth great-grandparents.[30]

Michel Dupuis married Marie Gautrot, daughter of François Gautrot and his first wife Marie, in 1664 in Port Royal. Michel and Marie had five children together, including three sons and two daughters, in addition to Marie's daughter from her earlier marriage to Jean Potot.[5,31] In the 1671 census, Michel Dupuis was thirty-seven and Marie thirty-four with four children at that time. They had six arpents of cultivated land, with five cattle and one sheep.[22]

Newlyweds were welcomed into the community with the French custom of *charivari*. Outside their house on their wedding night, visitors would serenade, beat kettles, and blow horns until they were invited in for refreshments. The couple would usually stay with one of their families initially. Once they gathered materials for their own home, the whole community would help with house-raising. All would help to clear a plot of land, build a house, and provide some cattle, pigs, and chickens for the couple's use to start out. Archeological work in the Port Royal area has found remains of houses built on fieldstone foundations, 350 to 1,000 square feet, built with wooden beams and thatched roofs. Inside, walls were plastered and insulated with seagrass, making it airtight and bright. One room was furnished sparsely, with a fireplace and bake-oven on one end.[32] This sounds charming, but imagine a family with ten children in this space.

A unique Acadian culture was emerging, free from a social hierarchy. Their entertainment consisted of gathering together to tell stories or gossip. They enjoyed mimicry and lampooning one another, and especially the Yankees, whom they considered standoffish and hard-nosed. They enjoyed heroic stories, ending with a rescue from some impossible situation or with irony, as a clumsy hero saved the day. Instead of a happy ending or punishment of the villain, they enjoyed a laugh at the scoundrel's expense. Many stories took the form of ballads. They loved music and dancing. Holidays were for community feasting and dancing. The New Year's celebration included a procession of men and boys going house to house, embracing and kissing the women, to symbolize the end of old arguments between neighbors and the beginning of a new year of peace and harmony. Other holidays merged Catholic and Mikmaq traditions, such as the spring festival, *le retour des oies*, the return of the geese, which celebrates the joy of coming spring with all fool's day, and the traditions of Catholic Easter.[32] As someone with standoffish Yankee ancestry, I like this side of my family.

Some also married into the Miqmak community. For example, Claude Petitpas Jr.—third son of Claude Petitpas and Catherine Bugaret, brother of Isabelle, and my sixth great-uncle— married a Miqmak woman, Marie-Thérèse, around 1686. The couple had at least seven children, according to the 1708 census. It was common to find mixed families and *métis* children living among the French families. The French policy encouraged by Champlain was that Indigenous people who were baptized Catholic were considered French citizens. Somewhat later, Claude and Marie lived among her people in Muskoudoboit, on the east coast near present-day Halifax. This location brought them into regular contact with French and New England fishermen. Claude Jr. was a schooner captain and became an interpreter with his son Barthélemy. They were proficient in three languages—Mikmaq, French, and English. Claude Jr. was recognized for his "tender regard to sundry English captives during the late Indian war," as he paid their ransom out of his own pocket. For this benevolence, he was granted a hundred English pounds from the Boston Legislative Council on June 30, 1720. He managed to straddle the delicate balance across the three cultures.[33]

BACK AND FORTH BETWEEN
FRENCH AND ENGLISH RULE

By 1671, the area was ceded back to France by treaty. This ushered in a period of further French immigration and expansion to communities in other parts of the peninsula. The French initiated the area's first official census in 1671, which yielded 392 people, most of whom were in Port Royal.[22]

René Landry arrived in Port Royal with his wife, Marie Bernard, between the censuses of 1671 and 1678. Ultimately, they had fifteen children,[34] two of whom, Marie and Antoine, appear separately in my family tree. René and Marie's daughter Marie Landry married Martin Dupuis, son of Michel Dupuis and Marie Gautrot, in 1686 in Port Royal.[35] Antoine Landry married Ann Marie Thibideau in 1681 and started their family in Port Royal.[36] Later on, in 1710, Antoine and Ann Marie's daughter Françoise Landry married into the Leblanc family to Pierre LeBlanc (son of Antoine Leblanc and grandson of Daniel Leblanc)[37]; Françoise and Pierre would become my fifth great-grandparents. You can see how the web of relationships grows.

In 1672, Jacques Bourgeois and Jeanne Trahan sold part of their land in Port Royal to establish the "Bourgeois colony" in the Chignecto isthmus, near the present-day border of New Brunswick and Nova Scotia. They built a farm, flour, and sawmill in what became the very prosperous Beaubassin region. Their farm was near the Shediac portage, a strategic relay station between Acadia and Quebec. While two of their sons remained in Beaubassin, Jacques and Jeanne returned to Port Royal by 1699.[38]

By 1682, several families migrated north, up the coast to the Minas basin, to form the community of Grand Pré. Among them were the four oldest sons in the Leblanc family, including my ancestors Antoine Leblanc and Marie Bourgeois, Martin Dupuis and Marie Landry, and in-laws Antoine Landry and Anne Marie Thibideau. They all settled in the Gaspareau River valley, a great meadow stretching eighteen miles upriver from Grand Pré.[39] This is where most of Martin and Marie's

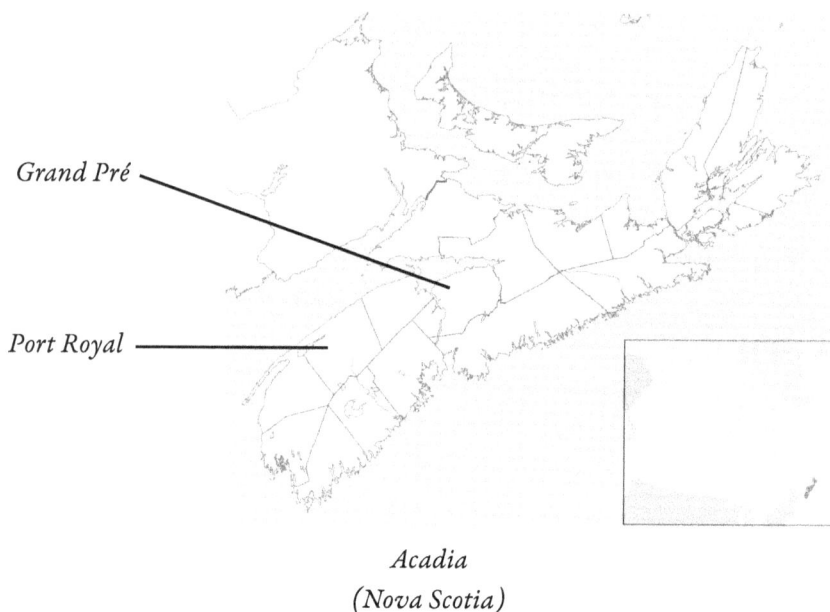

Grand Pré

Port Royal

Acadia
(Nova Scotia)

thirteen children were born. By 1701, the family would have six arpents of land, fifteen cattle, fifteen sheep, and fifteen hogs.[40] The settlers employed their dike building to the salt marshes there, reclaiming thousands of acres of productive farmland. The population grew, and soon, this became the largest settlement and the breadbasket of Acadia.[39]

The New England trade continued as French governors licensed it to make a profit for themselves. But over time, different French governors would impose a monopoly on trade, pushing out any English competitors. The Acadians preferred to trade with New Englanders, and clandestine trade continued. However, the Acadians were caught between the imperial interests of France and England, as neither wanted the other in North America. Tensions were mounting.[41]

After the King William's War broke out in Europe, Sir William Phipps from Boston set his sights on the prize of Acadia. In May 1690, he brought seven ships with sixty-four cannons and 736 soldiers to Port Royal. Within a half-hour, the meager French forces of about seventy soldiers capitulated. But Phipps did not honor the usual capitulation agreement. He encouraged his men to burn and loot the village and destroy the church and all emblems of their Catholic religion. Over several days, they methodically burned barns, ransacked homes and gardens for any buried treasure, and slaughtered the livestock. As the looting and burning continued, Phipps demanded that the villagers come in from where they were hiding in the woods to subject themselves to the Crown of England. Once again, the captors demanded allegiance to England. Phipps created a peacekeeping council of six well-respected Acadians chosen by their peers, including René Landry and Daniel Leblanc, who were then elders in the community. Phipps returned to Boston, where he was rewarded for his victory by becoming the Massachusetts governor.[42,43]

This new English rule ushered in a more unsettled time for residents. New England vessels came to trade but often looted the villages at will. When the English were not around, French privateers also came to the port, attempting to recruit young men as crew and outfit their ships with local supplies, sometimes taken at will. While they needed the trade, local residents didn't appreciate either of these visitors.[42]

In 1697, another treaty restored Acadia to France. By the 1701 census, there were about 1,134 settlers spread across the area.[40] But in 1703, yet another war with the British ensued, and the British attacked Grand Pré this time. Even while the Acadians and Mikmaq Indians fiercely defended the village, the church, village, and fields were all burned. The dikes were cut down, and their fields were flooded. Despite frequent burning and looting throughout Acadia, the French sent no new troops or supplies, as they were financially strapped by their war in Europe.[44]

In 1710, the final attack in this war brought 1,500 New England soldiers in a fleet of ships to defeat the Acadians, a significant escalation in troops and terror.[45] The new regime quickly made their new orders clear to the official representatives of the Minas Basin area (including my ancestors Antoine Landry, his brothers Jean and Pierre Landry, Pierre Thériot, Charles Bourgeois, and Antoine Leblanc) that "by the fate of war they have become prisoners at discretion and that both their persons and effects are absolutely at the disposal of the Conquerors."[46]

NO PEACE TO BE HAD

With the Treaty of Utrecht in 1713, this area was officially ceded to England—never again returning to France. However, this treaty did not end the tensions. The Acadians were once again given the choice to repatriate to France, go to the French colony of Quebec, or swear allegiance to the British Crown, which included fighting for the British crown if called upon. Most decided to stay, but they refused to sign the oath. They had now lived in Acadia for many generations. With the frequent change of rulers, each ruler demanded allegiance. Thus far, they had negotiated neutrality and refused to take up arms against either the French or the English. They had become known disparagingly as the "French neutrals." While this tactic had worked for earlier governors, it would increasingly become a sore point.[47] I imagine it was like living with rival gangs in the neighborhood, each vying for loyalty to their side. The Acadians just wanted to stay out of the fray by keeping their heads down and going on with their routines. But they couldn't avoid the mayhem. The destruction of property had become an emblem of the victors' triumph.

Between 1713 and 1755, intermittent wars between France and England continued in Europe. The Maritimes remained a theatre in the war of conquest of New France, which still had colonies at Ile St. Jean (now Prince Edwards Island) and Ile Royale (now Cape Breton) in northern Nova Scotia. The French set out to reclaim Acadian assets with assaults in Grand Pré and elsewhere. The Acadians lived in continual fear of attacks.

Even during these turbulent years, families rebuilt, and more children were born. Martin and Marie's oldest son, Jean Baptiste Dupuis (1687-1779), married Marguerite Richard on January 1, 1713, in Port Royal.[48] Marguerite was the daughter of Alexandre Richards and Isabelle Petit-pas. Jean's father, Martin Dupuis, died in August of 1713;[49] his widow and ten other children continued to live in *La Riviere des Gaspereau.*[50] Jean and Marguerite settled in the Grand Pré area, in the hamlet of *La Riviere des Habitants,*[51] where they ultimately had ten children, one of whom was my fourth great-grandfather Sylvain Dupuis (1721-1799).[52] Sylvain would marry Françoise LeBlanc in 1747;[53] Françoise was the great-granddaughter of Daniel LeBlanc, granddaughter of Antoine, and daughter of Pierre LeBlanc. (Sylvain and Françoise would become parents of Norbert Dupuis, featured in Chapter 10.) Somehow, families carried on during this turbulence.

With the death of English King George I and the accession of George II in 1727, another oath of allegiance was sought for the new monarch. This time, there would be no exemptions for neutrality to not take up arms. The council deputies in Port Royal, Guilliaume Bourgeois and Charles Landry (also my distant cousins), presented a statement signed by seventy-one heads of households explaining the necessity of maintaining neutrality. For their "insolence," Bourgeois and Landry were imprisoned and laid in irons. Landry fell ill in the miserable conditions of the dungeon. Charles Landry died within a month despite his wife's pleas for release.[54]

The Mikmaq were also feeling the tension as the English attempted to survey all of their provincial lands in the 1730s, including the "unclaimed land" that the Mikmaq had claimed as their own. The Mikmaq interrupted the survey work and threatened Acadians who appeared to be cooperating with the English, including a Minas notary, René Leblanc (a cousin and nephew of Antoine Leblanc). The Mikmaq believed such cooperation was a threat to their future and the once close relationship between the Indigenous people and the Acadians was diminishing.[55] Later, in 1749, the British leaders at Minas were attacked by a large force of Native fighters. They took René Leblanc as a prisoner and held him in captivity for several years before he was ransomed. Several Minas residents joined in the attack, many of whom had Mikmaq blood themselves. To avoid arrest, they fled with their families to French territory.[56] I discovered that some of Françoise Leblanc's siblings went to Ile Saint-Jean; they may have fled during this fighting (see Chapter 12).

Among the Acadians who moved to Isle Royale in French territory was Claude Petitpas (junior). After the death of his Mikmaq wife, Claude remarried an Acadian woman from Port Royal, Françoise Laverne. She was only seventeen, while Claude was fifty-seven. She bore him four more children. On Isle Royale, they lived in Port Toulouse, a settlement created specifically for the Acadian migrants. Claude seems to have been working for both sides. He was apparently trying to influence the young Mikmaq in favor of the British, but in 1728, the French governor found out and sent him to France to get rid of him. However, within a couple of years, he returned and accepted an appointment as an Indian interpreter for the French. Before his death in 1731, Claude recommended the same position for his son, Barthélomy, who had also worked across sides. Back in 1720, when Claude received his commendation from the legislative council in Boston, the council also resolved to pay tuition fees for Claude's son at Harvard.[33] It is unclear whether Barthélomy ever attended Harvard, but he spent three years in Boston at English expense. The intention was that he would be a Protestant missionary for the Mikmaq "to win over this nation and make it change its religion." Instead, after he returned to Acadia, his schooner was caught by the French as it was selling contraband products in Louisbourg on Isle Royale. Recognizing his education, they sent him to a Quebec seminary to re-channel his missionary efforts for the Catholics. But he didn't pursue that either. He was serving as a ship pilot in French waters in 1745 when the New Englanders captured Louisbourg. Barthélomy was captured and sent to prison in Boston. While Massachusetts Governor William Shirley exchanged other prisoners, he retained Barthélomy for throwing off his English allegiance to work for the French. Barthélomy died in 1747 in the Boston prison.[57] Perhaps to press his point, Governor Shirley honored Berthélomy's father, Claude Petitpas, in 1747, long after his death, as a "faithful servant of the crown of Great Britain."[33] More likely, Claude and Barthélomy had greater loyalty to the Native people over either of their rulers. It seems that neither the French nor the British inspired their loyalty.

When William Shirley became governor in Massachusetts in 1741 for England, he saw the Maritimes as the key to English supremacy in

North America. He set out not only to ensure victory but to remove the French altogether from this region. He was angry at the Acadians for not taking up arms. He also sought to replace the Acadian population with Protestants. As a step in that direction, Shirley and colleagues overtook the French colony at Louisburg on Ile Royale in 1745 and deported more than 4,000 to France, including 2,000 Acadians who had resettled there after the British conquest in 1710.[58] In 1749, Nova Scotia became the fourteenth British colony in North America. Then, over 2,500 new colonists from Scotland and Northern Ireland were transported to the new capital, called Halifax, on the east coast. Many of them, however, soon chose to move to other American colonies with a more hospitable climate.[59]

New intimidation tactics were used to coerce Acadians to take up arms against the French. Communities were again asked to select representatives to attend a meeting in Halifax in 1749. They selected their most respected elders, including Claude LeBlanc (a more distant cousin) from Grand Pré. But when these leaders again insisted that they retain their neutrality, they were all jailed to set an example. All Acadians were then stripped of their neutrality rights; they could no longer hold public meetings or elect their own leaders. Several hundred more Acadians fled to French territories, but most still refused to leave. Those who fled were forced by the French to sign an oath to take up arms against the English or face the punishment of death. The Acadians were used as pawns on both sides.[59]

Governor Shirley continued to plot a way to deport the Acadians, although the authorities in England did not deem this move to be legal or political. Then, in 1753, Lt. Colonel Charles Lawrence was appointed as governor of Nova Scotia. He proved to be as sinister as Massachusetts Governor Shirley. They would be good partners. Over the next two years, they developed a secret plan. Although it was unauthorized, it would be "a great and noble scheme" to rid the colony of Acadians.[60]

LE GRAND DÉRANGEMENT: THE GREAT DISPLACEMENT

and the journey of Sylvain Dupuis and Françoise Leblanc

❧

I FEEL A PARTICULAR KINSHIP WITH MY FOURTH GREAT-GRAND-parents, Françoise Leblanc (1717-1802) and Sylvain Dupuis (1721-1799). They were born into a time when their Acadian homeland was in turmoil. They endured so much anguish. While Acadia had been under English rule since 1713, the ongoing wars between England and France over North American territories put them in the crossfire. Françoise and Sylvain married around 1747 in Grand Pré when Acadia was becoming increasingly militarized.[1] Acadians were regularly intimidated by both the English and French to sign an unconditional oath to take up arms against the other, but the Acadians continued to insist on their neutrality. Nonetheless, Françoise and Sylvain had five children in the first seven years of their marriage (Paul b. 1748, Françoise b. 1749, Augustin b. 1751, Jean Baptiste b. 1753, and Marguerite b. 1754).[2] But their family life thereafter would be disrupted beyond imagination.

A COLONY ON EDGE

In the summer of 1754, Lieutenant-Governor Charles Lawrence instituted a policy that forcibly demanded provisions and labor from the inhabitants for their rulers and troops. He also embargoed all exports from the province, punishable by fines and confiscation of their vessels. He posted armed guards at bridges and crossroads to prevent communication between districts. Everyone was on edge. Then, in the summer of 1755, the "Great and Noble Scheme" to rid the province of the French was fully underway.[3]

On the evening of June 2nd, 200 troops were ordered by Governor Lawrence to raid and ransack homes across the Minas basin region simultaneously at midnight to seize arms and ammunition. In the

Pisquid and Grand Pré area, they took in 400 muskets and other arms. After that, a proclamation was issued that anyone found possessing firearms "should be treated as Rebels to His Majesty." Another 3,000 weapons were surrendered. The local residents attempted to fight back. On June 10, twenty-five deputies from the Minas hamlets petitioned the lieutenant governor "to make known the annoying circumstance in which we are placed, to the prejudice of the tranquility we ought to enjoy." They pleaded for the return of their firearms that were "absolutely necessary to defend our cattle when attacked by the wild beasts and for the protection of our children and ourselves ... We are grieved, Sir, at seeing ourselves guilty without being aware of having disobeyed." The petition was signed by more than 300 residents. "We still entertain, Sir, the same pure and sincere disposition to prove under any circumstances our unshaken fidelity to His Majesty, provided that His Majesty shall allow us the same liberty that he has granted us."[3] On receipt of the petition, Lawrence ordered the deputies to Halifax, to explain their "audacity in subscribing and presenting so impertinent a paper." Once in Halifax, their attempts to mollify the authorities did no good. They endured Lawrence's onslaught of insults. Again, they were asked to take the Oath, pledging they would take up arms on behalf of England. Again, they resisted. As a result, the deputies were sent to the dungeon on Georges Island, where they remained.[4] Nothing would derail the expulsion plans already in motion.

On August 4, Lawrence ordered the arrest of parish priests in Minas and Port Royal. Soon, troops seized the parish registers and papers, then marched the priests into the market square, where they were subjected to the soldiers' mockery and insults. Later that day, the priests were marched to awaiting warships and taken away.[5]

The full expulsion plan was meant to be kept secret. But on August 9, an anonymous Halifax correspondent wrote to Boston about the decision to act. It was published widely in the colonial press, including the Pennsylvania Gazette:

...We are now upon a great and noble Scheme of sending the neutral French out of the Province, who have always been secret Enemies, and have encouraged our Savages to cut our Throats. If we effect their Expulsion, it will be one of the greatest Things that ever the English did in America; for by all Accounts, that Part of the Country they possess, is as good Land as any in the World: In case therefore we could get some good English Farmers in their Room, this Province would abound all Kinds of Provision.[6]

It is unclear how much of this plan had leaked out among the Acadians, but nonetheless, what happened next would be terrifying. The task of removing the Acadians from the Minas basin area fell to Lieutenant-Colonel John Winslow from Massachusetts. The orders were to transport them to distant colonies in groups not exceeding one thousand persons so that "they cannot easily collect themselves together again." The intention was to fracture the community and destroy their identity as a distinct people.[7] Winslow accepted his assignment, but he didn't relish his role. Fortunately, his journal provides a detailed view of the Acadian removal from his point of view.[8]

THE ANNOUNCEMENT

On August 19, Winslow arrived with three armed ships at the mouth of the Gaspereux River in the village of Grand Pré. Everyone watched with anticipation as Winslow and 300 men came ashore. The soldiers established an encampment on the church grounds, turning the now-empty priest's house into the commander's headquarters. Winslow called for a meeting of deputies for the next day. As their elected deputies were already imprisoned in Halifax, a number of elders made their way to the priest's house. They included François Landry, in his late sixties, who was English speaking, and René Leblanc, the notary from Grand Pré, now age seventy-five. Both had previously served as intermediaries with the provincial government, and both are my distant cousins. René Leblanc had spent two years as a captive with the Mikmaq because he was deemed to be too close to the English. He was returned in a prisoner exchange. Winslow ordered the community to continue with their harvest because it would be needed to feed his troops until his provision vessel arrived. This was all they were told. The elders responded that they would happily arrange this.[9]

Over the next week, the weather was sunny, cool, and dry, perfect for threshing of wheat. But while they worked, the residents observed four sloops and a schooner arrive, riding high in the water, curiously empty. On Friday, August 29, Winslow informed his three captains of their mission for the first time, swearing them to secrecy. They were instructed to carry out the plan ruthlessly. On the following Friday, Winslow arranged for a local collaborator to read a summons in French throughout the countryside. It ordered all the men and boys over age ten "to attend at the church at Grand Pré on Friday the fifth instant at Three of the Clock in the afternoon, that we may impart to them what we are ordered to communicate."[8,10]

The meeting announcement was very unsettling. My fourth great-uncle, Augustin Leblanc, came home after hearing the summons. His wife Françoise later described his face as disfigured in fear. "He remained seated for a long time in front of the hearth, his head in his hands. When he stood up, his face was entirely bathed in tears. He said not a single word but began to collect all the objects that could be carried with them." The couple went to the woods with their two young sons. They were not alone in leaving. But most considered it unthinkable to abandon their homes.[8,10]

At midday on Friday, François Landry in western Minas and René Leblanc in Grand Pré held two large meetings. The elders counseled, what else could they do? Usually, their cooperation had softened the British. They decided to comply. That afternoon, 418 men and boys assembled at the church of Saint-Charles-des-Mines in Grand Pré, where many of them had been baptized and married. They included a number of familiar clans—Leblanc, Landry, Hébert, Richard, Gautreau, Trahan, Thériault, and Dupuis. Sylvain Dupuis was then age thirty-four. None of his children were old enough to accompany him. All remained home with his wife. Once inside, the doors were barred, and troops surrounded the building.[10]

Through an interpreter, Winslow read the orders from His Excellency, Governor Lawrence. It began with Lawrence's habitual insults of the disagreeable nature of the French inhabitants but quickly turned to instructions: "That your Lands and Tenements, Cattle of all kinds, and Livestock of all sorts are forfeited to the Crown and all other [of] your Effects, saving your Money and Household Goods. And that you yourselves are to be removed from this province. Thus, it is peremptorily His Majesty's order, that the whole French Inhabitants of these Districts be removed." Winslow recorded in his diary that all present were "greatly struck"; they were in shock.[8,10]

Winslow compiled an inventory of residents and livestock. "Silvan Dupuis" was among them, and he listed "three sons, two daughters, four bullocks, three cows, three young cattle, ten sheep, seven hogs, and one horse."[11]

Winslow immediately left the church, leaving them in their prison while they waited for sufficient transports for their deportation. François Landry and René Leblanc quickly formed a delegation and asked to see Winslow. They were admitted to his quarters. Their greatest concern was for their wives and children. They asked if a smaller group could remain hostage while the majority returned home. This request was denied. But Winslow did allow a group of twenty men to return to their hamlets to convey the news. The rest would be "answerable" if these men did not return the following morning. These men would also tell the women they were responsible for feeding and clothing the prisoners as they provisioned the troops. Winslow also demanded a list of any inhabitants that did not come in.[10]

Lawrence had instructed his agents to be ruthless with anyone who fled. François Landry provided a comprehensive list of Minas residents, which indicated that three dozen men were at large. Fearing he might be attacked, Winslow sent his troops out to find and arrest the missing men. As the Yankees had a hatred of French Catholics, they went on a religious crusade. They shouted epithets as they forced the families of missing men from their homes, plundered their properties, and threatened their lives. When the prisoners heard of this terror from the women delivering food, they feared more for their families' safety.[12]

On September 10, while the men were allowed to stretch their legs in the churchyard, a number of young men attempted to overwhelm the guard, perhaps to escape. The troops quickly re-established order, but Winslow decided there were too many prisoners for his guards to handle. He ordered all the unmarried men and boys, as well as some of the married men, to board the five ships in the harbor, using them as prison ships until the other transports arrived. François Landry was shocked. He and René Leblanc had hoped that by being cooperative, all the removal talk would be just talk. But now it appeared that the young men might be separated from their fathers, defying Winslow's promise of keeping families together. Winslow waived the questions away. "It must be done," he said. He gave Landry one hour to prepare the men.[12]

THE REMOVAL

On the morning of September 11, approximately 450 Acadians left the church and assembled as a group along the road before the ships' landing. On the left flank were the young men and boys. Facing them were 300 armed soldiers. One of the young men shouted, "Non! Pas sans nos pères"—not without our fathers. Winslow asked for a translation, and Landry complied. Winslow declared, "The King's command is to me absolute and should be absolutely obeyed." He ordered his troops to fix bayonets and advance. Winslow walked to the young man who had shouted, grabbed him by the shoulders, and pushed him to the road. "He obeyed", Winslow wrote in his journal.[8,12] The rest followed.

The women heard the clamor, and they lined up along the distance from the landing to the church. The young men went off praying, singing, and crying. Their mothers, sisters, and fiancées reached out for a last embrace. According to Acadian tradition, the women began singing, and the young men joined in the dirge,

> *Let us bear the cross.*
> *Without choice, without regret, without complaint,*
> *Let us bear the cross,*
> *However bitter and hard.*[8,13]

Winslow wrote in his journal, "It was a "scene of sorrow." Before the turn of the tide, 230 prisoners were aboard the transports. Once again, Landry and Leblanc tried to negotiate, to intercede with His Majesty for those who have kept the fidelity and submission promised. They provided documents from notarial files of their oath of fidelity, signed in 1730. If they must be removed, they asked that they be delivered to places where they would find their kindred. Perhaps because he was rattled by the emotional display earlier in the day, Winslow agreed to send the translated documents to Lawrence, but he refused any intercession or commitment to their destination. He was aware but did not reveal, that Lawrence intended to send the Acadians to widely dispersed locations.[8,13]

On Saturday, October 4, Winslow instructed the women and children to be ready with their household goods. He would begin boarding the vessels ready in the harbor while waiting for other transports to arrive. On Monday and Tuesday, a cold, hard rain postponed the embarkation. On Tuesday evening, in the storm's confusion, a group of twenty-four young men escaped from their transport. They were disguised as women delivering food. Winslow was furious. He resolved that the women and children would board the transports regardless of the weather. On Wednesday, October 8, a cold but clear day, Winslow ordered his men to fan out and drive the women and children, the sick and infirm, into the village. As they assembled, Winslow made a spectacle intended to terrorize all, to punish the ringleader of the escape from the night before. François Hébert was bound and dragged to his home, where he and all the community were forced to watch the burning of his home, barn, and all his possessions. Winslow also warned that if other fugitives did not surrender, their friends would see the same result, and the escapees themselves would be shot on sight.[8,14]

At the landing, the scene was chaos. Winslow had instructed his officers to keep families together. But because the men had been held at the church and the young men were already on board the transports, attempting to unite families was complicated. During the loading, the troops shuttled prisoners from one vessel to another as families called out with desperate pleas to soldiers who could not understand their language. In the confusion, mothers called out for missing children, wives refused to board without their husbands, and angry husbands resisted the soldiers' orders.[14]

Winslow described the scene in his diary: They "began to Embarke the Inhabitants who went verry solentarily and Unwillingly. the women in Great Distress Carrying Their Children In their arms."[8,15] My fourth great-grandmother, Françoise Leblanc, and her five young children would have been among them. Others, wrote Winslow, "carried their decrepit parents in carts in scenes of confusion, woe, and distress." Many families remained separated, parents from children, husbands from wives, and boarded onto separate ships destined for different colonies from Massachusetts to Georgia.[15]

On Monday, October 13, all the Acadians at Grand Pré had been boarded onto the five available transports. The ships were outfitted to carry human cargo, with holds divided into two or three levels about four feet high, similar to what was used for the African slave trade. Winslow's instructions were to load two people per marine ton, the equivalent of 100 cubic feet—a space of about four feet high, four feet wide, and six feet long. Families, including children, were locked below decks, with no provision for light, ventilation, heat, or sanitation. Food and water were inadequate. On October 20, the four transports from Pisquid, further up the Minas Basin, arrived downriver to Grand Pré. Those transports were seriously overcrowded. Their maximum carrying capacity of 650 persons held 920 Acadians. Winslow was able to commandeer a trading vessel into service and shifted 200 people to it to ease things up a bit.[16]

On Tuesday, October 21, fourteen vessels pulled anchor in the late afternoon, carrying 2,648 Acadians from several dozen villages and hamlets in Minas Basin. On the next morning, they joined other vessels in the Annapolis Basin. Finally, on October 27, after many weeks of preparation, the convoy of twenty-two transports, carrying 4,000 Acadians, headed south. As they departed Annapolis Royal, if they could see the shore, they would have seen flames and smoke as the troops torched the buildings. The work of destruction was the final step in the removal, as Governor Lawrence wanted to ensure there was nothing left for the Acadians to return to. In Winslow's final diary entry, he wrote, "Buildings Burnt by Lieutenant-Colonel Winslow in Districts of Minas"—255 homes, 276 barns, 11 mills, and one "mass house"(church).[8,16]

EXILE—THE DUPUIS FAMILY IN MASSACHUSETTS

Between 1755 and 1763, more than 14,000 Acadians were deported from the entire maritime region, although the number varies across different reports. Approximately one-third perished, including 650 from two unseaworthy ships. Others died of diseases that rapidly spread in the confined space on board. Some 2,000 escaped to the woods and were hunted down; a few made their way on foot to Quebec.[17]

Many were transported to cities all along the East Coast of the English colonies. Some were taken to England as prisoners of war. Others were sent on ships to France and the Caribbean islands. As they arrived in these places, most of the local authorities had no advanced notice they were coming. It was the middle of the French and Indian

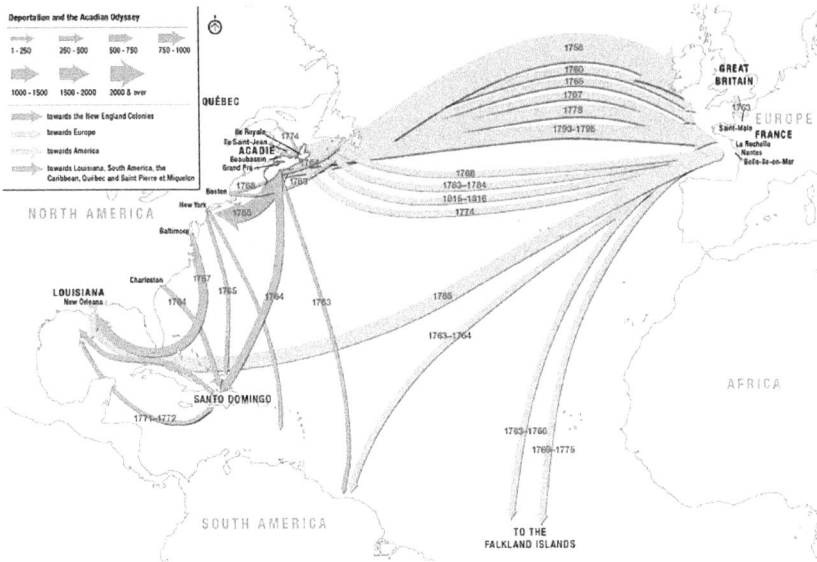

Acadian Deportation Map

War in the English colonies, and these French were considered enemies, not to be trusted. They were unwanted, often mistreated, and many were pushed on elsewhere.

About 2,000 refugees landed in Massachusetts, and some Massachusetts officials tried to get rid of them. In May 1756, Thomas Hancock outfitted a ship to take some to North Carolina, but the Acadian exiles overpowered the crew and made their way back. Massachusetts asked New Hampshire to take some exiles, but New Hampshire refused.[15]

Immigration records show that Sylvain Dupuis and Françoise Leblanc, with five young children (Paul, Françoise, Augustin, Jean-Baptiste, Marguerite), arrived in Boston in 1755.[18,19] It's unclear on which ship they arrived. The first ships to arrive in the Boston Harbor on November 5, 1755, were six ships destined for ports further south. They took refuge in a storm. Many of these passengers were sick from hunger, lack of water, or poor water quality, in addition to seasickness from the storm. They suffered from the ships' overloading, the stress of deportation, and not knowing what was ahead. After hearing about the poor conditions on board the ships, Boston authorities ordered that 132 passengers be allowed to disembark in order to reach the recommended capacity of two persons per ton. Those ships then continued on their way.[20] The passengers allowed off were the lucky ones.

On November 15, the ship Seaflower arrived with 160 Acadians from Pisquid in the Minas Basin. Two other ships from Grand Pré, the Swallow and the Racehorse, arrived in Boston in December with 238 and 120 passengers, respectively.[21] Arrival didn't mean they were allowed to disembark, however. While the Massachusetts government knew of their coming, no provisions were made for the Acadians' support. They were quarantined aboard the ships for fear of contagion. Slowly, passengers were allowed to disembark and take up temporary quarters in Boston.[20]

The General Court (as the Massachusetts legislature was called) ruled in March 1756 that the Acadians would be parceled out to the colony's 98 towns, giving the town's selectmen and overseers of the poor the authority to employ, bind out as indentured servants, or support the Acadian families at the province's expense. The legislators attempted to get assurances for reimbursement from the Nova Scotia government but without success.[20] The Acadians were initially given freedom, but some exiles took jobs as sailors and attempted to return to Canada. As a result, the General Court passed a new law in April 1756 forbidding the hiring of Acadians as sailors. Soon after, another law forbade them to leave their assigned towns.[15] After a short period of town support, they were expected to support themselves. Ultimately, nearly 2,000 exiles would be settled in Massachusetts.[20]

Conditions in other colonies were worse. In Maryland and New York, the government didn't approve any support, reducing the exiles to begging on the street. After complaints about "Acadian vagabonds," Maryland laws authorized jail for indigent Acadians, and in both Maryland and New York, the majority of Acadian children were forcibly taken away and put into service.[22] In Virginia, the exiles were kept on their transport ships through the winter, and then they were shipped to England, where they were treated as prisoners. In South Carolina and Georgia, the exiles were shipped back north. Some of these "boat people" turned up on the shores of New York and Massachusetts, where they were taken in. Others were unaccounted for.[23]

Sylvain, Françoise, and their children were assigned to Worcester County, in the town of Shrewsbury, Massachusetts, about fifty miles west of Boston.[24] Records show the town submitted for support and later payment of expenses for the family of "Sylvanus Dupee" and "Silvane Dupee" on December 6, 1757, and January 27, 1761, respectively.[25] Françoise's parents, Pierre Leblanc and Marie-Françoise Landry, were also assigned to Shrewsbury and included on the December 6, 1757, Shrewsbury list, along with Françoise's unmarried sister Mary Rose (age twenty-two) and brother Pierre Jr. (known as Pierre Hillaire, age nineteen); their French names were translated to English in these records: Peter White Sr, Mary White, Mary Rose White and Peter White Jr.[26] The parents were age seventy and sixty-two, respectively, in 1755, when they were deported. I'm sure all were grateful to have the three generations of family together. No details on their lives in Massachusetts were recorded. But other reports give us an idea of what their experience might have been.

A letter to the editor of the Boston Gazette in August 1756 described the writer's fear that the French exiles would escape in stolen ships or, worse, set fire to their town or attack them in the middle of the night, as they were "heated with passion or Popish zeal."[20] Most Acadians had been successful farmers or tradesmen with property, but they had to leave with only what they could carry on their person. In exile, they could not afford the necessities of life. Now, the destitute families were dependent on the goodwill of town officials to find means to earn their keep. Goodwill was sometimes hard to come by. Their low wages, or sometimes no wages, left them not much better off than slaves. The language barrier made things worse. An Acadian fisherman named Belloni Melancon was assigned to the inland town of Lancaster. His son was apprenticed to an artisan, but the artisan beat him so badly that the boy lost the use of his arm. The townspeople took Melancon's crippled wife from her bed and threw her in a cart. Melancon then petitioned the General Court to let him move to a seacoast town where he could earn his living as a fisherman. The General Court allowed him to move to Weymouth and fish; the state paid for his rent and wood.[15]

Jean-Simon Leblanc and his wife Jeanne Dupuis, cousins of both Sylvain and Françoise, were deported with two daughters from Port Royal. Their other six children had been sent on other ships. They were assigned to Westborough, Mass.[27] We know more about this Leblanc family because of a friendship he developed with the pastor, Rev. Ebenezer Parkman, of the Congregational Church in Westborough. Rev. Parkman kept a detailed diary, which has been preserved by the Massachusetts Historical Society. Parkman made clear his views that the war on France was just, and he believed the Catholic church was doing the work of the devil. But he was compassionate. On October 16, 1756, he wrote, "I am informed that a Family of French Neutrals ... are come into Town & Dwell in Mr. Hammonds House." Parkman could read and write in French. Jean-Simon Leblanc was a deputy at Port Royal and spoke fluent English. Over the next ten years, there were 150 entries in Parkman's diary referring to the Acadian exiles, giving a perspective on how they lived. Parkman treated the French warmly, and he was frequently visited by Leblanc and others in neighboring towns.[28]

The Leblanc family was first assigned to the Hammond household for a short time. They moved from there to the home of Cornelius Bigelow, and then on January 12, 1757, they moved to a schoolhouse where other Acadians were being sheltered. During the first six months after their arrival, Parkman visited the Leblancs at least once a week, and members of the family visited Parkman's parsonage. The first visit was for Thanksgiving Day, November 25, 1756, when Madame Leblanc and daughter Marie dined at Rev. Parkman's. Unfortunately, according to the diary, Monsieur Leblanc, who had also been invited, was not well enough to come. Although he was only thirty-five, Simon Leblanc was described as "Rheumatic." The traumatic experience of deportation was hard on the health of many Acadians. They arrived in weak condition.

Parkman also noted that Madame Leblanc was frequently sick, with illness lasting a few weeks during December of 1756 and again in January 1757.[28]

The two Leblanc daughters, Marie and Magdalena, became friends with Parkman's daughters, and the Leblanc girls were frequent guests at the Parkman table. Apparently, the Leblancs were reunited with at least two of their sons, Amand and Pierre. Amand worked for Parkman "in the corn field, the tobacco patch, the orchard, plowing, planting, hoeing, mowing, reaping," or "digging a water well to well water the cattle." Pierre was able to borrow or purchase a yoke of oxen to go farm to farm, plowing and planting fields. Their sisters also worked for the Parkmans. On May 18, 1757, Parkman noted, "The French girls bring 33 yards of cloth which Magdalena has spun and wove for us." He paid a dollar for the cloth. A government report of the day wrote that "French Acadians … [labor] at much lower wages" than those commonly paid others. Two other Leblanc sons and a daughter were married, and with their own families, they were also deported to Massachusetts. They also visited their parents and the Parkman family. Both Simon and his son Joseph Leblanc dined with Rev. Parkman on several occasions, mentioning that Joseph was visiting from Cambridge.[27,28] Another Leblanc daughter and her husband had escaped to the woods during the deportation process, and Leblanc didn't know of their fate—later, he learned they had safely made their way to Quebec.[29]

One of the exiles' hardships was searching for family and friends who had been sent on different ships. However, they were forbidden to travel from one place to another without a government permit. The permit would permit travel for no more than six days and could not include "the Lord's Day." This was one way the Acadians were prevented from gathering together or attending worship services. Catholic services were not available anyway. Punishment for these transgressions was imprisonment.[27]

It seems that some of these host community residents simply hated the exiles for their nationality, as the "enemy," or for their Catholic religion. Others could not get past their destitute appearance, to which the Acadians had been reduced. The host communities did not consent to the Acadians' support. They were angry and afraid. Yet others saw Acadians with compassion, recognizing they were unfortunate refugees who were spoils of a war, not of their making. I currently reside in Massachusetts and have ancestors from the Massachusetts Yankees and the Acadian refugees. I hope my Yankee ancestors were compassionate. This is not unlike the plight of refugees who arrive unbidden in other countries today, coming from wars and other disasters in their home-land. Not all migrations are voluntary.

RESETTLEMENT IN QUEBEC

Once the British conquered all of New France and made it official with the Treaty of Paris in 1763, the Acadians were allowed to leave Mas-sachusetts and the other colonies where they had landed. But permission was required. Petitions with more than 1,000 names began arriving at the General Court of Massachusetts in 1763. They sought permission to depart Massachusetts and settle in other French-speaking regions, including France, St. Dominique (present-day Haiti), and Quebec.[20] The Massachusetts archives show Silvain Dupuis, Françoise Dupuis, and their children desiring to relocate to France on August 24, 1763.[25] Other lists in these archives show French neutrals seeking to relocate to Haiti, Quebec, and Canada. Some names are on more than one of these lists. Perhaps the exiles were hedging their bets in hopes that one of the requests would come through. I was unable to find Sylvain and Françoise Dupuis on the other lists in the archives, although they eventually relocated to Quebec.

Governor James Murray of the new British colony of Quebec invited the Acadians to settle in Quebec. He would offer them land, but he was unable to provide funds to get them there. Therefore, the Massachusetts exiles applied to the Massachusetts Court for relocation funds. They would have a long wait for an answer. Forwarding several petitions to the House of Representatives in January 1766, Massachusetts Governor Bernard urged that permission be allowed and funds be granted for the transport of Acadians, as they were "industrious British subjects, temporarily disadvantaged by circumstance." But in June 1766, after their deliberation, the House of Representatives ruled that further aid for resettlement was denied because the province already had great expense in supporting the Acadians. As a result, the Acadians left in small groups on their own. Those with funds went by ship. Most traveled overland on foot.[20] Most likely, my Dupuis and Leblanc relatives were among those walking from Massachusetts to Quebec, a distance of over 300 miles.

Sylvain Dupuis and Françoise Leblanc first appear on Quebec records in 1767 in St. Sulpice for the baptisms of their newborn son Pierre, four-year-old son Charles, and three-year-old daughter Marie, all on August 9. With no Catholic church available in Massachusetts, they were catching up on baptisms. A funeral for two-month-old son Pierre Sylvain is also recorded there on August 15 of the same year. The family apparently then moved to nearby L'Assomption, Quebec, where another son, Simon Pierre, was born and baptized on August 26, 1768, followed by baptisms of twelve-year-old Joseph and ten-year-old daughter Elizabeth on August 28, 1768. The family then moved to Montreal. This is where their oldest daughter, Françoise (recorded as Dupuy), died at age twenty on October 17, 1769; her funeral in Montreal was on October 18. On November 4, 1769, their son Simon Pierre, age one, died, and his funeral was on November 6.[30] Then, my third great-grandfather, Norbert (recorded as Norbert Dupuy), was born and baptized on June 5, 1771, in Montreal (Basilica Notre Dame),[31] followed by daughter Anastasie Dupuis who was born and baptized on October 6, 1773, in Montreal.[30]

Consider the number of moves this family endured after they lost their homeland and were deported from Grand Pré in 1755. They left with only what they could carry and spent several months crammed into a tiny space on board a ship. They were without a home for twelve years. Eight more babies came after leaving Acadia, including four born in Massachusetts, two while transitioning within Quebec, and two more after arriving in Montreal. Sadly, three children died, including the two sons born during the Quebec transitions, and the oldest daughter, Françoise, at age twenty. The trauma is unimaginable. But they remained together, and eleven of their fourteen children survived.

The family moved for the last time to the new Acadian community of L'Acadie in Quebec. It is about 30 miles south of Montreal, midway between Montreal and Vermont. This is where my fourth great-grand-father Sylvain Dupuis died at age seventy-seven, on May 28, 1799.[32] His wife, Françoise Leblanc, remarried in L'Acadie on September 28, 1801 to Antoine Boudreau,[33] widower of Françoise's sister Marie Josephe Leblanc. Françoise Leblanc died there a year later, on November 24, 1802, at age seventy-five.[34] They were of hearty stock! If this is not resilience, I don't know what is.

THE DIASPORA OF ACADIANS AND DUPUIS

Once the Acadian exiles were allowed to move after the war, most took the opportunity. A few chose to stay in the area of their exile, but most chose to move to where they were free to speak their language and worship their Catholic faith. They were also eager to find family members from whom they had been separated during the deportations.

To stay or move into any of the British colonies required taking a new oath of allegiance. In Massachusetts in 1766, 890 men volunteered to sign the oath in order to migrate to Quebec or Nova Scotia. The next year, there was a similar exodus from Connecticut. Those returning to Nova Scotia would have found their original farms taken over by New Englanders who had been recruited to move there. But the Acadians created new communities in coastal towns along the Bay of Fundy and the Gaspé peninsula. In Quebec, many settled along the St. Lawrence

River between Montreal and Quebec City. By 1770, at least 4,000 people were settled in predominantly Acadian communities in Quebec, with another 2,000 along the north shore, on the Gaspé peninsula, or New Brunswick.[35]

While Sylvain and Françoise's immediate family made their way back to French-speaking Canada, what happened to their siblings? Their dispersal during deportation and in subsequent moves resembles the larger Acadian diaspora. Sylvain was one of ten siblings, and Françoise was one of fourteen, although only ten were alive at the time of deportation. Most were living in the area of Grand Pré at the time of the Acadian deportation. They went in many directions.

Sylvain's father, Jean Baptiste Dupuis's deportation destination is unknown, but he apparently made his way back to Quebec, as he died in 1779 at age ninety-two in St. Philippe, Quebec.[36] Sylvain's mother may have died before deportation; her death date and location are unknown. Sylvain's oldest sibling, Germain, and his wife, Marie-Marguerite Granger, were among those initially deported to Virginia. More than 1,200 exiles arrived there in November 1755 as a surprise to Virginia authorities, who were also miffed that one colonial governor would send such a large number to another without permission. Concerned by the danger posed by receiving enemies of war, they kept most of the exiles on board their transport ships all winter. Imagine spending October to May in the cramped spaces on board these ships! By Spring, the Virginia authorities decided to ship them all off to England. They went to ports in Bristol, Southampton, Liverpool, and Falmouth, England, where they also arrived unannounced.[37]

Germain, Marie-Marguerite, and their newborn daughter, Anne Marthe, were among the Acadians who arrived in Falmouth on the coast of Cornwall, England, in June 1756. Some exiles reportedly found irregular employment there. Some of the younger men apprenticed with English tradesmen, with whom their families lodged. Others begged for food. Reports of their poor treatment reached the French government, which eventually arranged for their passage to France. On May 26, 1763,

TRAVELS OF SYLVAIN DUPUIS, HIS PARENTS, AND SIBLINGS FROM DEPORTATION

Family Member	Spouse	Exiled to	Final Settlement
Jean Baptiste (father)	Marguerite Richard	Unknown	St. Phillipe, Quebec (father only)
Germain	Marguerite Granger	Virginia->England	Brittany, France
Fabien	Judith Hébert	Connecticut	Fabien died in Connecticut. Judith died in Haiti
Elizabeth	Pierre Hébert	Guilford, Connecticut	St. Phillipe, Quebec
Sylvain	Francoise Leblanc	Shrewsbury, Massachusetts	L'Acadie, Quebec
Jean Baptiste	Marie-Josephe Granger	Unkown	Both died in Haiti
Cecile	Olivier Hébert	Connecticut	LaPrairie, Quebec
Euphrasine	Jean Baptiste Hébert	Connecticut	Both died in Haiti
Amand	Marie-Blanche Landry	Andover, Massachusetts	St. Jacques, Quebec
Joseph	Marguerite Bourgeous	Unknown	Quebec
Alexandre	unknown	Unknown	LaPrairie, Quebec

Germain's family boarded the ship *La Fauvette* for Morlaix, France, on the Brittany coast.[38] They were among 159 people out of the 250 that had arrived seven years earlier in Falmouth, England. They were lucky to survive. It appears that the family had several more children between 1764 and 1778, and they spent the rest of their lives in this area.[39]

When word got out that France was repatriating the English prisoners, exiles everywhere sought to go to France. This apparently led to the appeals sent to the Massachusetts legislature from the Massachusetts exiles, including the family of Sylvain and Françoise. France quickly clarified that their invitation was for English prisoners only. The French did not wish "to interfere" with the removal of the Acadians in the English colonies. With that door closed, other French colonies became attractive, including St. Dominique (present-day Haiti), Cayenne

(French Guiana), Iles Malouines (Falkland Islands), and Martinique. Those proved disastrous for the exiles that pursued them.[40]

Four of Sylvain Dupuis's siblings were deported to Connecticut, including Fabian, Elizabeth, Cecile, and Euphrasine, all of whom had married Hébert siblings: three sons and one daughter of René Hebert and Marie Boudreau, who were also deported there.[41] Connecticut generally treated their Acadian exiles with respect. Unlike other colonies, Connecticut authorities knew about the Acadian deportations and passed a law in advance for how the exiles would be distributed. Some were housed with local families. Others were assigned in family groups to unoccupied houses. The elder Héberts were assigned to such a house in Guilford, Connecticut. Their son, Pierre, and his wife, Elizabeth Dupuis, and their children were also in Guilford. It is unclear if other of their married children resided in the same community.

Once they were free to leave at the end of the war, the Connecticut exiles went in different directions. Fabien Dupuis reportedly died in Connecticut; his widow Judith Hébert and their children went to Mirebalais, St. Dominique (Haiti). Going with them were Judith's brother, Jean-Baptiste Hébert, and his wife Euphrasine Dupuis and their children. It is unknown where another sibling, Jean-Baptiste Dupuis, and his wife, Marie-Josephe Granger, had been deported, but they also went on to Haiti. All of them died in Mirebalais between 1764-1766,[42-44] although it appears that two of Euphrasine's daughters later married in St Dominique.[45] Acadians had been recruited by the French governor of St. Dominique with the promise of land and transportation paid. However, the exiles didn't know they were being recruited to work camps. Some were put to work clearing the jungle to build a naval base. The Mirebalais Acadian settlers worked as laborers on plantations. Many died of tropical diseases like yellow fever and malaria. This may have been the fate of my ancestors in Haiti. Others escaped and made their way to New Orleans. Louisiana.[46]

Louisiana had long been a French colony. But in 1762, France ceded the territory to Spain, yet France remained in a caretaker role until 1766.

By 1765, there were nearly 500 Acadians living there. As other exiles heard about Acadians in Louisiana, they sailed there directly. Family connections grew the population. This includes many familiar surnames from the Port Royal and Grand Pré area, including Dupuis, Leblanc, Landry, and Richards families. None of Sylvain's or Françoise's siblings were among them, although later generations migrated there. By 1803, this area was purchased by the new United States in the Louisiana Purchase, and in 1812, it became the state of Louisiana. By 1900, more than 4,000 Acadians had settled there. The Acadian's pronunciation of their name sounded like "Cajun." Therefore, in Louisiana, this is how they came to be known.[47]

The other Hébert and Dupuis siblings who had been exiled in Connecticut—Pierre Hébert and Elizabeth Dupuis, Oliver Hébert and Cecile Dupuis, along with the Hébert parents—made their way to Quebec. Olivier, Cecile, and their children traveled by ship, sailing in May 1768, first to Boston, then on to Quebec, where they arrived in July 1768. Olivier and Cecile settled in La Prairie, Quebec,[48] along with Alexandre Dupuis.[49] La Prairie is southwest of Montreal, at the confluence of the St. Lawrence and St. Jacques Rivers. Elizabeth Dupuis and Pierre Hébert settled in St. Phillipe, Quebec,[49] along with Elizabeth's father, Jean-Baptiste Dupuis.[36] St. Phillipe and La Prairie are next to one another. Sylvain and Françoise settled a little south of there in L'Acadie, a community of other Acadian settlers. Amand Dupuis and his family had been exiled in Andover, Massachusetts,[50] and they settled in St. Jacques, Quebec, northeast of Montreal.[49] This community was another that was founded by Acadians who had been exiled in the Boston, Massachusetts area. Thus, six of the ten Dupuis siblings, including Sylvain himself, made their way to Quebec, ending up in the greater Montreal area.

Among Françoise Leblanc's ten siblings alive at the time of deportation, four were deported directly to France in 1758 with their families. At that time, the British had taken Fort Louisbourg on Ile Royale, defeating the last French base in the Maritimes. They decided to deport the remaining French directly to France rather than to the American colonies. This included Acadians from Ile Saint-Jean (present-day Prince Edward Island, NS) and Ile Royale (Cape Breton Island, NS). As noted earlier, many Acadians fled to these French-held territories during British harassment and burning of homes in their original communities. This was likely the case for four of the Leblanc siblings, as all had married and begun their families in Grand Pré. They endured the terror of fleeing their homes, only to find a worse terror on their deportation to France.

The Acadians from Ile Saint Jean began arriving in France in November 1758. However, among the 3,100 who left Ile Saint-Jean, only 1,649 survived the voyage, dying from exposure or disease. At least three ships wrecked or sank en route.[51] Ursule Lablanc, her husband Joseph Broussard, and their children were among the arrivals in Cherbourg, France, in 1758; however, both Ursule and Joseph died there on December 4, 1758, and January 19, 1759, respectively.[52,53] There were fifty-three deaths registered in Cherbourg alone between December 1 and February 22, 1759.[54] Their children survived, and at least two of them, Charles and Agnes, married in France and migrated to Louisiana in 1785.[55,56]

Joseph Leblanc, his wife Anne Moyse, and their children were on another ship from Ile Saint Jean that landed in St. Malo, France, in early 1759. Joseph, age thirty-three, died soon after arrival;[57] their two sons, ages three and one, died at sea.[58,59] Anne Moyse survived and remarried another Acadian in St. Malo, Claude Guidry, who had also lost his wife and two children soon after the voyage.[60] This new Guidry family migrated in 1785 to Louisiana, but that ship ran aground at the mouth of the Mississippi River. They ran out of food, three dozen people got sick, and fifteen died. The ship finally reached New Orleans after 113 days at sea.[61] This journey must have felt like déja vu for Anne Moyse, but this time her family survived.

Marguerite Monique Leblanc, her husband Charles Hébert, and her children may have been on one of the same ships that landed in St. Malo, France. Their two children, Pierre and Marie, died at sea.[62,63] Marie Monique and Charles died soon after in St. Malo on January 25 and February 22, 1759, respectively.[64,65] These families had already

TRAVELS OF FRANÇOISE LEBLANC, HER PARENTS AND SIBLINGS, FROM DEPORTATION

Family Member	Spouse	Exiled to	Final Settlement
Pierre Leblanc (father_	Francoise Landry	Shrewsbury, Massachusetts	Lavaltrie, Quebec
Ursule	Joseph Broussard	Cherboug, France	Both died on arrival
Anne	Charles Dugas	Unknown	Carelton, Quebec
Angelique	Germain Dupuis	Boston, Massachusetts	St. Jacques, Quebec
Augustin	Françoise Hébert	Worcester, Massachusetts	Yamachiche, Quebec
Francoise	Sylvain Dupuis	Shrewsbury, Massachusetts	L'Acadie, Quebec
Joseph	Marie-Anne Moyse	St. Milo, France	Joseph died en route Marie -> Louisiana
Maire-Rose	Jean-Baptiste Hébert	Shrewsbury, Massachusetts	Becancour, Quebec
Marguerite-Monique	Charles Hébert	St. Milo, France	Died in St. Milo
Pierre Hillaire	Eliz-Isabelle Hébert	Massachusetts -> Connecticut	L'Acadie Quebec
Marie-Magdaleine	unknown	St. Milo, France?	Died there?

experienced so much terror in fleeing their Grand Pré homes, as refugees in Saint-Jean, and in finally being rounded up for deportation. Their wintertime Atlantic voyage to France was unimaginable. Another sibling, Marie Magdaleine Leblanc, may also have died in Saint-Servan, a village two miles from the port in St. Malo, according to others' reports on Ancestry.com, but I was unable to verify her exile or death.

It is unclear where Anne Leblanc and her husband, Charles Dugas, were deported, but eventually, they settled on the Gaspé peninsula in Carleton, Quebec.[66] This village was originally called Saint-Joseph de Tracadièche when it was founded in 1766 by Charles Dugas and his son-in-law, Benjamin Leblanc (a cousin of Françoise and son of Grand Pré's René Leblanc, described above). On behalf of twenty-five others, they co-signed a letter to the Quebec lieutenant governor to request permission to settle the area to make a living from fishing and farming. Without waiting for an answer, they settled their families in this territory. The village name was later changed to Carleton.[67]

The remaining five Leblanc siblings had all landed in Massachusetts for their exile. As noted above, Pierre Hillaire and Mary Rose were in exile with Françoise and her family and Françoise's parents in Shrewsbury, Worcester County.[26] Also in Worcester County were brother Augustin Leblanc, his wife Françoise Hébert, and Françoise Hêbert's brother Jean Baptist Hébert.[68] Augustin Leblanc and his wife Françoise were described earlier in this chapter when, after hearing Winslow's announcement in Grand Pré, the couple gathered their two sons and fled to the woods. Apparently, they were removed from others in their family. The proximity of family in the Worcester area must have led to romance, as Jean Baptist Hébert and Mary Rose Leblanc married in 1762 while in exile in Massachusetts.[69] Françoise's brother, Pierre Hillaire Leblanc, apparently connected with other Grand Pré families in Connecticut. In 1762, he married Marie Elizabeth Isabelle Hébert,[69] the daughter of Pierre Hébert and Elizabeth Dupuis, Sylvain's sister, who was in exile in Guilford, Connecticut, as mentioned above. This Hébert family were cousins of the Hébert family who married the other Leblanc siblings. Also in Massachusetts, assigned to Nantucket, were Angelique Leblanc and her husband Germain Dupuis (cousin of Sylvain Dupuis).[70] Angelique and Germain, with their children, reportedly sailed from Boston, along with Angelique's parents Pierre Leblanc and Françoise Landry, on the Schooner Abigail, landing in Quebec on June 18, 1767.[71]

These Leblanc siblings all resettled in Quebec. Pierre Hillaire Leblanc and Marie Elizabeth Isabelle Hebert settled in L'Acadie,[69] where Françoise and Sylvain Dupuis also settled. Marie Rose and Jean Baptiste Hébert settled in Bécancour,[69] further downstream on the St. Lawrence, just south of Trois Riviere. A little further south of Trois Riviere is Yamachiche, where Augustin Leblanc and Francoise Hébert settled.[69] Both these communities grew quickly with Acadian settlers. Yamachiche drew Massachusetts exiles in particular. St. Jacques is northeast of Montreal and inland; it was another community founded by Acadian settlers who had been exiled in the Boston area. Angelique Leblanc and Germain Dupuis settled there.[71] It is in the same region as Lavaltrie, Quebec, where Françoise's parents apparently settled: Pierre Leblanc and Marie Françoise Landry. It is where Marie Françoise Landry was buried in October 1767,[72] while Pierre Leblanc died two years later in Quebec City.[73]

The web of Acadian families spread far and wide, but the connections were still strong. Many found others in their family. Now, this is my heritage web. Now, these are my people, too.

The Acadian deportation, *le grande dérangement*, is now viewed in the context of other forced migrations, such as with the partition of India and Pakistan in 1947 and with the violent breakup of Yugoslavia in the 1990s. With the latter, the term "ethnic cleansing" was coined. At that time, a United Nations Commission of Experts defined this term as *"a purposeful policy designed by one ethnic or religious group to remove by violent and terror-inspiring means the civilian population of another ethnic or religious group from certain geographic areas."*[74]

In John Mack Faragher's thorough and scholarly book on Acadian history, he concludes this definition well defines the expulsion of the Acadians.[75] I agree. The terror comes through from their stories 400 years later.

❧

Epilogue

As I found my way through this French-Canadian history via my ancestors' stories, I was changed in turn. My cultural identity has changed, although French-Canadian is now one of several cultural heritages in my greater ancestry. More than that, this virtual travel has helped me integrate earlier memories, experiences, and perspectives with this heritage.

One of the earliest memories I still hold in my bones is the simple act of walking—a smaller version of migration. I remember the rhythm of walking and its soothing sensations. Growing up in the country, I would walk to my best friend's house, which was a mile away. We lived on a dirt road then. It followed the rolling landscape, bordered by pastures and woods in various shades of green. Along the way, I found blue cornflowers and purple thistle on the roadside, birds that jumped from fencepost to fencepost, cows that noisily munched their clover and swatted flies with their tails, and breezes that carried all the cow-pasture distinct smell my way. Curiously, it wasn't a bad smell—it smelled like home. As I've said, I come from a long line of farmers. Perhaps this walking memory also connects me with my ancestors on a deeper level, as their migrations took them, often on foot, to find new opportunities from one home to another.

As a child, I was also curious about what was around the corner or over the next hill, just beyond my view. What were the people's lives like in those places? I have since crossed several oceans and met people in many other countries. I have met many migrants and ex-patriots who have chosen to live in a new region or new country. They sometimes described their forever in-between status, no longer fitting in back home nor fully fitting in with their new chosen home. They often felt they didn't fully "belong" in either place.

It seems the urge to migrate is a mixture of gumption to take on the new and of loss for what was left behind. I know something of that from my personal experience. I moved from my childhood home on that farm in western New York. After college, I settled in New England, where I have remained for more than fifty years. Maybe I was driven to leave the farm like my mother did, even though I didn't know her full story until much later. I chose to leave my family behind and knit together a new adopted family from new friends found here. Yet, do I belong here? New England has been my home longer than I lived in my childhood home. Still, I have always felt sad about leaving my family—for not being there for them and nurturing those relationships. I don't know the adults my nieces, nephews, and cousins have become; their children hardly know my name. While my original family connections are thin, they and that home base are certainly a part of me and my foundation. My education and professional roles have put me in new places, but I am still a country girl at heart. This background remains the lens from which I see the larger world. I can relate to my ancestors who chose to migrate hundreds of miles for new opportunities, a better life, new adventures, and new perspectives. That migration also comes with new relationships. I married in Massachusetts, but I chose to keep my maiden name. Who knew that in doing so, I was honoring a French custom I didn't know about at the time?

But my ancestors' legacies are about more than movement alone and about more than their losses.

I came from a long line of hard workers. Until the early 1900s, subsistence farming was required of most families. As land became scarce for new generations (as with François and Jacques Allard, Norbert Dupuis, and John Dupee), they sought new land opportunities by pushing further westward. The process involved packing up, moving, and starting over. Then forests were cleared, and new homes and farms were built. This sometimes occurred more than once in a generation and sometimes skipped generations. They were strivers. They knew how to start over and make a new life from scratch. They usually came with family, or some went ahead, and others followed. Family ties offered many hands for the hard work and support to navigate the many challenges. Their new homes brought new neighbors and new marriage partners. The families and community ties expanded, bringing more family and community support. More is possible when a community is working together, as with the Acadian communities when their imperial rulers left them alone. They found joy in the community.

There were entrepreneurs. I think of Jacques Campeau and Cécile Catin, who brought goods from Montreal to sell in the rugged outpost of Detroit via multiple canoe voyages. They brought their young children on each of the 650-mile trips, and Cécille gave birth on the Niagara Portage. Jacques set up a prosperous business in early eighteenth-century Detroit. My grandparents' generation left farming at the beginning of the Michigan auto-industry boom in 1910. They were all strivers, too, and persistent. They all benefited from their extended family's support, which made their transformation successful.

There were very few noblemen or noblewomen in my family. I think of Sir Hubert Leroux, who came to Montreal as a fur trader in 1672. His wife, Ann Marie Van Zeigt, had become a *Fille du Roi* following her nobleman father's death and turn of fortune. But after she was widowed twice and left with debts, she had to scramble to support her family. It was never an easy nor noble life for her. I had many *Filles du Roi* among my ancestors; all were incredibly brave to cross the Atlantic in hopes of better prospects than what they left behind. Most of them succeeded in that.

I found ancestors who fought in wars for their country, even when the boundaries of that country or its ruler had just changed, and they were now fighting on the other side. This applied to Norbert Dupuis in Ontario and Joseph Allard in Michigan, both in the War of 1812. With my mix of American, English, and French-Canadian ancestry, I found my loyalties on both sides of these battles. They fulfilled their duties. The promise of new land was a reward for Norbert.

My Acadian ancestors taught me what it was like being buffeted between rulers as the spoils of imperial wars. They were living in terror. Even keeping their heads down, out of political conflict, was not enough. Their exile taught me about what it was like to be a refugee. Not all migration is voluntary. They were unwanted where they landed. Families were separated, but they sought out connections as best they could. They suffered great hardships and demonstrated great resilience. Again, family connections and a few kind people in the communities where they landed made a difference. They are an inspiration! The world we live in today still offers hardships and even terror. Our generations may well need this inspiration for the unknowns that lie ahead.

When I reflect on my own travel experiences, they taught me as much about my American culture as they did about the people and places that I visited at the time. Our value in individualism is uniquely American. We tout this as if we don't need or care about others' help. Americans often overlook our own history, which offers many examples of the extra strength we get from family and community. Many Americans traveled in wagon trains for mutual support in their westward migration. Neighbors have helped neighbors recover from hard times. Church groups have assisted refugees in resettlement even in modern times. Our American value of individualism is often used to deny the social support we all need. It is usually social support that helps us all to succeed.

Today, more people live outside their countries of origin than at any time in history.[1] They migrated for many reasons, including escape from floods, draughts, and other disasters. These situations, in turn, impact local economies as people are unable to grow food. This often pushes farmers into cities to look for other work. Climate change threatens to create many more weather migrants in years to come. Policies can mitigate these migrations, however. Policies that improve building codes or incentivize agricultural practices for the new conditions make it possible for people to stay. When there is water scarcity, countries have often cooperated to share water resources across boundaries, reducing conflict and migration.[2] My French-Canadian ancestors left France because the feudal system restricted land ownership to the gentry and even restricted access to the peasants' own food crops. In New France, they could work toward owning their land and keep much of the profits from their business and farm production. They were well-fed and healthier as a result. Nonetheless, once land became scarce for new generations in North America, people migrated westward. People are still seeking new opportunities, and they are still on the move.

Today, we are more likely to put up walls on our borders than welcome newcomers. We are afraid of people who seem different or foreign. In the U.S., we were put off by each wave of immigrants, including the French-Canadians, the Irish, the Italians, and Eastern Europeans. More recently, we have been fearful of Central Americans, Caribbean, Arab and African immigrants. Yet, as we get to know each wave of newcomers, we share in one another's cultural practices and food (corned beef and cabbage, spaghetti and pizza, tacos and enchiladas). We soon become neighbors, helping one another. It is natural to be fearful of change, but our heritage tells us we don't need to let that stop us from embracing change. We are stronger than that. Fear of ethnic differences should not be a reason to restrict immigration, but sadly, that fear seems to be the main reason for blocking entry. Sadly, the fear of difference and ethnic cleansing repeats itself around the world.

My DNA includes a mix of cultural ancestry. While I discovered some of what it means to be French-Canadian, I also have heritage from some First Nations people and from the English and other European seekers to American shores. These migrations brought a mix of cultures together, and marriages across cultures enriched subsequent generations. Humans have been migrating across continents for thousands of years, long before the new world was conquered. With each migration, they started over and built new families and communities. Like my Indigenous and French-Canadian ancestors, they shared cultural practices and generated new ones that better fit the new environment. Most definitely, there will be more migrations for the generations to come.

I think we are all a product of our ancestors' legacies. We may all have walking memories deep in our bones! May we and future generations also build on our ancestors' legacies as we find our own place in the world.

NOTES

❧

CHAPTER 1: LOOKING FOR A BETTER LIFE

1. U.S. Evangelical Lutheran Church, "Baptisms 1826-1945," accessed January 20, 2015, *Ancestry.com*. Olive Evalina Lillie Burroughs was born in Rothbury, Oceana, Michigan on 20 June, 1886, according to her baptism record on Feb. 20, 1887 with U.S., Evangelical Lutheran Church in America Church Records, 1826-1945,. *found on Ancestry.com*, 20 Jan, 2015. Olive's biological mother was Matilda Samine (Minnie) Johanson-Johnson and her father, George Lillie.

2. Olive was adopted by Rufus and Sarah Burroughs and was found living with them 1900 US census, in Collins, NY, when Olive was age 13.

3. Olive E Burroughs married Ray Dewey on 30 Dec. 8, 1908, recorded in New York State, Marriage Index (1881-1967), found on Ancestry.com, June 30, 2017.

4. Details on the passenger steamers—City of Detroit III, https://historicde-troit.org/buildings/city-of-detroit-iii. Details on the passenger steamers. Accessed on October 26, 2020.

5. Gillette, Gary. "A sleeping giant: Detroit in the mid-1930's," a https://sabr. org/journal/article/a-sleeping-giant-detroit-in-the-mid-1930s. Accessed on Sept. 20, 2020.

6. Pauline Dewey married Leonard J DePue, 24 Apr 1937, in Detroit, Michigan. recorded in Michigan, County Marriages (1867-1952), published 2015. accessed Ancestry.com on August 26, 2020.

7. Edna Dewey married Onnie Lehto on, June 15, 1940 in Detroit, Michigan., recorded in Michigan, Marriage Records (1867-1952), Accessed on Ancestry. com on February 2015.

8. Leonard and Pauline DePue were found on 1940 United States Census on Lincoln Street in Detroit. Year: 1940; Census Place: Detroit, Wayne, Michigan; Roll: T627_1848; Page: 61A; Enumeration District: 84-261. Found on Ancestry.com on April 15, 2014.

9. Pauline Dewey Pfeffer died on 23 Dec 2017, with burial in Perrysburg NY. Recorded in U.S., Find A Grave Index (1700s-Current), Found on Ancestry. com on September 30, 2020.

CHAPTER 2: RIPPLE EFFECTS

1. Frederick Dupee's marriage to Lillian Allor, Feb 22, 1909, in St. Clair, Michigan. Recorded in Michigan, County Marriages, 1822-1940, published 2016. Accessed Ancestry.com on August 26, 2020.
2. WWI 1917-1918 draft record for Frederick James Depue. Registration State: Michigan; Registration County: Wayne; Roll: 2032417; Draft Board: 15. Accessed on Ancestry.com on August 26, 2020.
3. Fred Dupue was found as a boarder U.S. census in Detroit. Year: 1910; Census Place: Detroit Ward 17, Wayne, Michigan; Roll: T624_680; Page: 11B; Enumeration District: 0259; FHL microfilm: 1374693. Accessed on Ancestry.com on August 26, 2020.
4. Edward Depue's date of birth, 8 Jun 1910. Recorded in U.S. Public Records Index, Volume 1. Accessed Ancestry.com on August 26, 2020.
5. Alvoy I Depue's date of birth, 2 Feb 1912, and death date, 25 Sep 2006. Recorded in U.S., Social Security Applications and Claims Index, 1936-2007, claim date 21 Nov 1973. Accessed Ancestry.com on August 26, 2020.
6. Leonard DePue's date of birth, 09 Dec 1913. Recorded in U.S. Public Records Index, Volume 2, published 2010. Accessed Ancestry.com on August 26, 2020.
7. Lillian M. Depue's death date, 2 Jan 1914. Death record recorded in Michigan, Death Records, 1867-1950, published 2015. Accessed Ancestry.com on August 26, 2020.
8. Maternal death rates: CDC, https://www.cdc.gov/nchs/maternal-mortality/index.htm, retrieved on September 17, 2020.
9. Fred Dupee in U.S. census in Columbus, St. Clair Michigan. Year: 1920; Census Place: Columbus, St Clair, Michigan; Roll: T625_795; Page: 3B; Enumeration District: 100; Image: 102. Accessed Ancestry.com on August 26, 2020.
10. Frederick Depue's marriage to Elizabeth Snoblen, 26 Jun 1917 in North Branch, Michigan. Recorded in Michigan, County Marriages, 1867-1952, published 2015. Accessed Ancestry.com on August 26, 2020.
11. Elizabeth A. Dupee's death date, 4 Jun 1920. Death recorded in Michigan, Death Records, 1897-1920, published 2010. Accessed Ancestry.com on August 26, 2020.
12. Marian E. Dupee's death date, 1 Jun 1920 in Columbus, St. Clair, Michigan. Death recorded in Web: RootsWeb Death Index, 1796-2010, published 2012. Accessed Ancestry.com on August 26, 2020.
13. Frederick J. Dupee's marriage to Frances Blum, 24 Aug 1921 in Detroit, Michigan. Recorded in Michigan, County Marriages, 1867-1952, published 2015. Accessed Ancestry.com confirmed on August 26, 2020.

14. Frances Witkowski born 1 Dec 1886, in Detroit, Michigan. Recorded in Michigan, Births and Christenings Index, 1867-1911, published 2015. Accessed Ancestry.com on August 26, 2020

15. Frances Miller's marriage to William Blum on 10 May 1907 in Wayne County, Michigan. Recorded in Michigan, County Marriages, 1822-1940, published 2016. Accessed Ancestry.com on August 26, 2020.

16. Birth date of Frances Blum on 4 Oct 1907, death date on 5 Aug 1908 in Detroit, Michigan. Both recorded in Michigan, Death Records, 1867-1950, published 2015. Accessed Ancestry.com on August 26, 2020.

17. Birth date of Lucille Helen Blum on 8 Mar 1915, death date on 1 Jan 1921 in Detroit, Michigan. Michigan, Death Records, 1867-1950, published 2015. Accessed Ancestry.com on August 26, 2020.

18. Death of William George Blum on 23 Jun 1919 in Detroit Michigan. Recorded in U.S., Find A Grave Index, 1700s-Current, published 2012. Accessed Ancestry.com on August 28, 2020.

19. Depue, Roger L., *Between Good and Evil, a Master Profiler's Hunt for Society's Most Violent Predators.* Warner Books. New York, NY. 2005, p. 23.

20. Adverse Childhood Experiences research conducted by CDC and Kaiser-Permanente is summarized online at Centers for Disease Control https://www.cdc.gov/violenceprevention/aces/index.html, accessed on March 18, 2023.

21. Frederick Depue in U.S. census in Detroit, Michigan. Year: 1930; Census Place: Detroit, Wayne, Michigan; Roll: 1047; Page: 1B; Enumeration District: 0395; Image: 658.0; FHL microfilm: 2340782. Accessed on Ancestry.com on 26 Aug 2020.

22. Marriage of Dorothy R Blum to Robert D Bell on 29 Sep 1928 in Wood, Ohio. Recorded in Ohio, County Marriages, 1774-1993, published 2016. Accessed Ancestry.com on August 26, 2020.

23. Leonard DePue was found in the U.S. Census in Year: 1930; Census Place: Northville, Wayne, Michigan; Roll: 1075; Page: 24B; Enumeration District: 1032; Image: 491.0; FHL microfilm: 2340810. Accessed Ancestry.com on August 28, 2020.

24. Wayne County Child Developmental Center, Northville, Michigan, history found online at https://sites.rootsweb.com/~asylums/wccdc_mi/index.html, accessed on April 17, 2023.

25. Death of Leonard DePue on 17 Oct 1994 in Los Angeles, California. Recorded in California, Death Index, 1940-1997. Accessed Ancestry.com on August 28, 2020.

26. How Intergenerational Trauma Impacts Families. Apr 15, 2022. PsychCentral.com. https://psychcentral.com/lib/

how-intergenerational-trauma-impacts-families#how-its-passed-down, accessed on June 14, 2023.

27. Edward and Alvoy DePue were found in the U.S. census for Isadore Allor. Year: 1930; Census Place: Detroit, Wayne, Michigan; Roll: 1037; Page: 16A; Enumeration District: 0159; Image: 512.0; FHL microfilm: 2340772. Accessed Ancestry.com on August 28, 2020.

28. Alvoy Isadore Depue arrival Ontario Canada on 10 May 1930. Recorded in Border Crossings: From U.S. to Canada, 1908-1935. Accessed Ancestry.com on August 28, 2020.

29. Alvoy DePue in census Year: 1940; Census Place: Roseville, Macomb, Michigan; Roll: T627_1782; Page: 1B; Enumeration District: 50-18. Accessed Ancestry.com on August 28, 2020.

30. Marriage of Alvoy Depue and Viola Westrick on 27 Sep 1933 in St. Clair, Michigan. Recorded in Michigan, County Marriages, 1867-1952. Accessed Ancestry.com on August 28, 2020.

31. Alvoy Depue, 1942, East Detroit Michigan, City Directory. Recorded in U.S. City Directories, 1821-1989. Accessed Ancestry.com on August 28, 2020.

32. Alvoy Depue, Residence years 1993-1994, St. Clair, Michigan. Recorded in U.S. Phone and Address Directories, 1993-2002. Accessed Ancestry.com on August 28, 2020.

33. Death of Viola Ann Depue on 25 Feb 1995 in St. Clair, Michigan. Recorded in Michigan, Deaths, 1971-1996, published 1998; Accessed Ancestry.com on August 28, 2020.

34. Death of Alvoy I Depue on 25 Sep 2006 in St. Clair, Michigan. Recorded in U.S., Find A Grave Index, 1700s-Current. Accessed Ancestry.com on August 28, 2020.

35. Edward DePue in U.S. census Year: 1940; Census Place: Detroit, Wayne, Michigan; Roll: T627_1871; Page: 4A; Enumeration District: 84-1033. Accessed Ancestry.com on August 28, 2020.

36. Marriage of Edward F. DePue and Helen Marie Miller on 27 Jun 1936 in Detroit, Michigan. Recorded in Michigan, County Marriages, 1867-1952, published 2015. Accessed Ancestry.com on August 28, 2020.

37. Newspaper story on retirement of Edward DePue in The Chronicle Telegram (Elyria, Ohio) 22 Aug 1975.

38. Death of Walter E Julien in Olathe, Kansas, as reported in 30 Nov 2000 obituary, recorded in Web: Obituary Daily Times Index, 1995-Current, published 2012. Accessed Ancestry.com confirmed on August 28, 2020.

39. Death of Helen Marie Julien on 8 Aug 2011 in Olathe, Kansas, recorded in U.S. Cemetery and Funeral Home Collection, published 2011. Accessed Ancestry.com on August 28, 2020.

40. Death of Edward F DePue on 2 Sep 2001 in Detroit, Michigan. Recorded in U.S., Social Security Death Index, 1935-Current. Accessed Ancestry.com on August 28, 2020.
41. Death of Doris Marie DePue on 12 Nov 2013 in Beverly Hills, Michigan. Recorded in U.S., Social Security Death Index, 1935-Current, published 2011; Accessed Ancestry.com on August 28, 2020.
42. Fred DePue in U.S. census Year: 1940; Census Place: Detroit, Wayne, Michigan; Roll: T627_1861; Page: 6B; Enumeration District: 84-714. Accessed on Ancestry.com on Aug 28, 2020.
43. Death of Frances DePue on 1 Apr 1952. Recorded in Michigan, Death Records, 1867-1950. Accessed on Ancestry.com on Aug 28, 2020.
44. Death notice for Frederick DePue on 25 May 1954 in The Times Herald, Port Huron, Michigan. Retrieved on Feb 15, 2021.
45. Burial of Frederick DePue on 24 May 1954. Recorded in U.S., Find A Grave Index, 1700s-Current. Accessed on Ancestry.com on Aug 28, 2020.

CHAPTER 3: TRANSITIONS

1. 2022 population estimate for St. Clair County found at https://www.census.gov/quickfacts/stclaircountymichigan, accessed on Aug 30, 2020.
2. 2021 population estimate for St. Clair City found at https://www.census.gov/quickfacts/stclaircitymichigan, accessed on Aug 30, 2020.
3. St. Clair Historical Museum site offers "Educators' Resources," including slides of the shipbuilding history and a narrative of "The Town at the Turn of the Century," from which my summary was derived: https://www.historicstclair.com. Accessed on August 30, 2020.
4. William Dupee's (Sr.) birth on 6 Oct 1846 in Bayfield, Ontario and death on 16 Jul 1922 in Columbus, St. Clair, Michigan. Recorded in Michigan, Death Records, 1867-1950. Accessed at Ancestry.com on Feb 12, 2021.
5. William Dupee (Sr.) and his wife Mary Jane's family story is summarized here from several U.S. census reports in 1870, 1880, 1900, 1910, and 1920. Year of marriage, immigration year, residence and occupation, children home at the time, language used, and neighbors, among other details, are given on different census years and compiled here in story form.
6. Mary Jane (Herrick) Dupee's birth on 5 Sep 1854 in Columbus, St. Clair, Michigan and death on 8 Apr 1910 in Columbus St. Clair, Michigan. Recorded in Michigan, Death Records, 1897-1920. Accessed at Ancestry.com on Feb 12, 2021.
7. William Dupee's death notice on 21 Jul 1922 mentioned he suffered from a

broken hip bone and that he was a veteran thresherman in Detroit Free Press, Detroit, Michigan.

8. Birth of Luther Dupee on 8 Oct 1875 in Columbus, St. Clair, Michigan. Recorded in Michigan, Births and Christenings Index, 1867-1911, published 2011; Accessed Ancestry.com on August 30, 2020.

9. Birth of Lucy Bell Dupee on 8 May 1877 in Columbus, St. Clair, Michigan. Recorded in Michigan, Births and Christenings Index, 1867-1911, published 2011; Accessed Ancestry.com on August 30, 2020.

10. Birth of Nellie Dupee on 27 May 1879 in Columbus, St. Clair, Michigan. Recorded in Michigan, Births and Christenings Index, 1867-1911, published 2011; Accessed Ancestry.com on August 30, 2020.

11. Birth of Frederick Dupee on 4 Apr 1881 in Columbus, St. Clair, Michigan. Recorded in Michigan, Births and Christenings Index, 1867-1911, published 2011; Accessed Ancestry.com on August 30, 2020.

12. Birth of William R. Dupee (Jr.), on 16 Nov 1885 in Columbus, St. Clair, Michigan. Recorded in Michigan, Births and Christenings Index, 1867-1911, published 2011; Accessed Ancestry.com on August 30, 2020.

13. Marriage of Lucy Dupee and Adolphus Shirkey on 15 Nov 1898. Recorded in Michigan, County Marriages, 1822-1940. Accessed on Ancestry.com on August 30, 2020.

14. Adolph and Lucy Chortie Shirkey in U.S. Census in St. Clair, Michigan. Year: 1900; Census Place: Saint Clair, Saint Clair, Michigan; Page: 3; Enumeration District: 0111; FHL microfilm: 1240742. Accessed on Ancestry.com on August 30, 2020.

15. Adolph and Lucy Shirkey in U.S. census in St. Clair, Michigan. Year: 1920; Census Place: St Clair, St Clair, Michigan; Roll: T625_795; Page: 3B; Enumeration District: 133; Image: 522. Accessed on Ancestry.com on August 30, 2020.

16. Marriage of Nellie Dupee and Ellis Whitaker on 7 Mar 1906 in Port Huron, Michigan. Recorded in Michigan, Marriage Records, 1822-1940. Accessed at Ancestry.com on August 30, 2020.

17. Nellie and Ellis Whitaker and family in U.S. census Year: 1910; Census Place: Columbus, Saint Clair, Michigan; Roll: T624_673; Page: 4B; Enumeration District: 0095; FHL microfilm: 1374686. Accessed at Ancestry.com on August 30, 2020.

18. First Marriage of Ellis Whitaker to Dorothy Shirkey on 29 Dec 1891 in Port Huron, Michigan. Recorded in Web: St. Clair County, Michigan, Marriage Index, 1838-1898. Accessed at Ancestry.com on August 30, 2020.

19. Map of Columbus, Michigan, 1916 in Standard atlas of St. Clair County, Michigan, compiled and published by Geo. A. Ogle & Co. found at

University of Michigan, County histories and atlases collection. Online at https://quod.lib.umich.edu/m/micounty/3927951.0001.001/58?page=-root;rgn=subject;size=100;view=image;q1=Atlases. Accessed on Feb 12, 2021.

20. Frederick Dupee's marriage to Lillian Allor, 22 Feb 1909 in St. Clair, Michigan. Recorded in Michigan, County Marriages, 1822-1940, published 2016. Accessed Ancestry.com on August 26, 2020.

21. Marriage of William R. Dupee (Jr.) and Julia Hyslop on 29 Jun 1909. Recorded in Michigan, County Marriages, 1822-1940. Accessed at Ancestry.com on August 30, 2020.

22. Luther Dupee's marriage to Anna Carl on 24 Jan 1918 in St. Clair, Michigan. Recorded in Michigan, Marriage Records, 1867-1952. Accessed Ancestry.com confirmed on August 30, 2020.

23. Ford Motor Company history, at Encyclopedia of Detroit online, at https://detroithistorical.org/learn/encyclopedia-of-detroit/ford-motor-company, accessed on June 27, 2023.

24. Ford Highland Park Plant, at Encyclopedia of Detroit online at https://detroithistorical.org/learn/enclopedia-of-detroit/ford-highland-park-plant, accessed on June 27, 2023.

25. Ford, Henry. Henry Ford on Mass Production. 1926. Essay in Britannica online at https://www.britannica.com/topic/Henry-Ford-on-mass-production-2215524, accessed on June 28, 2023.

26. Meyer, Stephen. The Five Dollar Day: Labor, Management, and Social Control in the Ford Motor Company, 1908-1921. State University of New York Press, 1981.

27. Meyer, Stephen. The Degration of Work Revisited: Workers and Technology in the American Auto Industry, 1900-2000. Online at Automobile in American Life and Society, University of Michigan. http://www.autolife.umd.umich.edu/Labor/L_Overview/L_Overview3.htm, Accessed on June 27, 2023.

28. Sugrue, Thomas J. "From Motor City to Motor Metropolis: How the Automobile Industry Reshaped Urban America, Automobile in American Life and Society, http://www.autolife.umd.umich.edu/Race/R_Overview/R_Overview.htm. Accessed on Jan. 12, 2021.

29. WWI 1917-1918 draft record for Frederick James Depue. Registration State: Michigan; Registration County: Wayne; Roll: 2032417; Draft Board: 15. Accessed on Ancestry.com on August 26, 2020.

30. Milwaukee Junction and the birth of Detroit's Auto Industry. The Historical Marker Database, online at https://www.hmdb.org/m.asp?m=172664, accessed on June 28, 2023.

31. Frederick Depue in U.S. census in Detroit, Michigan. Year: 1930; Census Place: Detroit, Wayne, Michigan; Roll: 1047; Page: 1B; Enumeration District: 0395; Image: 658.0; FHL microfilm: 2340782. Accessed on Ancestry.com on 26 Aug 2020.

32. Fred DePue in U.S. census Year: 1940; Census Place: Detroit, Wayne, Michigan; Roll: T627_1861; Page: 6B; Enumeration District: 84-714. Accessed on Ancestry.com on Aug 28, 2020.

33. Sadler, Bob. Detroit Electric and its place in automotive history, published online Jan 26, 2022, at https://www.motorcities.org/story-of-the-week/2022/the-detroit-electric-and-its-place-in-automotive-history, accessed on Jul 2, 2023.

34. Frederick DePue obituary on 25 May 1954 in The Times Herald, Port Huron, Michigan. Retrieved on Feb 15, 2021.

35. Theobald, Mark. 2004. Briggs Manufacturing Co. 1909-1954. Online at http://www.coachbuilt.com/bui/b/briggs/briggs.htm, accessed on June 29, 2023.

36. Obituary of William Roy Dupee (Jr.) on 4 Jun 1962, p. 13, The Times Herald, Port Huron, Michigan. Recorded in http://www.legacy.com. Publication Date: 1/ May/ 2013; Publication Place: New Baltimore, Michigan; Accessed Ancestry.com on August 30, 2020.

37. William R Dupee in U.S. census in Detroit, Michigan. Year: 1930; Census Place: Detroit, Wayne, Michigan; Roll: 1041; Page: 17A; Enumeration District: 0267; Image: 762.0; FHL microfilm: 2340776. Accessed at Ancestry.com on August 30, 2020.

38. William R Dupee in U.S. census in Detroit, Michigan. Year: 1940; Census Place: Detroit, Wayne, Michigan; Roll: m-t0627-01866; Page: 1B; Enumeration District: 84-886. Accessed at Ancestry.com on August 30, 2020.

39. Encyclopedia Britannica. General Motors American Company, online at https://www.britannica.com/topic/General-Motors-Corporation, accessed on June 29, 2023.

40. William Dupee in U.S. census in Columbus, St. Clair County, Michigan. Year: 1910; Census Place: Columbus, Saint Clair, Michigan; Roll: T624_673; Page: 2A; Enumeration District: 0095; FHL microfilm: 1374686. Accessed at Ancestry.com on Feb 12, 2021.

41. WWI Draft Registration Card for William Roy Dupee (Jr.) on 12 Sep 1918 in Detroit, Michigan. Recorded in U.S., World War I Draft Registration Cards, 1917-1918, published 2005; Accessed at Ancestry.com on August 30, 2020.

42. William R Dupee (Jr.) in US census in Columbus, Michigan. Year: 1920; Census Place: Columbus, St Clair, Michigan; Roll: T625_795; Page: 3A;

..

Enumeration District: 100; Image: 101. Accessed at Ancestry.com on August 30, 2020.

43. Luther Dupee, Year: 1920; Census Place: St Clair, St Clair, Michigan; Roll: T625_795; Page: 15A; Enumeration District: 132; Image: 503, Accessed at Ancestry.com on August 30, 2020.

44. Luther Dupee, Year: 1930; Census Place: St Clair, St Clair, Michigan; Roll: 1025; Page: 7A; Enumeration District: 0048; Image: 829.0; FHL microfilm: 2340760, Accessed at Ancestry.com on August 30, 2020.

45. Lucy Shirkey in U.S. census in Year: 1930; Census Place: St Clair, St Clair, Michigan; Roll: 1025; Page: 6A; Enumeration District: 0046; Image: 779.0; FHL microfilm: 2340760. Accessed on Ancestry.com on August 30, 2020.

46. Lucy Shirkey in U.S. census in Year: 1940; Census Place: St Clair, St Clair, Michigan; Roll: T627_1816; Page: 11A; Enumeration District: 74-59. Accessed on Ancestry.com on August 30, 2020.

47. St. Clair in Michigan history during the Great Depression in http://michiganhistory.leadr.msu.edu/the-great-depression. Retrieved on Feb 16, 2021.

48. Obituary of Luther Dupee in The Times Herald; Publication Date: 17/ May/ 1951; Publication Place: Port Huron, Michigan, United States of America; URL: https://www.newspapers.com. Accessed Ancestry.com on August 30, 2020.

49. Death of Anna L Dupee on 9 Mar 1961 in St. Clair, Michigan. Recorded in U.S., Find A Grave Index, 1700s-Current. Accessed at Ancestry.com on Feb 28, 2021.

50. Obituary of Lucy (Dupee) Shirkey in The Times Herald; Publication Date: 10/ Jul/ 1950; Publication Place: Port Huron, Michigan; URL: https://www.newspapers.com. Accessed at Ancestry.com on August 30, 2020.

51. Death of Adolphus Shirkey on 9 Jul 1950 in Kimball, St. Clair, Michigan. Recorded in Michigan Department of Community Health, Division for Vital Records and Health Statistics; Lansing, Michigan; Death Records 1867-1950. Accessed on Ancestry.com on Aug 28, 2020.

52. Death of Julia T. Dupee in 1964, burial in Richmond, Macomb County, Michigan. Recorded in U.S., Find A Grave Index, 1700s-Current. Accessed on Ancestry.com on Aug 28, 2020.

53. Death of Ellis Whittaker on 8 Apr 1940 in Columbus, St. Clair, Michigan. Recorded in Michigan, Death Records, 1867-1950. Accessed on Ancestry.com on Aug 30, 2020.

54. Obituary of Nellie (Dupee) Whitaker in The Times Herald; Publication Date: 23/ Dec/ 1964; Publication Place: Port Huron, Michigan, United States of America; URL: https://www.newspapers.com. Accessed at Ancestry.com on August 30, 2020.

CHAPTER 4: FAMILIES ON THE MOVE

1. Birth date of John Dupee in 1811 in Canada, death date on 29 May 1896 in Burlington, Michigan. Both dates were recorded in Michigan, Death Records, 1867-1950, published 2015; Accessed Ancestry.com on August 28, 2020.

2. Birth date of Catherine (O'Brien) Dupee in 1813 in Cornwall, Canada, death date on 30 Jun 1899 in North Branch, Michigan. Both dates were recorded in Michigan, Death Records, 1867-1950, published 2015; Accessed Ancestry.com on August 28, 2020.

3. John Dupee and family in Stanley, Ontario: 1861 Census of Canada, Library and Archives Canada; Ottawa, Ontario, Canada; Census Returns For 1861; Roll: C-1036. Accessed at Ancestry.com on July 30, 2020.

4. George Dupee in U.S. census Year: 1860; Census Place: St Clair, St Clair, Michigan; Roll: M653_559; Page: 616; Family History Library Film: 803559. Accessed at Ancestry.com on August 30, 2020.

5. St. Clair Historical Museum site offers "Educators' Resources," including slides of the shipbuilding history and a narrative of "The Town at the Turn of the Century," https://www.historicstclair.com. Accessed on August 30, 2020.

6. George Dupee Civil War Draft registration, July 1863. National Archives and Records Administration (NARA); Washington, D.C.; Consolidated Lists of Civil War Draft Registration Records (Provost Marshal General's Bureau; Consolidated Enrollment Lists, 1863-1865); Record Group: 110, Records of the Provost Marsha; Accessed Ancestry.com on August 30, 2020.

7. Marriage of George Dupee to Eliza A. Curie on 24 Jun 1871 in Sherbrooke, Guysborough, Nova Scotia, Canada. Recorded in: Nova Scotia Marriages, 1864-1918. Accessed at Familysearch.org on August 30, 2020.

8. History of Gold Mining in Nova Scotia. Online at: http://www.virtualmuseum.ca. Retrieved on Feb 10, 2021.

9. Marriage of Eliza A. Dupee to Samuel B. Blakley on 24 Mar 1889 in Sheet Harbor, Halifax, Nova Scotia, Canada. Recorded in: Canada Marriages, 1661-1949. Accessed at Familysearch.org on August 30, 2020.

10. John Dupee (Jr.) in the U.S., Civil War Soldier Records and Profiles, 1861-1865. Accessed at Ancestry.com on August 30, 2020.

11. John Dupee (Jr.) in U.S. census, Year: 1870; Census Place: Port Huron, St Clair, Michigan; Roll: M593_699; Page: 313A; Image: 34621; Family History Library Film: 552198. Accessed at Ancestry.com on August 30, 2020.

12. John Dupee (Jr.) in U.S. census, Year: 1880; Census Place: East Tawas, Iosco, Michigan; Roll: 584; Page: 390D; Enumeration District: 146. Accessed at Ancestry.com on August 30, 2020.

13. Death of John Dupee (Jr.) on 29 May 1886 in St Charles, Saginaw County, Michigan. Recorded in U.S., Find A Grave Index, 1700s-Current. Accessed at Ancestry.com on August 30, 2020.

14. David Dupee's report of his immigration year was included in U.S. census: Year: 1900; Census Place: Saint Charles, Saginaw, Michigan; Roll: 740; Page: 21B; Enumeration District: 0074; FHL microfilm: 1240740. Accessed at Ancestry.com on Feb 12, 2021.

15. David Dupee in U.S. census: Year: 1870; Census Place: Fremont, Saginaw, Michigan; Roll: M593_702; Page: 281A; Family History Library Film: 552201. Accessed at Ancestry.com on Feb 12, 2021.

16. Death of David Dupee on 1 Feb 1905 in St. Charles, Saginaw, Michigan. Recorded in Michigan, Death Records, 1867-1950. Accessed at Ancestry.com on Feb 12, 2021.

17. Death of Emma Dupee on 8 Oct 1878 in St. Charles, Saginaw, Michigan. Michigan, Death Records, 1867-1950. Accessed at Ancestry.com on Feb 12, 2021.

18. Birth record for Elmer Dupee on 6 Aug 1876 in Saginaw, Michigan, identifies his parents as Emma and David Dupee. Recorded in Michigan, U.S., Births and Christenings Index, 1867-1911, FHL Film 967180. Accessed at Ancestry.com on Feb 12, 2021.

19. Marriage of David Dupee and Ellen LaMarsh on 2 July 1879 in Saginaw, Michigan. Recorded in Michigan Department of Community Health, Division of Vital Records and Health Statistics; Lansing, Michigan; Michigan, Marriage Records, 1867-1952; Film: 18; Film Description: 1879 Lapeer-1879 Wexford. Accessed at Ancestry.com on Feb 12, 2021.

20. Schaetzl, Randall. White pine logging in Michigan background. Dept of Geography, Michigan State University. Online at https://project.geo.msu.edu/geogmich/loggingbackgrd.html. Retrieved on Feb 12, 2021.

21. John Dupee (Sr.) in U.S. census Year: 1880; Census Place: Burlington, Lapeer, Michigan. Accessed at Ancestry.com on August 30, 2020.

22. Death of John Dupee (Sr.)on 29 May 1896 in Burlington Lapeer County, Michigan. Recorded in Michigan, Death Records, 1867-1950, published 2015; Accessed at Ancestry.com on August 30, 2020.

23. Marriage of James Dupee and Katie Flake on 21 Oct 1897 in Traverse City, Michigan. Recorded in Michigan Department of Community Health, Division of Vital Records and Health Statistics; Lansing, Michigan; Michigan, Marriage Records, 1867-1952; Film: 59; Film Description: 1897 Arenac - 1897 Kalkaska. Accessed at Ancestry.com on August 30, 2020.

24. James Dupee in U.S. census Year: 1900; Census Place: Grant, Grand Traverse, Michigan; Page: 2; Enumeration District: 0035; FHL microfilm: 12407. Accessed at Ancestry.com on August 30, 2020.

25. Catherine (Dupee, Haines) Bowen died on March 31, 1932. Her obituary stated she was survived by a brother, James Dupee of Flint, Michigan, found in the Flint Daily Journal, in Flint, Michigan, April 1, 1932. P. 4.

26. Bélanger, Claude. French-Canadian Emigration to the United States 1840-1930. Department of History, Marianopolis College, University of Montreal, 23 Aug 2000. Online at http://faculty.marianopolis.edu/c.belanger/ quebechistory/readings/leaving.htm. P. 10. Retrieved Feb 13, 2021.

27. Marriage of Betsey (Dupee) O'Brian and Mathias Vincent on 12 Sept 1869 in Burlington, Lapeer County, Michigan. Recorded in Michigan, U.S., Marriage Records, 1867-1952, accessed at Ancestry.com on Apr 28, 2023.

28. Mathias Vincent and family were living in Burlington, Lapeer County, Michigan, at the time of the 1860 U.S. Federal Census. Mathias and other siblings were born in Canada. The National Archives in Washington D.C.; Record Group: Records of the Bureau of the Census; Record Group Number: 29; Series Number: M653; Residence Date: 1860; Home in 1860: Burlington, Lapeer, Michigan; Roll: M653_549; Page: 655; Family History Library F, accessed on Ancestry.com on Apr 28, 2023.

29. Betsey (Dupee) Vincent and family in U.S. census Year: 1880; Census Place: Burlington, Lapeer, Michigan; Roll: 589; Page: 146A; Enumeration District: 162, accessed at Ancestry.com on Apr 28, 2023.

30. Jane (Dupee) Vincent in U.S. census includes year of immigration, Year: 1900; Census Place: North Branch, Lapeer, Michigan; Page: 8; Enumeration District: 0046; FHL microfilm: 1240724. Accessed at Ancestry.com on August 30, 2020.

31. Marriage of Mary Dupee and Charles Duncan on 8 Jan 1864 in Middlesex, Ontario. Recorded in: Archives of Ontario; Toronto, Ontario, Canada; County Marriage Registers, 1858-June 1869; Reel: 15 and 16. Accessed at Ancestry.com on August 30, 2020.

32. Marriage of Anna (Dupee) Morden and Levi Cash on 8 June 1900 in Mackinac, Michigan. Recorded in Michigan Department of Community Health, Division of Vital Records and Health Statistics; Lansing, Michigan; Michigan, Marriage Records, 1867-1952; Film: 68; Film Description: 1900 Delta-1900 Mackinac. Accessed at Ancestry.com on Feb 15, 2021.

33. Only the marriage record for their daughter, Jennie Haines (born in Canada), to Daniel Duchter on 20 Mar 1890 in White Oak, Ingham, Michigan, verifies her parents as Catherine Dupee and William Haines. In Michigan, County Marriages, 1867-1952 Accessed at Ancestry.com on Mar 4, 2021. Subsequent MI censuses place Catherine and William Haines in Michigan.

34. Marriage of Jane Dupee and Thomas Ashbury on 6 Dec 1876 in York, Ontario.

Recorded in Archives of Ontario; Series: MS932; Reel: 21. Ontario, Canada, Marriages, 1801-1928. Accessed at Ancestry.com on Feb 15, 2021.

35. Immigration and residence of John and Catherine Dupee's daughters are based on public records and U.S. censuses for each, as available. Others' public trees listed daughter Phoebe, but I was unable to find any records for her; it's unclear whether she died young or was married before the family's 1861 Ontario census. Mary Dupee-Duncan-Burton's divorce and second marriage records place her in Lapeer County, Michigan, in 1904 and 1907; her 1930 obituary stated she had lived in Imlay City, Lapeer County. Michigan, for 22 years prior to her death. Birth records for children of Anna and Enos Morden indicate they moved to Burlington, Lapeer County, Michigan, around 1874 when their third child, Cornelius, was born; later children were also born here. After Enos Morden died in 1899, Anna remarried to Levi Cash. Census data showed they lived in Ohio for a while but moved to Ogemaw, Michigan, which is where Anna died in 1937. Census Records for Catherine (Dupee) and William Henry Haines place them in Presque Isle, Michigan, in 1900 and Alcona, Michigan, in 1910. Census records for Jane Dupee-Ashbury place her in Burlington, Michigan, in 1880. Following the death of Jane's husband, Thomas Ashbury, and remarriage in 1886 to Jonathan Vincent, Jane and her family lived in North Branch, Lapeer, Michigan, which is where Jane died in 1913.

36. Jane (Dupee) and Thomas Ashbury in U.S. census Year: 1880; Census Place: Burlington, Lapeer, Michigan; Roll: 589; Family History Film: 1254589; Page: 150B; Enumeration District: 162; Image: 0308. Accessed at Ancestry.com on Feb 15, 2021.

37. Jane (Dupee) Ashbury married Jonathan S. Vincent on 23 Dec 1886, in Oxford, Oakland County, Michigan. Michigan Department of Community Health, Division of Vital Records and Health Statistics; Lansing, Michigan; Michigan, Marriage Records, 1867-1952; Film: 32; Film Description: 1886 Lenawee-1886 Washtenaw, accessed on Ancestry.com on Feb 15, 2021.

38. Mary (Dupee), Charles Duncan, and family resided in Lockport, Niagara County, New York, on June 1, 1875. New York, State Census, 1875, accessed on Ancestry.com on June 26, 2023.

39. Divorce of Mary Dupee and Charles Duncan decreed on 4 Oct 1904 in Lapeer, Michigan. Recorded in Michigan Department of Community Health, Division for Vital Records and Health Statistics; Lansing, Michigan; Michigan. Divorce records 1897-1952. Accessed at Ancestry.com on August 30, 2020.

40. Marriage of Mary Dupee Duncan to Samuel Burton on 12 Oct 1904 in Lapeer, Michigan. Recorded in Michigan, Marriage Records, 1867-1952. Accessed at Ancestry.com on Nov 22, 2020.

41. Divorce of Mary Burton and Samuel H Burton on 7 Oct 1907 (withdrawn) Recorded in Michigan Department of Community Health, Division for Vital Records and Health Statistics; Lansing, Michigan; Michigan. Divorce records, 1897-1952. Accessed at Ancestry.com on Nov 22, 2020.

42. Samuel H Burton in U.S. Census Year: 1910; Census Place: Imlay, Lapeer, Michigan; Roll: T624_659; Page: 11A; Enumeration District: 0044; FHL microfilm: 1374672. Accessed via Ancestry.com on Nov 22, 2020.

43. Death of Hosiah S (Samuel) Burton on 5 April 1911 in Imlay, Lapeer, Michigan. Recorded in Michigan, U.S., Death Records, 1867-1952. Accessed via Ancestry.com on Feb 7, 2023.

44. Death of Mary (Dupee) Burton on May 14, 1930, in Imlay City, Lapeer, Michigan. Michigan Department of Community Health, Division for Vital Records and Health Statistics; Lansing, Michigan; Death Records. Accessed at Ancestry.com on Nov 22, 2020.

45. Michigan history of vital records on divorce. https://www.michigan.gov/libraryofmichigan/0,9327,7-381-88854_89996_90000-467352--,00.html. Accessed on Nov 22, 2020.

46. Divorce in Canada, between 1840 and 1968. https://www.bac-lac.gc.ca/eng/discover/vital-statistics-births-marriages-deaths/divorce-1841-1968/Pages/acts-divorce-1841-1968.aspx. Accessed on Nov 22, 2020.

47. Death of Catherine (O'Brien) Dupee on 25 Jun 1899 in North Branch, Lapeer, Michigan. Recorded in Michigan, Death Records, 1867-1950. Accessed at Ancestry.com on August 30, 2020.

48. Jacques Lacoursière, Jacques and Philpot, Robin (translation). *A People's History of Quebec*. Baraka Books, Montreal, Canada, 2002. P. 111.

49. Ibid, pp. 115-116.

50. Marriage of John Dupee to Catherine O'Brien on 1 Jan 1835 in Middlesex, Ontario, Canada. Recorded in Ontario, Canada, Marriages, 1801-1928, published 2010; Accessed on Ancestry.com on August 30, 2020. David O'Brien and Fanny Dupee were married on the same date and recorded in the same record. Both marriages were witnessed by Michael Dupee.

51. Death of Michael Dupee on 28 Oct 1893, age 98, in Enniskillen, Lambton, Ontario. Recorded in Ontario, Canada, Deaths, 1869-1938 and Deaths Overseas, 1939-1947. Archives of Ontario; Series: MS935; Reel: 68. Accessed at Ancestry.com on Aug 30, 2020.

52. Marriage of Sylvester Dupee (age 71) to Mary Phillips Donaghue on 23 Dec 1870, Huron, Ontario, Canada. Recorded in Ontario, Canada, Civil Marriage Registrations, 1869-1873, published 2002; Accessed on Ancestry.com, confirmed on August 30, 2020.

53. Mary Jane (Herrick) Dupee's birth on 5 Sep 1854 in Columbus, St. Clair,

Michigan, and death on 8 Apr 1910 in Columbus, St. Clair, Michigan. Recorded in Michigan, Death Records, 1897-1920. Accessed at Ancestry. com on Feb 12, 2021.

54. Birth date of Luther Herrick on 4 Nov 1829 in New York, death date on 10 Jan 1916 in St. Clair, Michigan. Both recorded in Michigan, Death Records, 1867-1950, published 2015; Accessed Ancestry.com on August 28, 2020.

55. Lucy (Babcock) Herrick birthdate of March 29, 1830, in Green Mountain, Vermont, was reported in her obituary, which was added to a Find-a-Grave memorial by Patricia Love and posted to Ancestry.com by Hannah Grant in 2010. Her death date from Find-a-Grave was 13 Mar 1896 in Columbus, St. Clair, Michigan. Accessed Ancestry.com on August 28, 2020.

56. Dunbar, Willis F., May, George S. *Michigan: A History of the Wolverine State.* Grand Rapids: W.B. Eerdmans Publishing Company, 1995. p. 91.

57. Michigan in Encyclopedia Britannica online. https://www.britannica.com/ place/Michigan. Retrieved on Feb 10, 2021.

58. Henry Herrick's arrival Place: Salem, Massachusetts; Year: 1629; Page Number: 143. Recorded in U.S. and Canada, Passenger and Immigration Lists Index, 1500s-1900s, published 2010; Accessed on Ancestry.com, on August 30, 2020.

59. Editha Laskin arrival Place: Salem, Massachusetts; Year: 1628; Page Number: 59. Recorded in U.S. and Canada, Passenger and Immigration Lists Index, 1500s-1900s, published 2010; Accessed on Ancestry.com, on August 30, 2020.

60. David O'Brien and family U.S. Federal census Year: 1860; Census Place: St Clair, St Clair, Michigan; Page: 644; Family History Library Film: 803559, accessed at Ancestry.com on July 26, 2023.

61. Vermette, David. "When an influx of French-Canadians immigrants struck fear into Americans." The Smithsonian Magazine. August 21, 2019. Accessed online Mar. 10, 2023.

62. Massmoments. Ku Klux Klan Rallies in Worcester. Primary source, Worcester Telegram and Gazette, Oct. 19, 1924. Accessed online, https://www. massmoments.org/moment-details/ku-klux-klan-rallies-in-worcester.html, on April 7, 2023.

CHAPTER 5: CLOSE FAMILY TIES

1. Marriage of Frederick Dupee and Lillian Allor on 22 Feb 1909 in St. Clair, Michigan. Recorded in Michigan, County Marriages, 1822-1940, published 2016. Accessed Ancestry.com on August 26, 2020.

2. Lillian M. (Allor) Depue's birth date on 28 Aug 1888 and death date, 2 Jan 1914. Death record recorded in Michigan, Death Records, 1867-1950, published 2015. Accessed Ancestry.com on August 26, 2020.

3. Birth date of Isadore Allor on 24 Aug 1856 in L'Anse Creuse, Michigan, death date on 5 Dec 1936 in Detroit, Michigan. Both recorded in Michigan, Death Records, 1867-1950, published 2015; Accessed Ancestry.com, on August 31, 2020.

4. Birth date of Mary Frances (Furton) Allor on 29 Feb 1860 in Mt. Clemens, Macomb County Michigan, death date on 26 Aug 1953 in Detroit Michigan. Both recorded in U.S., Find A Grave Index, 1700s-Current, published 2012; Accessed at Ancestry.com on August 31, 2020.

5. Marriage of Isadore Allor and Mary Forton on 30 May 1882 in Macomb, Michigan. Recorded in Michigan, County Marriages, 1822-1940. Accessed at Ancestry.com on August 31, 2020.

6. Isadore Allor and family in U.S. Census Year: 1900; Census Place: Saint Clair, Saint Clair, Michigan; Roll: 742; Page: 5B; Enumeration District: 0111; FHL microfilm: 1240742. Accessed at Ancestry.com on September 3, 2020.

7. Birth date of Elmer Allor on 28 Mar 1883, death date on Mar 1964. Both recorded in U.S., Social Security Death Index, 1935-Current, published 2011; Accessed at Ancestry.com on August 31, 2020.

8. Birth date of Francis Bernard Allor on 11 Sep 1884 in St. Clair, St. Clair County, Michigan, death date on 5 Sep 1952 in St. Clair, St. Clair County, Michigan. Both recorded in U.S., Find A Grave Index, 1700s-Current, published 2012; Accessed at Ancestry.com on August 31, 2020.

9. Birth date of Arthur Allor on 4 Feb 1887 in Erin, Michigan, death date on 27 Jan 1890 in Erin, Macomb County, Michigan. Both recorded in Michigan, Death Records, 1867-1950, published 2015; Accessed at Ancestry.com on August 31, 2020.

10. Birth date of Rev. Fr. Edward William Allor on 20 Apr 1890 in Michigan, USA, death date on 12 Feb 1974 in Toronto, Ontario, Canada. Both recorded in Canada, Find A Grave Index, 1600s-Current, published 2012; Accessed at Ancestry.com on August 31, 2020.

11. Birth date of Martha (Allor) Kendall on 30 Mar 1893, death date on 4 Oct 1982 in Detroit, Wayne County, Michigan. Both recorded in Michigan, Death Records, 1971-1996, published 1998; Accessed at Ancestry.com on August 31, 2020.

12. Birth date of Viola (Allor) Mertz on 6 Jan 1904 in St. Clair, St. Clair County, Michigan, death date on 16 Aug 1928 in Detroit, Wayne County, Michigan. Both recorded in Michigan, Death Records, 1867-1950, published 2015; Accessed at Ancestry.com on August 31, 2020.

13. Isadore Allor and family in U.S. Census Year: 1910; Census Place: St Clair, Saint Clair, Michigan; Roll: T624_673; Page: 13B; Enumeration District: 0124; FHL microfilm: 1374686. Accessed at Ancestry.com on September 3, 2020.

14. Isadore Allor and family in U.S. Census Year: 1920; Census Place: Detroit Ward 6, Wayne, Michigan; Roll: T625_806; Page: 16A; Enumeration District: 209; Image: 646. Accessed at Ancestry.com on September 3, 2020.

15. Marriage of Elmer Allor and Emma Brines on 20 Feb 1909 in Detroit, Michigan. Recorded in Michigan, County Marriages, 1822-1940. Accessed at Ancestry.com on September 3, 2020.

16. Marriage of Frank B. Allor and Nellie Fitten on 1 Jun 1909 in St. Clair, St. Clair, Michigan. Recorded in Michigan, County Marriages, 1822-1940. Accessed at Ancestry.com on September 3, 2020.

17. Marriage of Martha E Allor and Charles E Kendall on 22 Nov 1910 in Detroit, Michigan. Recorded in Michigan, County Marriages, 1822-1940. Accessed at Ancestry.com on September 3, 2020.

18. Sugrue, Thomas J. "From Motor City to Motor Metropolis: How the Automobile Industry Reshaped Urban America, Automobile in American Life and Society, http://www.autolife.umd.umich.edu/Race/R_Overview/R_Overview.htm. Accessed on Jan. 12, 2021.

19. Meyer, Stephen. The Five Dollar Day: Labor, Management, and Social Control in the Ford Motor Company, 1908-1921. State University of New York Press, 1981.

20. Elmer and Emma Allor in U.S. Census Year: 1910; Census Place: Detroit Ward 11, Wayne, Michigan; Roll: T624_685; Page: 2B; Enumeration District: 0164; FHL microfilm: 1374698. Accessed at Ancestry.com on September 3, 2020.

21. Elmer Allor. U.S., World War I Draft Registration Cards, 1917-1918, Registration State: Michigan; Registration County: Wayne; Roll: 2024029; Draft Board: 7, Accessed at Ancestry.com on Sept 3, 2020.

22. Elmer Allor. U.S., World War II Draft Registration Cards, 1942. The National Archives at St. Louis; St. Louis, Missouri; World War II Draft Cards (4th Registration) for the State of Michigan; State Headquarters: Michigan, Accessed at Ancestry.com on Jul 3, 2023.

23. Frank and Nellie Allor in U.S. Census Year: 1910; Census Place: Detroit Ward 9, Wayne, Michigan; Roll: T624_684; Page: 17A; Enumeration District: 0143; FHL microfilm: 1374697. Accessed at Ancestry.com on September 3, 2020.

24. Charles Kendall in U.S. Census Year: 1910; Census Place: Hamtramck, Wayne, Michigan; Roll: T624_678; Page: 1B; Enumeration District: 0292; FHL microfilm: 1374691. Accessed at Ancestry.com on September 3, 2020.

25. Charles Kendall, U.S., World War I Draft Registration Cards, 1917-1918, Registration State: Michigan; Registration County: Wayne, Accessed at Ancestry.com on September 3, 2020.

26. Charles Kendall, World War II Draft Registration Cards, 1942. The National Archives at St. Louis; St. Louis, Missouri; World War II Draft Cards (4th Registration) for the State of Michigan; Record Group Title: Records of the Selective Service System; Record Group Number: 147, accessed at Ancestry.com on July 3, 2023.

27. Fred Dupee U.S. census in Detroit. Year: 1910; Census Place: Detroit Ward 17, Wayne, Michigan; Roll: T624_680; Page: 11B; Enumeration District: 0259; FHL microfilm: 1374693. Accessed on Ancestry.com on August 26, 2020.

28. WWI 1917-1918 draft record for Frederick James Depue. Registration State: Michigan; Registration County: Wayne; Roll: 2032417; Draft Board: 15. Accessed on Ancestry.com on August 26, 2020.

29. Sadler, Bob. Detroit Electric and its place in automotive history, published online Jan 26, 2022, at https://www.motorcities.org/story-of-the-week/2022/the-detroit-electric-and-its-place-in-automotive-history, accessed on Jul 2, 2023.

30. Edward Allor's role as a foreman at Ford Motor Company was described in Gervais, Marty. *Faces of Windsor, My Town*. Winsor, Ontario, Canada. 2006. Chapter "Garage Sale Find" pp. 53-54.

31. Women in Industry and at home in WWI. The Henry Ford Museum online at https://www.thehenryford.org/explore/blog/women-in-industry-and-at-home-in-wwi, accessed on Jul 2, 2023.

32. Henry Ford Hospital – Historical Highlights: Influenza Ward, 1919. Online at https://henryford.libguides.com/hfharchives_historicalhighlights/fluward, accessed on Jul 2, 2023.

33. Marriage of Viola M. Allor and Joseph L Mertz on 3 Nov 1926 in Detroit, Michigan. Recorded in Michigan Department of Community Health, Division of Vital Records and Health Statistics; Lansing, Michigan, USA; Michigan, Marriage Records, 1867-1952; Film: 237; Film Description: Wayne (March - June 1927). Accessed at Ancestry.com on March 8, 2021.

34. Grunow, Frances M. "A brief history of housing in Detroit," published Nov 17, 2015, on the website: https://www.modeldmedia.com/features/detroit-housing-pt1-111715.aspx. Accessed Nov 6, 2020.

35. Elmer and Emma Allor in U.S. Census Year: 1920; Census Place: Detroit Ward 6, Wayne, Michigan; Roll: T625_806; Page: 14A; Enumeration District: 209; Image: 642. Accessed at Ancestry.com on September 3, 2020.

36. Charles and Martha Kendall in U.S. Census Year: 1920; Census Place:

Detroit Ward 15, Wayne, Michigan; Roll: T625_814; Page: 1A; Enumeration District: 475. Accessed at Ancestry.com on September 3, 2020.

37. Elmer and Emma Allor in U.S. Census Year: Year: 1930; Census Place: Detroit, Wayne, Michigan; Roll: 1068; Page: 13A; Enumeration District: 0851; Image: 675.0; FHL microfilm: 2340803, Accessed at Ancestry.com on September 3, 2020.

38. Elmer and Emma Allor in U.S. Census Year: 1940; Census Place: Detroit, Wayne, Michigan; Roll: T627_1891; Page: 63A; Enumeration District: 84-1638, Accessed at Ancestry.com on September 3, 2020.

39. Death and burial date of Emma B Allor in 1962, burial in Michigan Memorial Part, Wayne County, Michigan. Recorded in U.S., Find A Grave Index, 1700s-Current. Accessed at Ancestry.com on Feb 8, 2023.

40. Charles and Martha Kendal in U.S. Census Year: Year: 1940; Census Place: Detroit, Wayne, Michigan; Roll: T627_1891; Page: 63A; Enumeration District: 84-1638, Accessed at Ancestry.com on September 3, 2020.

41. Death date of Charles Kendall on 2 May 1965 in Detroit, Michigan. Recorded in an obituary in Detroit Free Press 5, May 1965, accessed in Newspapers.com Obituary Index, 1800s-current, with Ancestry.com on Feb 8, 2023.

42. Frank Allor World War I draft registration, residence R.F.D 2, St. Clair County, Michigan. U.S., World War I Draft Registration Cards, 1917-1918. Registration State: Michigan; Registration County: St Clair; Roll: 1682812; Draft Board: 2. Accessed at Ancestry.com on Mar 8, 2021.

43. Frank Allor and family in U.S. Census Year: 1920; Census Place: China, St Clair, Michigan; Roll: T625_795; Page: 8B; Enumeration District: 96; Image: 20. Accessed at Ancestry.com on Mar 8, 2021.

44. Frank Allor and family in U.S. Census Year: 1930; Census Place: China, St Clair, Michigan; Roll: 1024; Page: 1B; Enumeration District: 0005; Image: 711.0; FHL microfilm: 2340759. Accessed at Ancestry.com on April 18, 2023.

45. Death date of Ellen Nellie (Fitton) Allor on 4 May 1989 in China, St. Clair, Michigan. Recorded in Michigan, Deaths, 1971-1996. Accessed at Ancestry.com on Feb 8, 2023.

46. Joseph Mertz and family in U.S. Census Year: 1930; Census Place: Detroit, Wayne, Michigan; Page: 56A; Enumeration District: 0827; FHL microfilm: 2340801. Accessed at Ancestry.com on March 8, 2021.

47. Joseph Mertz and family in U.S. Census Year: 1940; Census Place: Detroit, Wayne, Michigan; Roll: m-t0627-01885; Page: 61A; Enumeration District: 84-1497. Accessed at Ancestry.com on March 8, 2021.

48. Father Ed at Ford Motor Co., a public memory, referring to the letter by

Harry Hudson's letter on Ford stationery, posted on familysearch.org by P. Kehrer on 26 Feb 2016, linked to Edward William Allor. Retrieved on August 31, 2020.

49. Report on Fr. Allor's tenure 1926-1937 at St. Assumption parish was found on https://assumptionparish.ca/about/our-former-pastors, accessed/confirmed on August 31, 2020.

50. Fr Edward William Allor, Biography, pp. 17-19. In Dictionary of Basilian Biography, Lives of Members of the Congregation of Priests of Saint Basil from Its Origins in 1822 to 2002, 2nd ed. P. Wallace Platt. University of Toronto Press, 2005. pp. 17-19. Found online at https://www.basilian.org/wp-content/uploads/2014/08/DictionaryBasilianBiography-2017.pdf. Accessed on Aug. 31, 2020.

51. History of Ste Anne's Basilica in Detroit is found on the website: https://ste-anne.org/about-us/parish-history. Retrieved on March 9, 2021.

52. Edward William Allor multilingual, a public memory posted on familysearch.org by P. Kehrer on 26 Feb 2016, linked to Edward William Allor. Retrieved on Aug. 31, 2020.

53. Isadore Allor and family in U.S. Census Year: 1930; Census Place: Detroit, Wayne, Michigan; Roll: 1037; Page: 16A; Enumeration District: 0159; Image: 512.0; FHL microfilm: 2340772. Accessed at Ancestry.com on September 3, 2020.

54. Death of Isadore Allor on 2 Dec 1936 in Detroit, Michigan. Recorded in Michigan, Death Records, 1867-1950. Accessed at Ancestry.com on September 3, 2020.

55. Mary Allor in U.S. Census Year: 1940; Census Place: Detroit, Wayne, Michigan; Roll: T627_1848; Page: 62B; Enumeration District: 84-252. Accessed at Ancestry.com on September 3, 2020.

56. From Feb 1952 Newspaper clipping (newspaper name unknown) copied and posted on Ancestry.com by William Allor in June 2013, linked to Mary Frances Furton. Retrieved on March 9, 2021.

57. Death of Mary Allor on 26 Aug 1953, burial at Mt Olivet Cemetery, Detroit, Michigan. Recorded in U.S., Find A Grave Index, 1700s-Current. Accessed at Ancestry.com on September 3, 2020.

CHAPTER 6: *HABITANTS*

1. Habitant in Merriam-Webster Dictionary, online at https://www.merriam-webster.com/dictionary/habitant. Accessed on October 2, 2020.

2. Isadore Allor's marriage to Mary Furton on 30 May 1882 in Mt. Clemens,

Macomb County, Michigan. Recorded in Michigan Department of Community Health, Division of Vital Records and Health Statistics; Lansing, Michigan, USA; Michigan, Marriage Records, 1867-1952; published 2015. Accessed Ancestry.com, on August 31, 2020.

3. Marriage of James Allard and Marine Forton on 28 Feb 1854. Recorded in Michigan, County Marriages, 1822-1940. Accessed on Ancestory.com Jan. 28, 2021.

4. Marriage of Joseph Allard and Madeleine Tremblay in Detroit, Michigan, on 6 Oct. 1818, recorded in U.S. French Catholic Church Records (Drouin Collection) 1695-1954. Detroit, Ste Anne 1801-1842. Accessed on Ancestry.com, Jan. 28, 2021.

5. Marriage of Jacques Allard to Geneviève-Madeleine (Geneva) Laforest on 7 Jan 1780 in Detroit. Recorded in Quebec, Genealogical Dictionary of Canadian Families (Tanguay Collection), 1608-1890; Volume: Vol. 2 Sect. 1: Abe-Ble; Page: 23. Accessed at Ancestry.com on Sept 1, 2020.

6. Marriage of Pierre Allard to Marie Angelique Bergevin on 5 Nov 1743 in Charlesbourg, Quebec. Recorded in Quebec, Genealogical Dictionary of Canadian Families (Tanguay Collection), 1608-1890, Volume: Vol. 2 Sect. 1: Abe-Ble; Page: 21. Accessed at Ancestory.com on Jan. 28, 2021.

7. Marriage of Jean Baptiste Allard and Anne-Elizabeth Pageau on 23 Feb 1705 in Charlesbourg, Quebec. Recorded in Quebec, Genealogical Dictionary of Canadian Families (Tanguay Collection), 1608-1890, Volume: Vol. 2 Sect. 1: Abe-Ble; Page: 18. Accessed on Ancestry.com on Jan 28, 2021.

8. Marriage of François Allard and Jeanne Anguille on 1 Nov 1671 in Quebec. Recorded in L'Abbe D Tanguay, ADS, Dictionnaire Genealogique des Familles Canadiennes Depuis la Fondation de la Colonie Jusqu'a Nos Jours, Premier Volume, Depuis 1608 jusqu'a 1700, Eusebe Senecal, 1871. Accessed at Ancestry.com on Jan. 28, 2021.

9. Marriage of Jacques Allard and Jacqueline Frérot, Blacqueville Normandy, France. Date unknown. Recorded in L'Abbe D Tanguay, ADS, Dictionnaire Genealogique des Familles Canadiennes Depuis la Fondation de la Colonie Jusqu'a Nos Jours, Premier Volume, Depuis 1608 jusqu'a 1700, Eusebe Senecal, 1871. Accessed at Ancestry.com on Jan. 28, 2021.

10. Jacques's arrival in Detroit in 1774 was reported in *Researches after the descendants of Robert Navarre*. Compiled by Christian Dennison, Pastor of St. Charles Church. Detroit, Michigan, 1897. Accessed at Ancestry.com on Jan 30, 2021.

11. Notation of Jacques Allard as a voyageur was in his marriage record in French. Recorded in Early U.S. French Catholic Church Records (Drouin Collection), 1695-1954. Accessed at Ancestry.com on Jan. 28, 2021.

12. Lacoursierre, Jacques and Philpot, Robin. A People's History of Quebec. Baraka Books, Montreal, Quebec. 2002. Page 69-74.

13. Ibid. p. 52

14. Ibid. pp. 57-63

15. Death of Pierre Allard: 27 Dec 1759 in Charlesbourg, Quebec. Recorded in Quebec, Genealogical Dictionary of Canadian Families (Tanguay Collection), 1608-1890. Volume: Vol. 2 Sect. 1: Abe-Ble; Page: 18. Accessed at Ancestry.com on Jan 29, 2021.

16. Lacoursierre, Jacques and Philpot, Robin. A People's History of Quebec. Baraka Books, Montreal, Quebec. 2002. Pp. 71-73.

17. Surnames in French custom and laws apply to French-Canadian genealogy: Women retained their maiden names for official records. Thus, Marie Angelique Bergevin will keep her name even in her death records. However, in person, she would be likely be referred to with her husband's surname, as Madame Allard. Their children would get their father's name. Dit names: in French-speaking areas of Canada, where many people with the same surname, people often used the custom of a second surname. This distinguished different branches of the family or indicated where in France the family came from. Sometimes, the family dropped the original surname and used dit name thereafter. The masculine form of dit applies to males (Jean Cass dit St. Aubin), and the feminine form dite applies to females (e.g. Catherine Casse dite St. Aubin). See https://www.familysearch.org/wiki/en/Canada_Names,_Personal. Accessed on Jan. 29, 2021.

18. Marriage and family of Marie Angelique Bergevin and Louis Jacques are recorded in Quebec, Genealogical Dictionary of Canadian Families (Tanguay Collection), 1608-1890, Volume: Vol. 4 Sect. 2: Gli-Jin; Page: 574. Accessed on Jan. 29, 2021.

19. Morrissonneau, Christian. "The Chemin du Roi between Quebec City and Montreal". Encyclopedia of French Cultural Heritage in North America. http://www.ameriquefrancaise.org/en/article-550/The_Chemin_du_Roy_between_Quebec_City_and_Montreal.html. Accessed on Jan. 18, 2021.

20. De Bruler, Ray Jr., "Land Use and Settlement Patterns in Michigan, 1763-1837" (2007). Dissertations. 838. https://scholarworks.wmich.edu/dissertations/838. pp. 108-110.

21. Genealogy (births, deaths, marriages) of family James Alard and Mary Geneva Laforest, including the birth of Mary Geneva on 16 Jun 1764 in Detroit. Recorded in The Genealogy of the French Families of the Detroit River Region by Rev. Fr. Christian Denissen, p.3, Accessed via Detroit Society for Genealogical Research, at https://dsgr.org (for members only). Accessed/confirmed on Sept 1, 2020. See also ref #5 above.

22. 1778 Census of Detroit. At the time, it was the third-largest city in Quebec. Reported in Peterson, Jacqueline and Brown, Jennifer S.H. *Many Roads to Red River*. 2001, p. 69; also reported in De Bruler, Ray Jr. (noted in #20 above) p. 107, citing Russell, Nelson Vance. *The British Regime in Michigan and the Old Northwest: 1760-1796*. Northfield, Minnesota: Carleton College, 1939.

23. Dunbar, Willis and George S. May. *Michigan: A History of the Wolverine State* (rev). Grand Rapids: W.B. Eerdmans Publishing Company, 1995.

24. Birth of Joseph Allard on 29 Jul 1795 in Detroit and marriage of Joseph Allard and Magdelene Tremblay on 6 Oct 1818 in Detroit, Michigan Territory. Both recorded in The Genealogy of the French Families of the Detroit River Region by Rev. Fr. Christian Denissen, p.4, Accessed via Detroit Society for Genealogical Research at https://dsgr.org (for members only). Accessed on Sept 1, 2020.

25. Joseph Allard's 1812 War service record found in: U.S., War of 1812 Service Records, 1812-1815. Also: War of 1812 Pension Application Files Index, 1812-1815. Both accessed at Ancestry.com on Jan. 30, 2021

26. Pierre Allard's 1812 service record found in: U.S., War of 1812 Service Records, 1812-1815. Accessed at Ancestry.com on Jan. 30, 2021

27. Louis Allard's 1812 service record found in: U.S., War of 1812 Service Records, 1812-1815. Accessed at Ancestry.com on Jan. 30, 2021

28. Au, Dennis M. "'Best Troops in the World': The Michigan Territorial Milita in the Detroit River Theater During the War of 1812." March 20, 2011. Found on http://npshistory.com/series/symposia/george_rogers_clark/1991-1992/sec7.htm. Accessed on Dec. 12, 2020.

29. Joseph Allor census, Year: 1870; Census Place: Erin, Macomb, Michigan; Roll: M593_688; Page: 436A; Image: 323919; Family History Library Film: 552187. Accessed at Ancestry.com on Sept 2, 2020.

30. Conversion of Joseph Allor's farm value in 1870 to 2023 dollars. https://www.in2013dollars.com/us/inflation/1870?amount=16000. Accessed on April 17, 2023.

31. Birth of James Allard 1832 in L'Anse Creuse, Michigan, married to Marine Freton on 28 Feb 1854 in Mt. Clemons, Michigan. Both recorded in The Genealogy of the French Families of the Detroit River Region by Rev. Fr. Christian Denissen, p. 6, Accessed via Detroit Society for Genealogical Research at https://dsgr.org (for members only). Accessed on Sept 1, 2020.

32. James Allor census, Year: 1860; Census Place: Erin, Macomb, Michigan; Roll: M653_553; Page: 1017; Image: 591; Family History Library Film: 803553. Accessed at Ancestry.com on Sept 2, 2020.

33. James Allor census, Year: 1870; Census Place: Erin, Macomb, Michigan;

Roll: M593_688; Page: 436B; Image: 317; Family History Library Film: 552187. Accessed at Ancestry.com on Sept 2, 2020.

34. French-Canadian Heritage Society of Michigan, based in Mt. Clemens, Michigan, home page: https://habitantheritage.org. Accessed on Sept 2, 2020.

35. Marriage of Magliore Forton and Lucia Rivard on 31 Aug 1846 in Macomb, Michigan. Recorded in Michigan, County Marriages, 1822-1940. Accessed at Ancestry.com on Jan 30, 2021.

36. Marriage of Julien Fréton Jr. and Catherine Thibault on 20 May 1811. Recorded in Early U.S. French Catholic Church Records (Drouin Collection), 1695-1954. Accessed at Ancestry.com on Jan 30, 2021.

37. Marriage of Julien Fréton Sr. and Marie Josette Gastinon dit Duchene on 12 Feb 1759 in Detroit. Recorded in Quebec, Genealogical Dictionary of Canadian Families (Tanguay Collection), 1608-1890, Volume: Vol. 4 Sect. 1: Fab-Gle; Page: 111. Accessed at Ancestry.com on Jan 30, 2021.

38. Marriage of Pierre Fréton and Françoise Alliot in Nantes, Bretagne, France. Recorded in Quebec, Genealogical Dictionary of Canadian Families (Tanguay Collection), 1608-1890, Volume: Vol. 4 Sect. 1: Fab-Gle; Page: 111. Accessed at Ancestry.com on Jan 30, 2021.

39. The several members and generations of the Fréton family can be found in The Genealogy of the French Families of the Detroit River Region by Rev. Fr. Christian Denissen, pp. 494-496, Accessed via Detroit Society for Genealogical Research, at https://dsgr.org (for members only). Accessed/confirmed on Sept 1, 2020.

40. Marriage of Margaret Fortin to Leon Peltier on 9 Feb 1880 in Macomb, Michigan. Recorded in Michigan, County Marriages, 1822-1940. Accessed at Ancestry.com on Jan 30, 2021.

41. Julien Freton's story as a silversmith was reported in a thesis, "The Silversmiths of Old Detroit," by Walter E. Simmons II, submitted to the Office for Graduate Studies, Graduate Division of Wayne State University, Detroit, Michigan, in partial fulfillment for a Master of Arts degree in 1969. This story was found on Ancestry.com, submitted by Linda Ambroz62 on 8 Jun 2017, accessed/confirmed on Ancestry.com on Sept. 2, 2020.

42. Marriage of Francois Gastinon dit Duchene and Marie Josephe David on 29 Jan 1739 in Detroit. Recorded in Early U.S. French Catholic Church Records (Drouin Collection), 1695-1954; also on their family: Quebec, Genealogical Dictionary of Canadian Families (Tanguay Collection), 1608-1890, Volume: Vol. 4 Sect. 1: Fab-Gle; Page: 183. Accessed at Ancestry.com on Jan 30, 2021.

CHAPTER 7: *LE DÉTROIT*

1. The settling of Detroit is described online at www.historydetroit.com accessed on Jan. 6, 2020.

2. Boivin Sommerville, Suzanne. *Le Détroit du Lac Érié, 1701-1710*, Vol. 2. French-Canadian Heritage Society of Michigan. 2016. Royal Oak, Michigan. Pp. 19-21.

3. Moreau-DesHarnais, Gail and Wolford Sheppard, Diane. *Le Détroit du Lac Érié, 1701-1710*, Vol. 1. French-Canadian Heritage Society of Michigan. 2016. Royal Oak, Michigan. P. 45.

4. Lacoursierre, Jacques and Philpot, Robin. A People's History of Quebec. Baraka Books, Montreal, Quebec. 2002. Page 29-30.

5. A description of voyageurs' trips to Détroit via St. Lawrence and Great Lakes was found in slides from the presentation: 1 October 2016 - Detroit Historical Museum: *French Detroit's History and Culture and their Impact on Detroit's Founding Families*, by Diane Wolford Sheppard, found on https://habitantheritage.org/cpage.php?pt=15. Accessed confirmed on Sept 2, 2020.

6. Moreau-DesHarnais, Gail and Wolford Sheppard, Diane. *Le Détroit du Lac Érié, 1701-1710*, Vol. 1. French-Canadian Heritage Society of Michigan. 2016. Royal Oak, Michigan. Pp. 47-48, 466.

7. *Le Détroit du Lac Érié, 1701-1710*, Vol. 1. Pp. 145-150. Jacques Campeau's time in Detroit.

8. Jacques Campeau (Campot)(Campau) was an early arrival in Detroit, in the Dictionary of Canadian Biography online, http://www.biographi.ca/en/bio/campot_jacques_3E.html. Access confirmed on Sept 3, 2020.

9. *Le Détroit du Lac Érié, 1701-1710*, Vol. 1. Pp. 229-232. Jacob de Marsac in Detroit.

10. Jacob de Marsac's role as one of Cadillac's officers is found in "Legends of Le Detroit" by Marie Caroline Watson Hamlin, 1884, p. 290. Accessed at Ancestry.com on Sept 2, 2020.

11. *Le Détroit du Lac Érié, 1701-1710*, Vol. 1. Pp. 154-158. Jean Casse dit St. Aubin in Detroit.

12. Jean Casse dit St. Aubin's role in Cadillac's garrison and village, in C.M. Burton, Detroit, 1896, pp. 28, 33. Digitized by the Internet Archive in 2008 with funding from Microsoft Corporation http://www.archive.org/details/cadillacsvillage01burtuoft. Retrieved on Dec 18, 2019.

13. Descriptions of early buildings in Fort Ponchartrain in Cadillac's garrison and village, in C.M. Burton, Detroit, 1896, pp. 12-13, 29-30. Digitized by the Internet Archive in 2008 with funding from Microsoft Corporation http://www.archive.org/details/cadillacsvillage01burtuoft. Retrieved on Dec 18, 2019.

14. *Le Détroit du Lac Érié, 1701-1710*, Vol. 1, pp. 47, 454, 466-7.
15. Ibid. p. 148.
16. Ibid, p. 458.
17. Ibid, p. 59.
18. Ibid, p. 65.
19. Ibid, pp. 367-368.
20. An overview of Franco-Indian Alliances and Cohabitation was found on the Library of Congress website at http://international.loc.gov/intldl/fiahtml/fiatheme3d.html#track1. Accessed on Dec 6, 2020.
21. *Le Détroit du Lac Érié, 1701-1710*, Vol. 2, p. 92.
22. Ibid, pp. 187-189.
23. Ibid, pp. 66-67.
24. *Le Détroit du Lac Érié, 1701-1710*, Vol. 1, p. 59.
25. Births, marriages, and deaths are recorded for the family of Jacob de Marsac and Therese David in Quebec, Genealogical Dictionary of Canadian Families (Tanguay Collection), 1608-1890, Volume: Vol. 3 Sect. 2: Dej-Ezi; Page: 327. Accessed at Ancestry.com on Sept 2, 2020.
26. *Le Détroit du Lac Érié, 1701-1710*, Vol. 1. P. 62.
27. Ibid, p. 468.
28. Ibid, p. 245.
29. Jean Casse dit St. Aubin, born about 1659 in Bordeaux, France, died in Detroit 1759, his marriage to Mary Louisa Gaultier on 7 Feb 1707 in Quebec, and later generations in The Genealogy of the French Families of the Detroit River Region by Rev. Fr. Christian Denissen, pp. 1113-4, Accessed via Detroit Society for Genealogical Research, at https://dsgr.org (for members only). Accessed/confirmed on Sept 3, 2020.
30. An overview of the fur trade and lifestyle of voyageurs was found in *Le Détroit du Lac Érié, 1701-1710*, Vol. 2, pp. 181-186; also: Boivin Sommerville, Suzanne. *Michigan's Habitant Heritage*, the Journal of the French-Canadian Heritage Society of Michigan, Vol. 26, 4, October 2005, pp. 156-161.
31. Slideshow (pdf) by Wolford Sheppard, Diane. "The Forgotten *Voyageurs*" found at habitantheritage.org. Retrieved on Jan. 12, 2021.
32. Births, marriages, and deaths are recorded for the family of Thérèse Cécile Campeau and François de Marsac in Quebec, Genealogical Dictionary of Canadian Families (Tanguay Collection), 1608-1890, Volume: Vol. 2 Sect. 2: Ble-Cha; Page: 531. Accessed at Ancestry.com on Jan 30, 2021.
33. Description of ribbon farms in Farmer, Silas. *History of Detroit and Wayne County and Early Michigan: A Chronological Cyclopedia of the Past and Present.* Silas Farmer & Co., Detroit, 1888. P. 21. Accessed at Ancestry.com on Jan 29, 2020.

34. *Le Détroit du Lac Érié, 1701-1710*, Vol. 1. P. 67.

35. Ibid. p. 71.

36. Ibid, pp. 450-454.

37. De Bruler, Ray Jr., "Land Use and Settlement Patterns in Michigan, 1763-1837" (2007). Dissertations. 838. https://scholarworks.wmich.edu/dissertations/838. P. 89.

38. Pierre Meloche, born 1 Sep 1701 in Montreal, died 23 Aug 1760 in Detroit, married to Jeanne Caron on 16 Aug 1729 in Lachine, Quebec, and later generations in <u>The Genealogy of the French Families of the Detroit River Region</u> by Rev. Fr. Christian Denissen, p. 820-821, Accessed via Detroit Society for Genealogical Research, at https://dsgr.org (for members only). Accessed on Sept 3, 2020.

39. Pierre Meloche's story in Detroit in The Meloche Legacy: A Meloche Family History Dating Back to the Year 1575, by James Lawrence, Joseph Meloche, Roger Meloche, Association des families Meloche. Book published by Association des families Meloche, Canada, 2001. Accessed at Ancestry.com on Sept 3, 2020.

40. Chief Pontiac's camp on the Meloche farm, found in Ross, Robert B. and Catin, George B. *Landmarks of Wayne County and Detroit.* Revised by Clarence W. Burton. The Evening News Association, Detroit. 1898. P. 173. Accessed at Ancestry.com on Sept 3, 2020.

41. Pontiac's Rebellion summarized at cs.mcgill.ca. Retrieved on Feb 5, 2021.

CHAPTER 8: THE KING'S RATIONS

1. Dodenhoff, Jean, "Grosse Pointe's First Settlers: From Whence Did They Come?", found online at http://www.gphistorical.org/pdf-files/tonnancour/settlers.pdf. Accessed on Sept 2, 2020.

2. King Louis XV's proclamation, with features of the King's rations, is from Paré, Father George, "The Cicotte Book." Bulletin–Detroit Historical Society. Vol. XIV, No. 5, p. 10.

3. Genealogy (births, deaths, marriages) of family James Allard and Mary Geneva Laforest, including the birth of Mary Geneva on 16 Jun 1764 in Detroit. Recorded in <u>The Genealogy of the French Families of the Detroit River Region</u> by Rev. Fr. Christian Denissen, p. 3, Accessed via Detroit Society for Genealogical Research, at https://dsgr.org (for members only). Accessed/confirmed on Sept 1, 2020.

4. The Yax family story came from the book *The Germanic Influence In The Making of Michigan* by John Andrew Russell, A.M., LL.D, Dean of the

School of Commerce and Finance, University of Detroit. Published by the University of Detroit, 1927. Pp. 50-51. Accessed online at https://quod.lib.umich.edu/g/genpub/AFK0855.0001.001?rgn=main;view=fulltext, on March 18, 2023.

5. Another version of the Yax story came from the book *Tales of the Forgotten Village* by W.P. Sugars. University Lithoprinters, Inc., Ypsilanti Michigan., 1953. P. 4. Accessed online at https://catalog.hathitrust.org/Record/001265300, on March 18, 2023.

6. Translation of the text from Ste Anne's Detroit registry: Catherine Herbinne, wife of Michael Yax, converts from Lutheran to Catholicism on Passion Sunday, March 16, 1755 at Ste. Anne's in Detroit to Father Bocquet in the presence of M. Dumay, captain of the troops of his Majesty, Knight of the military order of St. Louis and commanding officer for the King in this fort and its dependencies, and of a great number of other persons. Accessed at Ancestry.com on March 12, 2021.

7. Family of Michael Yax and Catherine Herbinne in Quebec, Genealogical Dictionary of Canadian Families (Tanguay Collection), 1608-1890, Volume: Vol. 7 Sect. 2: Tre-Zis; Page: 491. Accessed at Ancestry.com on Feb 3, 2021.

8. Marriage of Marie Françoise Meny (Mesny) and Jean Baptiste Billoud dit Lespérance., in: Moreau-DesHarnais, Gail. French Soldiers Married in Detroit in 1758. *Michigan's Habitant Heritage*, Vol. 29, #4, Oct. 2008, pp. 188-9. Accessed at habitantheritage.org on Jan. 8, 2021.

9. Genealogy (births, deaths, marriages) of children of Jean Baptiste Billiau dit Lesperance and Mary Meny in Detroit. Recorded in The Genealogy of the French Families of the Detroit River Region by Rev. Fr. Christian Denissen, pp. 740-1, Accessed via Detroit Society for Genealogical Research, at https://dsgr.org (for members only). Accessed/confirmed on Sept 1, 2020.

10. Death of Marguerite Simard reported in, Moreau-DesHarnais, Gail. People Buried from Ste. Anne de Detroit (1766-1776): Part III. [Records found at www.ancestry.com, Early U.S. Catholic French Church Records (Drouin Collection) Détroit, Ste- Anne, 1702-1780, begin with image 134 of 238.], and in *Michigan's Habitant Heritage*, Vol. 31, #4, October 2010, p. 211. Accessed at habitantheritage.org on Jan. 8, 2021.

11. Personal email correspondence with Gail Moreau-DesHarnais, co-editor of *Michigan's Habitant Heritage,* on Jan. 11, 2021, drawing from her research of Marie Mesny's family in Detroit's Ste. Anne's church records in the original French language in Drouin.

12. Translation of Baptism of Antoine Lespérance. In article by Moreau-DesHarnais, Gail. Deciphering French and French-Canadian Baptismal, Marriage, and Burial Records, Part 1: Baptismal Records. *Michigan's Habitant*

Heritage, Vol. 35, #1, January 2014, p. 58. Accessed at habitantheritage.org on Jan. 8, 2021.

13. Death of Charles Morand dit Grimard on 23 Feb 1785. Recorded in Early U.S. French Catholic Church Records (Drouin Collection), 1695-1954. Accessed at Ancestry.com on Feb 3, 2021.

14. Marriage of Michel Houde to Marie Anne Mini on 4 Feb 1788. Recorded in Early U.S. French Catholic Church Records (Drouin Collection), 1695-1954. Accessed at Ancestry.com on Feb 3, 2021.

15. Death of Michel Houde on 20 Aug 1793 . Recorded in: Quebec, Genealogical Dictionary of Canadian Families (Tanguay Collection), 1608-1890, Volume: Vol. 4 Sect. 2: Gli-Jin; Page: 521. Accessed at Ancestry.com on Feb 3, 2021.

16. Marriage of Simon Drouillard to Marie Anne Mini on 14 May 1804. Recorded in Early U.S. French Catholic Church Records (Drouin Collection), 1695-1954. Accessed at Ancestry.com on March 12, 2021.

17. Death of Simon Drouillard on 26 July 1805 in Detroit, burial at Ste Anne's. Recorded in U.S., Find A Grave Index, 1700s-Current. Accessed at Ancestry.com on March 12, 2021.

18. Enrollees in the Confraternity of the Blessed Sacrament, 1805-1832: Ste Anne de Detroit, transcribed by Sharon Kelley and Gail Moreau-DesHarnais, in *Michigan's Habitant Heritage*, Vol. 31, #2, April 2010, p. 107. Accessed at habitantheritage.org on Jan. 8, 2021.

19. Burial of Marie Magdaleine Mini 1812 in Detroit, Recorded in Early U.S. French Catholic Church Records (Drouin Collection), 1695-1954. Accessed at Ancestry.com on Feb 4, 2021.

20. Marriage of Julien Fréton Sr. and Marie Josette Gastinon dit Duchene on 12 Feb 1759 in Detroit. Recorded in Quebec, Genealogical Dictionary of Canadian Families (Tanguay Collection), 1608-1890, Volume: Vol. 4 Sect. 1: Fab-Gle; Page: 111. Accessed at Ancestry.com on Jan 30, 2021.

21. Marriage of Jean-Baptiste Aide-Créquy and Marie-Madeleine Gastinon on 11 Jan 1762 in Detroit. Recorded in: Quebec, Genealogical Dictionary of Canadian Families (Tanguay Collection), 1608-1890, Volume: Vol. 4 Sect. 1: Fab-Gle; Page: 183. Accessed at Ancestry.com on Jan 30, 2021.

22. Marriage and family of Louis Beaufait and Therese de Marsac in Quebec, Genealogical Dictionary of Canadian Families (Tanguay Collection), 1608-1890, Volume: Vol. 3 Sect. 2: Dej-Ezi; Page: 327. Accessed at Ancestry.com on Feb 4, 2021.

23. Excerpt on Louis Beaufait's role in Detroit history is from Burton, Clarence M. The City of Detroit, Michigan, 1701-1922. Clarence M. Burton, editor-in-chief, William Stocking, associate editor, Gordon K. Miller, associate

editor. Vo. 5. E-book, University of Michigan, at http://name.umdl.umich.edu/BAD1447.0005.001. Pp. 1355-1356. Accessed on Feb 4, 2021.

24.   Marriage of Jean Baptiste Rivard and Catherine Yax on 15 Feb 1762. Recorded in Quebec, Genealogical Dictionary of Canadian Families (Tanguay Collection), 1608-1890, Volume: Vol. 6 Sect. 2: Per-Rob; Page: 583. Accessed on Feb 4, 2021.

25.   Marriage of Ignace Thibault to Catherine Casse St. Aubin on 1 Dec 1768. Recorded in: Quebec, Genealogical Dictionary of Canadian Families (Tanguay Collection), 1608-1890, Volume: Vol. 2 Sect. 2: Ble-Cha; Page: 577. Accessed on Feb 4, 2021.

CHAPTER 9: *QUÉBÉQOIS*—INHABITANT OF QUEBEC

1.   Arrival of François Allard in Quebec as reported in the biography of François Allard by Romeo Allard, F.M.S., In LaForest, Thomas J. *Our French-Canadian Ancestors*, Vol 3. Palm Harbor, FL: The Lisi Press, 1992, pp. 15-23. Accessed at FamilySearch.org on Aug. 30, 2020.
2.   McNelley, Susan. *Hélène's World, Hélène Desportes of Seventeenth-Century Quebec*. Etta Heritage Press. 2014. P. 1.
3.   Ibid, p. 10.
4.   Lacoursière, Jacques and Philpot, Robin (translation). *A People's History of Quebec*. Baraka Books, Montreal, Canada, 2002. Pp. 12-13.
5.   Ibid, pp. 9-11.
6.   Fischer, David Hackett. Champlain's Dream. Simon & Schuster, New York, 2008. P. 3. No paintings depicting Samuel de Champlain exist. The statue in Quebec City not based on any knowledge of what he looked like.
7.   Ibid, p. 243.
8.   McNelley, p. 5-6.
9.   Ibid, pp. 10-12. Habituation, 1st winter
10.   Ibid, p. 44. diet
11.   Ibid, pp. 241-243. Helene's life summary
12.   Fischer, David Hackett, p. 94.
13.   Tanner, Adrian. Innu (Montagnais-Naskapi), Sept 1, 2020. In The Canadian Encyclopedia, online at https://www.thecanadianencyclopedia.ca/en/article/innu-montagnais-naskapi, accessed on Feb 13, 2023.
14.   McNelley, pp. 18-19. Interactions with indigenous people
15.   Jesuits projects, Ibid, pp. 80-81.
16.   Ibid, p. 139.

17. The nuns' arrival, ibid, pp. 133-135.

18. Wendats, ibid, p. 20

19. Fischer, David Hackett. P. 280

20. McNelley, Iroquois attacks on Montreal, p. 224.

21. Death of Joseph Hebert, Ibid, p. 199.

22. Sr. Marie Morin's account of Iroquois raids on Montreal in Simpson, Patricia. *Marguerite Bourgeoys and Montreal, 1640-1665*. Montreal: McGill-Queens University Press.1977. pp. 173-174.

23. McNelley, pp. 141-142.

24. Ibid, p. 158.

25. Kaskaskia, an American Indian tribe, is described in the Encyclopedia of Oklahoma History and Culture online, https://www.okhistory.org. Accessed on Sept. 13, 2021.

26. Marriage and family of Marie-Suzanne Capei8suec8e and Jean Gautier. Recorded in Quebec Genealogical Dictionary of Canadian Families (Tanguay Collection), 1608-1890, Volume: Vol. 4 Sect. 1: Fab-Gle; Page: 206, published on Ancestry.com, accessed on Sept. 6, 2020.

27. Jean Gauthier's voyageur contracts and family profile are documented in: Sheppard, Diane Woolford. "Detroit River Region *métis* Families – Gauthier *dit* Saguingoira – Capciouékoué Family," at https://habitantheritage.org. Accessed on Sept. 13, 2021.

28. Marriage and family of Pierre Gauthier dit Sanuingoira and Charlotte Roussel is documented in Jetté, *Dictionnaire Généalogique des familles du Quebec; Programme de recherche en démographie historique* (PRDH), accessed online (membership required) on May 3, 2021.

29. Dickenson, John A. "Lachine Raid," published online in www.thecanadianencyclopedia.ca on Feb 7, 2006, edited Dec. 15, 2013. Accessed on Sept. 15, 2021.

30. Parrott, Zach and Marshall, Tabitha. "Iroquois Wars," published online in www.thecanadianencyclopedia.ca on Feb 7, 2006, edited July 31, 2019. Accessed on Sept. 15, 2021.

31. McNelley, p. 54

32. Marriage of Suzanne Gautier and Jacques Souchereau on 8 Aug 1732 in Montreal. Recorded in Quebec, Genealogical Dictionary of Canadian Families (Tanguay Collection), 1608-1890, Volume: Vol. 4 Sect. 1: Fab-Gle; Page: 209, published on Ancestry.com 2011; accessed on Sept. 6, 2020.

33. Marriage and family of Susanne Gauthier and Jacques Souchereau Langoumois are documented in Jetté, *Dictionnaire Généalogique des familles du Quebec; Programme de recherche en démographie historique* (PRDH), accessed online (membership required) on May 10, 2021.

34. Marriage of Françoise Souchereau dit Langoumois and Etienne (Stephen) Godfroy Balard dit Latour on 1 Oct. 1770 in Les Cèdres, Québec. Recorded in *Early U.S. French Catholic Church Records* (Drouin Collection), 1621-1967. Accessed at Ancestry.com on Sept 19, 2021.

35. Lacoursière, pp. 21-23.

36. *Seigneurial* system. McNelley, p. 219

37. Lacoursière, p. 16.

38. McNelley, p. 42.

39. Desjardins, François. Immigration from Old to New France. Le blog de l'institut Drouin, Généalogie et Histoire du Québec. Feb 14, 2018, p. 65. Online at https://www.genealogiequebec.com/blog/en/2018/02/14/immigration-from-old-to-new-france/. Accessed on Jan. 29, 2021.

40. Background on the Filles du Roi was drawn from the book *Along a River, The First French-Canadian Women* by Jan Noel. University of Toronto Press, Toronto. 2013, pp. 75-83.

41. The original source of many statistics on Filles du Roi is from the study and book (in French), Yves Landry, *Les Filles du roi au xvii'ème siècle* (The King's Daughters in the 17th century), published by Leméac in 1992 and subtitled, Orphans in France, Pioneers in Canada. A book review and synopsis (in English) is available by Toupin, Dave. "A Treasure Trove of Facts about Les Filles du roi." As published in *Sent By the King*, Spring 2019, Vol. XXII, Issue I. Accessed from www.habitantheritage.org on August 24, 2021.

42. There are conflicting records on the birthdate of François Allard. Tanguay reports it as 1637, while the François Allard biography in LaForest's book (ref 1, above) reports 1642. I will go with the Tanguay report. Quebec, Genealogical Dictionary of Canadian Families (Tanguay Collection), 1608-1890, Volume: Vol. 1 Sect. 1: A-Hel; Page: 3. Accessed from Ancestry.com on January 29, 2021.

43. Lacoursière, p. 16.

44. Arrival of Jeanne L'Anguille with the *filles du roi* on 1671 is documented in *La Sociétié des Filles du roi et soldats du Carignan, Inc.* Accessed online at https://fillesduroi.org on Sept. 6, 2021.

45. The death of Jeanne's father, Etienne L'Anguille, is unconfirmed. Other family trees list his death date in 1771, which would have been just before Jeanne's departure for Quebec. Yves Landry (ref #40 above) reported that 56.7% of *filles du roi* had a deceased father upon immigration, making it a high probability that this loss motivated her decision to go to Quebec.

46. There are also conflicting reports on the birth and baptism of Jeanne L'Anguille. Tanguay (referenced in #41 above) reports her birthdate as 1647, while her baptism is reported in fichier documents as 1643. For my summary,

I will draw from fichier, as it includes not only Jeanne's key dates but also her siblings and parents. Jeanne was baptized on 27 Apr 1643 at Artannes-sur-Indre St-Maurice, Indre-et-Loire, France, recorded in Canada, Quebec, Quebec Federation of Genealogical Societies, Family Origins, 1621-1865 at www.fichierorigine.com. Accessed from familysearch.org on Sept. 28, 2021.

47. A description of the *filles du roi* ocean voyage was provided in the podcast *"Filles du Roi,* The Perilous Journey,*"* by Bill Kane, Episode 044, Feb 23, 2016, on Maple Stars and Stripes, accessed online at https://maplestarsand-stripes.com, on Sept. 5, 2021.

48. A marriage contract for François Allard and Jeanne Anguille was signed on 18 Oct. 1671, witnessed by a notary and recorded in Quebec, Canada, Notarial Records, 1637-1935, Bibliothèque et Archives nationales du Québec; Montréal, Quebec, Canada; District: Québec; Title: Becquet, Romain (1665-1682). Accessed at Ancestry.com on Sept. 5, 2020.

49. Marriage of François Allard and Jeanne Anguille on 1 Nov 1671 in Quebec. Recorded in Quebec, *Genealogical Dictionary of Canadian Families* (Tanguay Collection), 1608-1890, Volume: Vol. 1 Sect. 1: A-Hel; Page: 3. Published 2011 by Ancestry.com; accessed on Sept 5, 2020.

50. Jeanne Anguille died on 11 March 1711 in Charlesbourg, Capitale-Nationale Region, Quebec, Canada, and was buried in Cimetière Saint-Charles-Bor-romée. Recorded in Canada, Find A Grave Index, 1600s-Current. Accessed on Ancestry.com on Sept. 5, 2020.

51. François Allard died in 25 Oct. 1726 in Charlesbourg, Captiale-Nationale Refion, Quebec, Canada, and was buried in Cimetière Saint-Charles-Bor-romée. Recorded in Canada, Find A Grave Index, 1600s-Current. Accessed on Ancestry.com on Sept. 5, 2020.

52. Charlesbourg, Quebec history was drawn from *The Canadian Encyclopedia*, accessed online https://www.thecanadianencyclopedia.ca/en/article/charlesbourg, accessed Jun 22, 2020.

53. Marriage of Jean Baptiste Allard and Anne-Elizabeth Pageau on 23 Feb 1705, Charlesbourg, Quebec. Recorded in *Genealogical Dictionary of Canadian Families* (Tanguay Collection), 1608-1890, Volume: Vol. 2 Sect. 1: Abe-Ble; Page: 18. Published 2011 by Ancestry.com; accessed/confirmed on Sept 5, 2020.

54. Thomas Pageau's story is in the *Histoire Des Canadiens-Français, État Gênéral des Habitants du Canada en 1666* (1666 census). Excerpt posted on Ancestry.com by jdpiq on 13 Jun 2016; accessed on Sept 5, 2020.

55. Mathurin Roy's arrival in 1646, Recorded in U.S. and Canada, Passenger and Immigration Lists Index, 1500s-1900s, Place: Quebec, Canada; Year: 1646; Page Number: 168, published by Ancestry.com. Accessed on Sept 5, 2020.

56. Marriage of Pierre Allard to Marie-Angélique Bergevin on 5 Nov 1743 in Charlesbourg, Quebec. Recorded in Quebec, Genealogical Dictionary of Canadian Families (Tanguay Collection), 1608-1890, Volume: Vol. 2 Sect. 1: Abe-Ble; Page: 21. Published 2011 by Ancestry.com. Accessed on Sept 5, 2020.

57. The history of Jean Bergevin and Marie Piton and their descendants was drawn from "Les Ancetres Beauportois 1634-1760)" by Michel Langlois, pp. 247-249, as summarized by Jerry Longeuay dit Bergevin (9/1/97) and posted on familysearch.org; accessed/confirmed on Sept 6, 2020.

58. Death of Pierre Allard: 27 Dec 1759 in Charlesbourg, Quebec. Recorded in Quebec, Genealogical Dictionary of Canadian Families (Tanguay Collection), 1608-1890. Volume: Vol. 2 Sect. 1: Abe-Ble; Page: 18. Accessed at Ancestry.com on Jan 29, 2021.

59. Marriage and family of Marie Angelique Bergevin and Louis Jacques are recorded in Quebec, Genealogical Dictionary of Canadian Families (Tanguay Collection), 1608-1890, Volume: Vol. 4 Sect. 2: Gli-Jin; Page: 574. Accessed on Jan. 29, 2021.

CHAPTER 10: FRANCO-ONTARIANS—MIGRATION FROM DUPUIS TO DUPEE

1. Norbert Dupuis was born and baptized on 5 June 1771 in Montreal, Quebec. Recorded in Quebec, Vital and Church Records (Drouin Collection) 1621-1967. Accessed at Ancestry.com on Sept 7, 2020.

2. Geneviève Leroux was born and baptized on 3 May 1773 in Les Cèdres, Quebec. Recorded in Quebec, Vital and Church Records (Drouin Collection), 1621-1967. Accessed at Ancestry.com on Sept 7, 2020.

3. Marriage and family of Michel Leroux Rousson and Catherine Poirier Desloges are documented in Jetté, *Dictionnaire Généalogique des familles du Quebec; Programme de recherche en démographie historique* (PRDH), accessed online (membership required) on Jan 7, 2021.

4. Unnamed son of Norbert Dupuis and Genevieve Rousson was born in 1795 and died on January 15, 1796, recorded in Recorded in Quebec, Vital and Church Records (Drouin Collection), 1621-1967, Accessed at Ancestry.com on Sept 7, 2020.

5. Norbert Dupuis (Jr.) was born on 20 Jul 1797 and baptized on 6 Oct 1797 in Les Cèdres, Quebec. Recorded in Quebec, Vital and Church Records (Drouin Collection), 1621-1967, Accessed at Ancestry.com on Sept 7, 2020.

6. Marguerite Dupuis was baptized in 1809 at St. Regis, Quebec. Recorded

in Quebec, Vital and Church Records (Drouin Collection), 1621-1967. Accessed at Ancestry.com on September 7, 2020.

7. Jean Baptiste Dupuis was baptized in 1811 at St. Regis, Quebec. Recorded in Quebec, Vital and Church Records (Drouin Collection), 1621-1967. Accessed at Ancestry.com on September 7, 2020.

8. Seller, Robert. The History of the County of Huntingdon and the Seigniories of Chataugay and Beauharnois from the First Settlement to the Year 1838. The Canadian Gleaner, Huntingdon, Quebec. 1888. Accessed on Ancestry.com on Feb 5, 2023. Pp. 16-19. This book contains some inaccurate accounts of (Augustin) Eustache Dupuis's journey from Acadia to Massachusetts to Quebec, but his residence in Huntingdon County is likely accurate, based on dates and places of his adult life events.

9. Birth 22 July 1792 and death 25 Oct 1884 dates for Norbert Dupuis (son of Augustin Dupuis) are recorded in Canada, Find A Grave Index, 1600s-Current, accessed via Ancestry.com on Feb 16, 2023.

10. Baptism of Roach Joachim Dupuis, son of Joseph Dupuis and Marie Anne Parent, on 9 Jul 1803 at Saint Régis, Le Haut-Saint-Laurent, Quebec, Canada, recorded in Quebec, Canada, Vital and Church Records (Drouin Collection), 1621-1968, accessed at Ancestry.com on Mar 14, 2023.

11. Baptism of Angelique Dupuy, daughter of Joseph Dupuy and Marianne Parent, on 1 Nov 1806, at St. Regis, Indian Lands. Recorded in the book translated by Duncan MacDonald, The Parish Registers of Births, Marriages, Deaths of St. Regis Roman Catholic Mission (Early Jesuit) 1784-1830 PART ONE (1989, 210), Milton, Ontario: Global Heritage Press, 2012. P. 22.

12. Marriage of Sylvester Dupee and Mary Donaghue on 23 Dec 1870, recorded in Ontario, Canada, Marriages, 1801-1928; Archives of Ontario; Series: MS932; Reel: 6. Accessed at Ancestry.com on Oct. 17, 2021.

13. J.A (John Alexander) MacDonell. *Sketches Illustrating the Early Settlement and History of Glengarry in Canada*. P. 150. Montreal. W. Foster, Brown & Co. 1893. Accessed online, as reported in Wikipedia on Oct. 26, 2021.

14. Feltoe, Richard. *Redcoated Ploughboys—the Volunteer Battalion of Incorporated Militia of Upper Canada, 1813-1815*. Dundurn Press, 2012. P. 524 in Kindle version.

15. Ibid. pp. 33-36.
16. Ibid. pp. 78-81.
17. Ibid. pp. 231-236.
18. Ibid. pp. 244-247.
19. Ibid. pp. 291-292.
20. Ibid. pp. 317-376.
21. Ibid. p. 421.

22. Ibid. p. 468.

23. Norbert Dupee's service in the War of 1812 was listed in The Upper Canada Land Grant Register, which confirmed that "Norbin Dupie received the East half of lot 8, Con 4 Nissouri Twp. for his service in the Incorporated Militia. He made his land claim as a laborer for York Twp."

24. Marriage of Geneviève Dupuis and Louis Saucier on 12 Feb. 1821 in Anicet, Quebec. Recorded in Quebec, Vital and Church Records (Drouin Collection), 1621-1967. Accessed at Ancestry.com on Sept. 7, 2020.

25. Marriage of Marguerite Dupuis and Joachim Chatel on 03 Feb 1823 in Anicet, Quebec. Recorded in Quebec, Vital and Church Records (Drouin Collection), 1621-1967. Accessed at Ancestry.com on Sept. 7, 2020.

26. Geneviève (Dupuis) Saucier's birth in 1807 and death in May 1867 in St. Anicet, Huntingdon, Quebec. was recorded in Canada, Find A Grave Index, 1600s-Current. Published on Ancestry.com, 2012. Accessed on Sept 7, 2020.

27. Marguerite Dupuis's birth in 1809 in St. Anicet, Quebec and death on 26 Mar 1891 in Prescott, Ontario. Recorded in Ontario, Canada, Deaths, 1869-1938 and Deaths Overseas, 1939-1947, published on Ancestry.com, 2010. Accessed/confirmed Sept 7, 2020.

28. Marriage of Norbert Dupuis to Josephte Chatel on 19 Feb 1816 in Les Cédres, Quebec. Recorded in Quebec, Canada, Vital and Church Records (Drouin Collection), 1621-1968, accessed via Ancestry.com on Feb 16, 2023.

29. Pre-confederation land map of West Nissouri, Ontario, showing Norbin Dupee on Concession 4, lot 8, with three other French surnames bordering his lot, found at http://ao.minisisinc.com/FS_IMAGES/I0050917.jpg. Accessed on Oct. 17, 2021

30. A copy of the land transfer of Lot No. 8 in Nissouri, Fourth Concession, West Half, from Wells Dupie to David Young on Nov 30, 1846, was shared by Rosalie Duffin on Ancestry.com on Oct. 17, 2021. Rosalie is the 4th great-granddaughter of Norbert Dupee.

31. Dupee sons' military service recorded in the book *Men of Upper Canada, Militia Nominal Rolls 1828-1829*, authors Bruce S Elliott, Dan Walker, and Fawne Stratford-Devai. Toronto: Ontario Genealogical Society, 1995. p. 75.

32. Marriage of John Dupee to Catherine O'Brien on 1 Jan 1835 in Middlesex, Ontario, Canada. Recorded in Ontario, Canada, Marriages, 1801-1928, published 2010; Accessed on Ancestry.com on August 30, 2020. David O'Brien and Fanny Dupee were married on the same date and recorded in the same record. Both marriages were witnessed by Michael Dupee.

33. Marriage of Sylvester Dupee and Susannah Stanton on 18 March 1838 in Middlesex, Ontario, Canada. Recorded in Archives of Ontario; Toronto, Ontario, Canada; District Marriage Registers, 1801-1858; Reel: 3. Accessed

via Ancestry.com on Feb 16, 2023.

34. Marriage of "Norbear Dupre" and Dorothy Marsh, both of Nissouri, on March 8, 1840. Recorded in Ontario, Canada, Marriages, 1801-1928, Archives of Ontario; Toronto, Ontario, Canada; District Marriage Registers, 1801-1858; Reel: 3, Accessed at Ancestry.com on Sept 8, 2020.

35. Census in 1851 for Wells Dupe: Year: 1851; Census Place: Nissouri East, Oxford County, Canada West (Ontario); Schedule: A; Roll: C_11745; Page: 15; Line: 4. Accessed at Ancestry.com on Jan 2, 2022.

36. Death of Sylvester Dupee on 02 Jan 1878, with burial in Bayfield, Huron County, Ontario, Canada. Recorded in Canada, Find A Grave Index, 1600s-Current. Access at Ancestry.com on Sept. 8, 2020.

37. Death of Michael Dupee on 28 Oct 1893, age 98, in Enniskillen, Lambton, Ontario. Recorded in Ontario, Canada, Deaths, 1869-1938 and Deaths Overseas, 1939-1947. Archives of Ontario; Series: MS935; Reel: 68. Accessed at Ancestry.com on Aug 30, 2020.

38. Marriage of Michel Leroux dit Rousson and Catherine Poirier dite Desloges 1769 in Les Cédres, Quebec. Scanned document from Drouin Collection, originally posted on Ancestry.com on 30 Aug 2019.

39. Burial of Michel Leroux 1775, Recorded in Catholic Parish Registers on Familysearch.org, Image 26 of 237 in Les Cedres, Saint Joseph de Soulanges records for 1775 – 1781. Accessed on Sept 8, 2020.

40. Family of Michel Leroux Rousse and Catherine Poirier Desloges in Jetté, *Dictionnaire Généalogique des familles du Quebec; Programme de recherche en démographie historique* (PRDH), accessed online (membership required) on Jan 1, 2021.

41. Catherine Poirier's family: Family of Jean-Baptiste Poirier Desloges and Marie Geneviève Henault Deschamps Huneau, in Jetté, *Dictionnaire Généalogique des familles du Quebec; Programme de recherche en démographie historique* (PRDH), accessed online (membership required) on Sept. 20, 2020.

42. Marriage of Catherine Poirier and Michel Coullerier on 10 Feb 1777 in Les Cédres, Québec. Recorded in Quebec, Vital and Church Records (Drouin Collection), 1621-1967, published on Ancestry.com 2008, accessed on Sept 8, 2020.

43. Family of Michel Coullerier and Catherine Poirier Desloges in Jetté, *Dictionnaire Généalogique des familles du Quebec; Programme de recherche en démographie historique* (PRDH), accessed online (membership required) on Jan 1, 2021.

44. Sprague, D.N.. "American Revolution – Invasion of Canada". *The Canadian Encyclopedia*, 04 March 2015, *Historica Canada*. www.

thecanadianencyclopedia.ca/en/article/american-revolution. Accessed January 4, 2022.

45. Many details on Hubert Leroux and his wife Anne-Marie Van Zeigt were found with Leroux genealogy at http://www.angelfire.com/de/LeRoux/ and originally posted on Ancestry.com on 18 May 2016. Facts chosen to include were those corroborated with other resources.

46. Dechêne, Louise. Habitants and Merchants in Seventeenth-Century Montreal. Translated by Liana Vardi. Montreal: McGill-Queen's University Press, 1992. P. 7.

47. Marriage of Hubert Leroux and Marie-Anne Phansèque on 20 Nov 1673 in Montreal. Recorded in Quebec, Genealogical Dictionary of Canadian Families (Tanguay Collection), 1608-1890, Accessed at Ancestry.com on Sept 8, 2020.

48. Marriage of Marie Vuantzegue and Gabriel Cardinal on 15 Mar 1682 in Montreal. Recorded in Quebec, Canada, Notarial Records, 1637-1935, Accessed at Ancestry.com, accessed on Sept. 8, 2020.

49. The source of "decadent lives of Anne Marie Vanzegue and daughter Anne Charlotte Leroux" Peter J. Gagne, *King's Daughters and Founding Mothers, The Filles du Roi, 1663-1673*, (Vol 2) p. 546. Excerpt originally posted 5 Feb 2009 on Ancestry.com.

50. Another history of Anne Marie Fansèque appears in the book, *L'Allemande, la scandaleuse histoire d'une Fille du Roy 1657-1722*, Rémi Tougas, Septentrion, 2003. As the book is in French, I found a summary of key events at WikiTree.com/wiki/Phansèque-1, accessed on Jan 15, 2022.

51. Anne Marie's death under the name "France Cardinal" on 4 Dec 1722 and burial on 5 Dec 1722 in Laval, Quebec, is documented in Quebec, Canada, Vital and Church Records (Drouin Collection), 1621-1968. Accessed at Ancestry.com on Jan 15, 2022.

52. Jean Baptiste Leroux and Louise Chaussé's family life was summarized at https://www.angelfire.com/de/LeRoux/jeanleroux.html, accessed on Jan 15, 2022.

CHAPTER 11: *LES ACADIENNES*—THE ACADIANS

1. Family of Norbert Dupuis and Genevieve Leroux Rousson in Jetté, *Dictionnaire Généalogique des familles du Quebec; Programme de recherche en démographie historique* (PRDH), accessed online (membership required) on Jan 7 2021.

2. Family of Sylvain Dupuis and Francoise Leblanc in Jetté, *Dictionnaire*

Généalogique des familles du Quebec; Programme de recherche en démographie historique (PRDH), accessed online (membership required) on Jan 7 2021.

3.   Family of Jean Dupuis and Marguerite Richard in Jetté, *Dictionnaire Généalogique des familles du Quebec; Programme de recherche en démographie historique* (PRDH), accessed online (membership required) on Jan 7 2021.

4.   Martin Dupuis' profile is found in the Acadian Project as one of Acadia's first families on https://www.wikitree.com/wiki/Dupuis-41. Accessed on July 26, 2020.

5.   Michel Dupuis' profile is found in the Acadian Project as one of Acadia's first families on https://www.wikitree.com/wiki/Dupuis-41. Accessed on Sept 8, 2020.

6.   Find A Grave lists Martin Dupuis's birth (1612 in France) and death (1671 and burial in Port Royal), along with the names of his wife Perrine, and his child Michel. Recorded in Canada, Find A Grave Index, 1600s-Current, published 2012 on Ancestry.com, accessed/confirmed on Sept 8, 2020.

7.   Landry, Nicolas; Chiasson, Père Anselme. History of Acadia. August 19, 2013, updated by Dominique Millette and Clayton Ma on Nov 23, 2020, in thecanadianencyclopedia.ca. Accessed on Feb 28, 2022.

8.   Faragher, John Mack. *A Great and Noble Scheme, The Tragic Story of the Expulsion of the French Acadians from their American Homeland.* W. W. Norton & Company, New York. 2005. Pp. 1-3.

9.   Ibid. pp. 7-14.

10.   Fischer, David Hackett. Champlain's Dream. Simon & Schuster, New York, 2008. Pp. 201-206.

11.   Ibid, pp. 217-221.

12.   Ibid, pp. 211-212.

13.   White, Stephen, Origins of the Pioneers of Acadia, According to the Despositions of Their Descendents. translation by Lucie LeBlanc Consentino, Accessed at Lucie LeBlanc Consentino, Acadian & French-Canadian Ancestral Home, online at https://acadian-ancestral-home.blogspot.com, on Mar. 12, 2022.

14.   St-Jehan Passenger List, Among the French who sailed on the St-Jehan on April 1, 1636, were some of the pioneers of Acadia. translation by Lucie LeBlanc Consentino, Accessed at Accessed at Lucie LeBlanc Consentino, Acadian & French-Canadian Ancestral Home, online at https://acadian-ancestral-home.blogspot.com, on Mar. 12, 2022.

15.   Catherine Bugaret's profile is found in the Acadian Project as one of the Acadian first families on https://www.wikitree.com/wiki/Bugaret-2, accessed on Feb 9, 2022.

16.   Radegond Lambert's profile is found in the Acadian Project as one of

the Acadian first families on https://www.wikitree.com/wiki/Bugaret-2, accessed on Feb 9, 2022.

17. François Gautrot's profile is found in the Acadian Project as one of the Acadian first families on https://www.wikitree.com/wiki/Gautrot-42, accessed on Feb 9, 2022

18. Jacques Bourgeois' profile is found in the Acadian Project as one of the Acadian first families on https://www.wikitree.com/wiki/Bourgeois-8, accessed on Feb 24, 2022.

19. Jacques Bourgeois in Dictionary of Canadian Biography, vol II (1701-1740), at Http://www.biographi.ca.en/bio/bourgeois_jacques_2E.html, accessed on Mar 28, 2022.

20. Daniel LeBlanc's profile is found on the Acadian Project as one of the Acadian first families on https://www.wikitree.com/wiki/LeBlanc-100, accessed on Feb 28, 2022.

21. Jean Gaudet's profile is found on the Acadian Project as one of the Acadian first families on https://www.wikitree.com/wiki/Gaudet-21, accessed on March 23, 2022.

22. Tim Hebert; Transcription of the 1671 Acadian Census, at Port-Royal, Acadie, found online at https://freepages.rootsweb.com/~acadiancajun/genealogy/1671cens.htm, accessed on Apr 26, 2022.

23. Pierre Thibodeau's profile is found on the Acadian Project as one of the Acadian first families on https://www.wikitree.com/wiki/Thibodeau-30, accessed on Feb 26, 2022.

24. Pierre Thibodeau in Dictionary of Canadian Biography, vol II (1701-1740), at http://www.biographi.ca/en/bio/tibaudeau_pierre_2E.html, accessed on Feb 26, 2022.

25. Faragher, pp. 44-46. (recruitment of settlers)

26. Michel Richard's profile is found on The Acadian Project as one of Acadia's first families at https://www.wikitree.com/web/Richards-74, accessed on Feb 9, 2022.

27. Faragher, pp. 58-69. (1654 attack)

28. Dunn, Brenda. A History of Port Royal Annapolis Royal 1605-1800. Nimbus Publishing, pp. 23-24 (Capture of Port Royal) pp. 25-27;29 (the English period 1654-1670).

29. Claude Petitpas' profile is found on The Acadian Project as one of Acadia's first families at https://www.wikitree.com/web/Petitpas-15, accessed on Feb 9, 2022.

30. Marriage of Alexander Richards and Isabelle Petitpas around 1690 was reported in White, Stephen A., Patrice Gallant, and Hector-J Hébert. *Dictionnaire Généalogique Des Familles Acadiennes.*; Moncton, N.-B.: Centre

D'études Acadiennes, Université De Moncton, 1999, Print, pp. 1295 & 1373.

31. Marriage (1664) and dates of birth for both Michel Dupuis (b 1634) and Marie Gautertot (B 1636) are recorded in Web: Netherlands, GenealogieOnline Trees Index, 1000-2015, published in 2014 on Ancestry.com. Accessed on Sept 8, 2020.

32. Faragher, pp. 185-90. (Acadian customs)

33. Claude Petitpas (1663-1732) in Dictionary of Canadian Biography Vol !! (1701-1740) found online at http://www.biographi.ca/en/bio/petit-pas_claude_2E.html, accessed on March 14, 2022.

34. Rene Landry's profile is found in the Acadian Project as one of the Acadian first families on https://www.wikitree.com/wiki/Landry-70, accessed on July 25, 2020.

35. Marriage (1686) and dates of birth for both Martin Dupuis (b 1665) and Marie Landry (b 1670) are recorded in U.S. and International Marriage Records, 1560-1900, accessed from Ancestry.com on Sept 8, 2020.

36. Marriage of Antoine Landry and Marie Thibideau in 1681 is recorded in U.S. and International Marriage Records, 1560-1900, accessed from Ancestry.com on April 16, 2022.

37. Marriage of Pierre LeBlanc and Françoise Landry in 1710 is recorded in U.S. and International Marriage Records, 1560-1900, accessed from Ancestry.com on April 16, 2022.

38. Jacques Bourgeois in Dictionary of Canadian Biography Vol !! (1701-1740) found online at http://wwwbiographi.ca/en/bio/bougeois_jacques_2E.html. Accessed on March 26, 2022.

39. Faragher, p. 76. (Gaspereau River valley)

40. Acadian census 1701, Martin Dupuis, his wife, 3 boys, 4 girls, 6 arpents, 15 cattle, 15 sheep, 15 hogs, 1 gun, in Rivière Des Gasparots [Gasperreau] translated by Lucie LeBlanc, accessed at Accessed at Lucie LeBlanc Consentino, Acadian & French-Canadian Ancestral Home, online at http://www.acadian-home.org/frames.html, on Apr 26, 2022.

41. Faragher, pp. 77-79

42. Ibid, pp. 87-92. (Phipps attack)

43. Dunn, Brenda. A History of Port Royal / Annapolis Royal 1605-1800. Nimbus Publishing, p. 38 (Phipps captures PR); p. 39 (Peacekeeping Council includes Daniel Leblanc and Rene Landry); p. 41,43 (Nominal English Rule, 1693 PR raid).

44. Faragher, pp. 110-112. (attack on Grand Pré)

45. Ibid, pp. 120-123. (1710 attack)

46. Ibid. pp. 128-129. (address to the "People of Minas")

47. Ibid, p. 136. (Treaty of Utrecht)

48. Jean Baptiste Dupuis (b 1687) married Marguerite Richard on 1 Jan 1713 in Port Royal. Recorded in Millennium File, accessed at Ancestry.com on Sept 8, 2020.
49. Death of Marin Dupuis (b1665) on August 8, 1713 in Grand Pré, Acadia. Recorded in Canada, Find A Grave Index, 1600s-Current, accessed at Ancestry.com on Apr 26, 2022.
50. The widow Dupuis, 3 sons, 7 daughters in the 1714 Acadian census in La Riviere Des Gaspard (Gaspereau). Accessed at Lucie LeBlanc Consentino, Acadian & French-Canadian Ancestral Home, online at http://www.acadian-home.org/frames.html, on Apr 26, 2022.
51. Jean Dupuis with his wife, in the 1714 Acadian census, in La Riviere Des Habitants. Accessed at Accessed at Lucie LeBlanc Consentino, Acadian & French-Canadian Ancestral Home, online at http://www.acadian-home.org/frames.html, on Apr 26, 2022.
52. Find A Grave lists Sylvain Dupuis's birth (1721) and death (1799 burial in L'Acadie, Quebec), along with the names of his wife, Françoise Leblanc, and their children. Recorded in Canada, Find A Grave Index, 1600s-Current, accessed at Ancestry.com on Sept 8, 2020.
53. Marriage of Sylvain Dupuis and Françoise Leblanc on 17 Jul 1747 in Grand-Pré. Recorded in Family Data Collection – Marriages, published 2001 on Ancestry.com, accessed/confirmed on Sept 8, 2020.
54. Faragher, pp. 170-171. (another oath for King George II)
55. Ibid. pp. 202-203 (Mikmaq threat)
56. Ibid. p. 262. (Rene LeBlanc captivity)
57. Barthélomy Petitpas in Dictionary of Canadian Biography Vol III (1741-1770) found online at http://biographi.ca/en/bio/petitpas_barthelomy_3E.html, accessed on Apr 26, 2022.
58. Faragher. P. 228.
59. Ibid. pp. 252-268
60. Ibid. p. 333.

CHAPTER 12: *LE GRAND DÉRANGEMENT*—THE GREAT DISPLACEMENT OF ACADIANS

1. Marriage of Sylvain Dupuis and Françoise Leblanc on 17 Jul 1747 in Grand-Pré. Recorded in Family Data Collection – Marriages, published 2001 on Ancestry.com, accessed on Sept 8, 2020.
2. Family of Sylvain Dupuis and Francoise Leblanc in Jetté, *Dictionnaire Généalogique des familles du Quebec; Programme de recherche en*

démographie historique (PRDH), accessed online (membership required) on Jan 7 2021.

3. Faragher, John Mack. *A Great and Noble Scheme, The Tragic Story of the Expulsion of the French Acadians from their American Homeland.* W. W. Norton & Company, New York. 2005. Pp. 313-15.

4. Ibid. p. 319.

5. Ibid. pp. 329-30.

6. Ibid. p. 333.

7. Ibid. p. 336.

8. Journal of Colonel John Winslow. In Acadian Heartland, Records of the Deportation and Le Grand Dérangement, 1714-1768. Found in Nova Scotia Archives. Accessed online at https://archives.novascotia.ca/deportation/archives/?Number=NSHSIV&Page=113 on Nov 1, 2022.

9. Faragher, pp. 340-41.

10. Ibid. pp. 342-46.

11. Journal of John Winslow, volumes 1-4. Collection of the Nova Scotia Historical Society 1870-1884. Grand Pre, September the 15th 1755. "Names of the French Inhabitants, belonging to Grand Pre, Minas Rivers Cannard Habitant & Places adjatient. Confined by Lieut Colo Winslow within his Camp in this Place after their Coming in on his Citation on the 5th of September" Accessed at Lucie LeBlanc Consentino, Acadian & French-Canadian Ancestral Home, online at http://www.acadian-home.org/Grand-Pre-Names-Deported0001.pdf, on Jul 19, 2022.

12. Faragher, pp. 352-53.

13. Ibid. pp. 354-55

14. Ibid. pp. 358-59

15. "Hope and Despair of Acadian Exiles, 1755-1766." New England Historical Society. Accessed at https://www.newenglandhistoricalsociety.com/hope-despair-acadian-exiles-1755-1766/#comments, on Jul 19, 2022.

16. Faragher, pp. 361-63.

17. White, Stephen A. (2005). "The True Number of Acadians." In Ronnie Gilles LeBlanc (ed.). *Du Grand Dérangement à la Déportation: nouvelles perspectives historiques.* Université de Moncton. Pp. 21–56.

18. Sylvain Dupuis and Françoise Leblanc, with their children, are listed, with their assignment to Worcester County in Dafford, Robert. "Arrival of the Acadians in Massachusetts." Accessed at Lucie LeBlanc Consentino, Acadian & French-Canadian Ancestral Home, online at http://www.acadian-home.org/acadians-massachusetts-2.html. Accessed Jan 21, 2020.

19. Sylvain Dupuis and François Leblanc's 1755 arrival in Boston, recorded in U.S. and Canada, Passenger and Immigration Lists Index, 1500s-1900s,

Place: New England; Year: 1755; Page Number: 18. Accessed on Ancestry.com on Sept 11, 2020.

20. "Le Grand Derangement, the Acadian Exile in Massachusetts 177-1766." Accessed at https://www.sec.state.ma.us/mus/onlineexhibits/acadia/acadian-exhibit.html, on Jul 19, 2022.

21. Delaney, Paul. The Chronology of the Deportations and Migrations of the Acadians 1755-1816. Accessed at http://www.acadian-home.org/frames, on Jul 19, 2022.

22. Faragher, pp. 375-76.

23. Ibid. pp. 381-82.

24. Sylvain Dupuy and family are listed as having been distributed to Worcester County, Dafford, Robert. "Arrival of the Acadians in Massachusetts." Accessed at Lucie LeBlanc Consentino, Acadian & French-Canadian Ancestral Home, online at http://www.acadian-home.org/frames, on Jul 19, 2022.

25. Silvane Dupee or Silvan Dupuis or other spellings are listed in archives collection from the Secretary of the Commonwealth of Massachusetts related to the French neutrals, with accounts for their support from the province and for desiring to relocate to France. Accessed at https://www.sec.state.ma.us/ArchivesSearch/, on Jul 25, 2022.

26. Pierre Leblanc and Marie-Françoise Landry, their son Pierre, and daughter Mary Rose were also listed in archives collection from the Secretary of the Commonwealth of Massachusetts related to the French neutrals. Their names were sometimes translated as Peter White Sr, Mary White, Mary Rose White, and Peter White Jr Accessed at https://www.sec.state.ma.us/ArchivesSearch/, on Jul 25, 2022.

27. Bradshaw, Jim. "Simon LeBlanc family lived in poverty in Massachusetts, Minister's diary records tale of Acadian Families." Accessed at Lucie LeBlanc Consentino, Acadian & French-Canadian Ancestral Home, online at http://www.acadian-home.org/frames, on Jul 19, 2022.

28. The relationship of Jean-Simon Leblanc and his family with Rev. Ebenezer Parkman is documented in The Diary of Ebenezer Parkman, accessed at https://diary.ebenezerparkman.org on July 19, 2022.

29. Faragher, pp. 389-91.

30. Births and baptisms of children, marriages, and deaths of Dupuis children (Joseph, Elizabeth, Pierre, Charles, Marie, Simon-Pierre, Norbert, and Anastasie) are reported and documented in Françoise Leblanc's wikitree biography, referring to Drouin Collection church records. https://www.wikitree.com/wiki/Leblanc-2690. Accessed Jan 21, 2020.

31. Baptism of Norbert Dupuy on 5 June 1771 at Basilica Notre Dame,

Montreal, Quebec, Vital and Church Records (Drouin Collection), 1621-1967, accessed at Ancestry.com on Jan 31, 2020.

32. Death of Sylvain Dupuis on 28 May 1799 in L'Acadie, Quebec, is recorded in Canada, Find A Grave Index, 1600s-Current, accessed at Ancestry.com on Jan 31, 2020.

33. Marriage of Françoise Leblanc and Antoine Boudreau on 28 Sept 1801 in L'Acadie, Quebec is recorded in Dictionnaire généalogique des familles acadiennes, Author: Stephen A. White: Publication: University of Moncton, Centre d'études acadiennes; Online, p. 211. Accessed Jan 21, 2020.

34. Death of Françoise Leblanc on 24 Nov 1802 in L'Acadie, Quebec, is recorded in Canada, Find A Grave Index, 1600s-Current, accessed at Ancestry.com on Jan 31, 2020.

35. Faragher, p. 437.

36. Death of Jean Baptiste Dupuis (Sr.) on 23 Apr 1779 in St. Philippe, Quebec, recorded in Canada, Find A Grave Index, 1600s-Current, accessed via Ancestry.com on Jan 31, 2020.

37. Faragher, p. 381-383.

38. Germain Dupuy, Marie-Marguerite Dupuy, and Anne Marthe Dupuy sailed from Falmouth, England, to Morlaix, France, on May 26, 1763, recorded in Acadian-Cajun Genealogy & History, accessed online http://www.acadian-cajun.com/falmth.htm, accessed on Aug 3, 2022.

39. The specific birthdates and locations of the children of Germain Dupuis and Marie-Marguerite Granger, born in France, are listed in WikiTree for members of this family, which in turn cites Karen Theriot Reader's family tree on Geneanet, accessed at https://gw.geneanet.org/katheriot?lang=en&pz=-frederick+joseph&nz=theriot&ocz=1&p=germain&n=dupuis, on Jan 23, 2023.

40. Faragher, p. 425-6.

41. Family of Rene Hébert, exiled in Guilford, Connecticut, listed in Lucie LeBlanc Consentino's Acadian & French Canadian Ancestral Home online at http://www.acadian-home.org/frames, accessed on Jan 7, 2023.

42. Listings of specific death dates and burials in Mirebalais, St. Dominique (Haiti) are given in multiple Ancestry trees and in WikiTrees for Judith Hébert, Jean-Baptiste Hébert, and his wife Euphrasine Dupuis, while none provide specific sources, although other researchers have found their relatives' burials in Haiti's National Archives online, as listed below. For Jean-Baptiste Dupuis (reference 44) and his wife Marie Josephe Granger (reference 45).

43. Burial for Jean-Baptiste Dupuis on 27 Jan 1765 in Merebalais, St. Dominque, Haiti is recorded in ANOM: St. Domingue: Mirebalais, p. 5, accessed

via WikiTree online at http://anom.archivesnationales.culture.gouv.fr/caomec2/osd.php?territoire=SAINT-DOMINGUE&commune=MIRE-BALAIS&annee=1765, on Jan 9, 2022.

44. Burial for Marie Josephe Granger (wife of Jean-Baptiste Dupuis on 26 Nov 1764 is recorded in ANOM: St-Domingue: 1764, pé 44 Burial 26 Nov 1764, accessed online via WikiTree at http://anom.archivesnationales.culture.gouv.fr/caomec2/osd.php?territoire=SAINT-DOMINGUE&commune=MIREBALAIS&annee=1764, on Jan 9, 2022.

45. The marriage and descendants of Marguerite Hébert and Gabriel Dusseaux are documented in a story, "Ancestors of Constance Dusseaux," attached to Ancestry family tree by hailynn1 on Nov 2019, citing source: Rootsweb post by Bill Fonferek 16 Mar 2006.

46. Exile Destination: St. Dominique is described at Acadian-Cajun Genealogy & History, accessed at http://www.acadian-cajun.com/exsd.htm, on Aug 8, 2022.

47. Faragher, pp. 426-33.

48. The Connecticut exile and resettlement in Quebec for the family of Olivier Hébert and Cecile Dupuis is summarized with sources in WikiTree.com, as part of the Acadian Project, accessed at https://www.wikitree.com/wiki/Hebert-554, on Aug 5, 2022.

49. Death places for Elizabeth (St-Philippe), Amand (St-Jacques), and Alexandre Dupuis (La Praire) are listed with family of Jean Dupuis and Marguerite Richard in Jetté, *Dictionnaire Généalogique des familles du Quebec; Programme de recherche en démographie historique* (PRDH), accessed online (membership required) on Jan 7 2021.

50. Amand Dupuis and his family appear on a list of French Inhabitants in Andover, Essex County, listed in Dafford, Robert. Arrival of the Acadians in Massachusetts, in Lucie LeBlanc Consentino's Acadian & French Canadian Ancestral Home online at http://www.acadian-home.org/frames, accessed on Jan 7, 2023.

51. Faragher, pp. 403-4.

52. Death of Ursule Leblanc on 4 Dec 1758 in Cherbourg, France, recorded at Global, Find a Grave Index for Burials at Sea and other Select Burial Locations, 1300s-Current, accessed via Ancestry.com on Aug 15, 2022.

53. Death of Joseph Broussard on 19 Jan 1759 in Cherbourg, France, recorded at Global, Find a Grave Index for Burials at Sea and other Select Burial Locations, 1300s-Current, accessed via Ancestry.com on Aug 15, 2022.

54. Acadian arrivals in 1758 from Cherbourg, France at http://www.acadian-cajun.com/cherbourg.htm accessed on Aug. 15, 2022.

55. Arrival of Charles Broussard in Louisiana U.S. and Canada, Passenger and

Immigration Lists Index, 1500-1900s. Place: New Orleans, Louisiana; Year: 1785; Page Number: 7. Accessed at Ancestry.com on Jan 23, 2023.

56. Arrival of Agnes Broussard Potier in Louisiana U.S. and Canada, Passenger, and Immigration Lists Index, 1500-1900s. Place: New Orleans, Louisiana; Year: 1785; Page Number: 28. Accessed at Ancestry.com on Jan 23, 2023.

57. Death of Joseph Leblanc, age 33, on 18 Feb 1759 in St-Milo, France, was recorded in Find-A-Grave at https://www.findagrave.com/memorial/139591740/joseph-leblanc.Accessed via Ancestry.com on Jan 23, 2023.

58. Death of Joseph Leblanc (Jr.), age 3, at sea in 1759 was recorded in Find-A-Grave at https://www.findagrave.com/memorial/139591795/joseph-leblanc. Accessed via Ancestry.com on Jan 23, 2023.

59. Death of Francois Leblanc, age 1, at sea in 1759 was recorded in Find-A-Grave at https://www.findagrave.com/memorial/139591832/francois-leblanc. Accessed via Ancestry.com on Jan 23, 2023.

60. Marriage of Anne Moyse and Claude Guidry on 3 Feb 1762, recorded in Upper Brittany, France Marriages, 1536-1907, accessed at Ancestry.com on Jan 23, 2023.

61. Story of "Anne Moyse's Travels" on La Ville d'Archangel, a large 600-ton ship that left St. Malo, France on August 12, 1785, posted by priscillaberthalot on 18 Mar 2017 on Ancestry.com, accessed on Jan 23, 2023.

62. Death of child Pierre Hebert at sea in 1759, recorded in Find-A-Grave at https://www.findagrave.com/memorial/140014548/pierre-hebert. Accessed via Ancestry.com on Jan 23, 2023.

63. Death of child Marie Hebert at sea, in 1759, recorded in Find-A-Grave at https://www.findagrave.com/memorial/140014402/marie-hebert, Accessed via Ancestry.com on Jan 23, 2023.

64. Death of Marguerite-Monique Leblanc, age 24, on 25 Jan 1759 in St-Milo, France, was recorded in Find-A-Grave at https://www.findagrave.com/memorial/140014329/marguerite-monique-leblanc, accessed at Ancestry.com on Jan 23, 2023.

65. Death of Charles Hebert, age 32, on 22 Feb 1759 in St-Milo, France, was recorded in Find-A-Grave at https://www.findagrave.com/memorial/140014174/charles-hebert, accessed at Ancestry.com on Jan 23, 2023.

66. Death places for Anne Leblanc and Charles Dugas's family are listed in Jetté, *Dictionnaire Généalogique des familles du Quebec; Programme de recherche en démographie historique* (PRDH), accessed online (membership required) on Nov 9, 2022.

67. Founding of Carleton-sur-Mer by Charles Dugas and others described in Wikipedia at https://en.wikipedia.org/wiki/Carleton-sur-Mer. Accessed on Jan 23, 2023.

68. Augustin Leblanc (White), Françoise (Frances) Herbert, and Jean (John) Hebert were listed in archives collection from the Secretary of the Commonwealth of Massachusetts related to the French neutrals assigned to Worcester County. Their names were sometimes translated as Augustin White, and their first names were translated to English. Accessed at https://www.sec.state.ma.us/ArchivesSearch/, on Aug 3, 2022.

69. Marriage places and death places for Marie Rose and Pierre Hillaire, children of Pierre Leblanc and Marie Francoise Landry, are listed in Jetté, *Dictionnaire Généalogique des familles du Quebec; Programme de recherche en démographie historique* (PRDH), accessed online (membership required) on Nov 9, 2022.

70. Germain (Germon) Dupuis and Angelique (Ann) Dupuis were listed in archives collection from the Secretary of the Commonwealth of Massachusetts related to the French neutrals assigned to Nantucket. Their names were sometimes translated to English. Accessed at https://www.sec.state.ma.us/ArchivesSearch/, on Jul 25, 2022.

71. Profile of Marie Angelique Leblanc (1722-1787) found in WikiTree with the Acadian Project with Source listed on sailing from Boston to Quebec in book in French by André-Carl Vachon, *Les Acadiens déportés qui acceptèrent l'offre de Murray* (Tracadie-Sheila, N-B., La Grande Marée, 216 Kindle edition), pp. 128, 224. Her date and place of death (Jan 20, 1787, St. Jacques, Quebec) is listed here and in several Ancestry trees, but with no source to confirm this.

72. Death of Marie Francoise Landry on 13 Oct 1767 in Lavaltree, Quebec, is listed in Quebec, Vital and Church Records (Drouin Collection), 1621-1967, accessed via Ancestry.com on Jan 26, 2023.

73. Death of Pierre Leblanc dit Pineau on 22 Oct 1769 in Quebec, Capitale Nationale Region, listed in Canada, Find A Grave Index, 1600s-Current, accessed at Ancestry.com on Jan 26, 2023.

74. The UN definition of ethnic cleansing can be found at https://www.un.org/en/genocideprevention/ethnic-cleansing.shtml, accessed March 18, 2023.

75. Faragher, pp. 468-469, for discussion on applying the term of ethnic cleansing on Acadia.

EPILOGUE

1. Shah, Sonia. *The Next Great Migration, The Beauty and Terror of Life on the Move*. Bloomsbury Publishing, New York, 2020. P. 10.
2. Ibid. pp. 280-281.

PHOTO CREDITS

1. Chapter 1: Photo: "Leonard DePue" – as a young man
   Author: DePue family photo
   Source: DePue family photo
   License: provided by author
2. Chapter 1: Photo: "My father, Leonard, with Loretta and David in front of Holden Street house"
   Author: DePue family photo
   Source: DePue family photo
   License: provided by author
3. Chapter 2: Photo: Lillian and Fred's wedding photo in 1909
   Author unknown
   Source: courtesy of William Allor
   License: public domain, circa 1909
4. Chapter 3: Map "Columbus Township, St. Clair County, Michigan"
   Author: Notorius4life
   Source: Wikipedia https://commons.wikimedia.org/wiki/File:Columbus_Township_(St._Clair),_MI_location.png
   License: Creative Commons CCO 1.0 Universal Public Domain
5. Chapter 3: Photo "Detroit, Michigan and Griswald Streets, circa 1920"
   Author: Unknown author
   Source: Early Detroit Images from Burton Historical Collection, Detroit Public Library https://commons.wikimedia.org/wiki/File:Michigan_%26_Griswold_circa_1920.jpg
   License: Public domain (old) in U.S. first published before Jan. 1, 1928
6. Chapter 4: Map "Huron County, Ontario"
   Author: Videoman
   Source: Wikipedia
   https://commons.wikimedia.org/wiki/File:Map_of_Ontario_HURON.svg
   License: Creative Commons, public domain
7. Chapter 4: Map "Lapeer County, Michigan"
   Author: David Benbennick
   Source: Wikipedia https://commons.wikimedia.org/wiki/File:Map_of_Michigan_highlighting_Lapeer_County.svg
   License: Creative Commons, public domain
8. Chapter 5: photo of Lillian M Allor
   Author: unknown
   Source: courtesy of William Allor
   License: public domain, circa before 1909

9. Chapter 5: Photo of Isadore and Mary Frances Allor
Author: unknown
Source: courtesy of William Allor
License: public domain before 1925
10. Chapter 5: Photo of Lillian with brother Edward
Author: unknown
Source: courtesy of William Allor
License: public domain, circa before 1909
11. Chapter 5: wedding photo of Lillian Allor and Fred Dupee
Author: unknown
Source: courtesy of William Allor
License: public domain, circa 1909
12. Chapter 5: photo of "aunt Mary" Mary Frances Allor
Author: unknown
Source: courtesy of William Allor
License: public domain, circa 1919
13. Chapter 5: Photo of Father Edward Allor
Author: unknown
Source: courtesy of William Allor
License: public domain, circa 1920
14. Chapter 5: Photo "Basilica Sainte-Anne de Détroit"
Author: Andrew Jamison
Source Wikipedia Commons https://commons.wikimedia.org/wiki/File:Ste_Anne_de_Detroit.jpg
License: Creative Commons Attribution-Share Alike 3.0 Unported (CC BY-SA 3.0)
15. Chapter 6: "Relief map of USA Michigan" [Name of Lake St. Clair was added]
Author: Nzeemin
Source: Wikipedia https://commons.wikimedia.org/wiki/File:Relief_map_of_USA_Michigan.png
License: Creative Commons Attribution-Share Alike 3.0 Unported (CC BY-SA 3.0)
16. Chapter 6: Map "Macomb County, Michigan"
Author: David Benbennick
Source: Wikipedia https://commons.wikimedia.org/wiki/File:Map_of_Michigan_highlighting_Macomb_County.svg
License: Creative Commons, public domain
17. Chapter 7: Drawing "Fort Pontchartrain du Détroit in 1710"
Author: Pierre Descomps

Source: Wikipedia Commons https://commons.wikimedia.org/wiki/
File:Fort_Détroit.jpg
License: Creative Commons Attribution-Share Alike 3.0 Unported (CC
BY-SA 3.0)

18. Chapter 8: Photo: "Evidence of ribbon farms today"
Author: Judy DePue
Source: Judy DePue
License: provided by author

19. Chapter 8: Map "French colonization in 1750," ("shaded dark" added)
[image title: Non-Native American Nations Control over N America, 1750]
Author: Esemono
Source: Wikipedia Commons https://commons.wikimedia.org/wiki/
File:Non-Native_American_Nations_Control_over_N_America_1750.png
License: all rights released (public domain) worldwide

20. Chapter 9: Photo "Champlain statue in Quebec City"
Author: Judy DePue
Source: Judy DePue
License: provided by author

21. Chapter 9: Drawing: Champlain's "Habitation de Quebec"
Author: Samuel de Champlain, circa 1608
Source: Wikipedia Commons https://commons.wikimedia.org/wiki/
File:Champlain_Habitation_de_Quebec.jpg
License: The author died in 1635, so this work is in the public domain in the
country of origin; in the US, the public domain tag is PD-1996.

22. Chapter 9: Painting "Arrival of the French Girls at Quebec, 1667"
Author: C.W. Jeffries
Source: Wikipedia Commons
https://commons.wikimedia.org/wiki/File:The_Arrival_of_the_French_
Girls_at_Quebec,_1667_-_C.W._Jefferys.jpg
License: public domain in Canada, in US PD 1996.

23. Chapter 9: Photo Charlesbourg, Quebec, "The Trait-Carré, Aerial View in
1937"
Author: W.B. Edwards, Archives de la Ville de Québec, fonds Edwards, nég.
19052
Source: Wikipedia Commons https://en.wikipedia.org/wiki/Charles-
bourg,_Quebec_City#/media/File:Le_Trait-Carre_de_Charlesbourg,_vue_
aerienne_de_1937.png
License: public domain in the US, PD 1996.

24. Chapter 10: Photo "Sainte-Jacques Street in old Montreal today"
Author: Judy DePue

❧

Source: Judy DePue
License: provided by author

25. Chapter 11: Map - Canada Nova Scotia location map (Labeled "Acadia (Nova Scotia)" [arrows for Port Royal and Grand Pré added]
Author: Hanhil
Source: Wikipedia Creative Commons
https://commons.wikimedia.org/wiki/File:Canada_Nova_Scotia_location_map_2.svg
License: Creative Commons Attribution-Share Alike 3.0 Unported (CC BY-SA 3.0)

26. Chapter 12: Map - "Acadian deportation map"
Author: Maestrobistro
Source: Wikipedia Creative Commons
https://commons.wikimedia.org/wiki/File:Acadian_deportation_map.jpg
License: Attribution-Share Alike 4.0 International CC-BY-SA 4.0

ACKNOWLEDGMENTS

WHILE I HAD AN INTEREST IN FAMILY HISTORY FOR MANY YEARS, I picked up more serious genealogy pursuits after I retired from full-time work. Initially, I shared my findings with family members in the form of brief stories via email. For me, it was always about finding the stories, learning who our ancestors were, and what shaped their lives. But I have to thank my brother Dave, who suggested I publish my stories in a book for a broader audience. So, it became a challenge to raise my game. Could I make it interesting to readers outside my immediate family? He also resurrected a long-time dream of mine to write a book. I was an English major in college and always an avid reader. Isn't writing a book a secret dream of every book lover? It remains a secret until you are confident you can actually do it. Seriously, I told very few people initially. Therefore, getting this far is proof that we can still fulfill our dreams, even in our senior years. Some call our retirement years our second or third act. I strongly believe that we should not stop nurturing our dreams—or even coming up with new dreams—as we grow older. It's also good to nurture our curiosity and continue learning.

Of course, fulfilling dreams and writing books are never done alone. I have benefitted from the support of many people. First, I want to thank members of my Genealogy Club and our leader, Eleni Tsoukatos, at the Attleboro Public Library. We help one another find resources and problem-solve around breaking through genealogical brick walls. Everyone in this group demonstrates the necessary staying power to continue on our quests. Another valuable genealogical resource has been the French-Canadian Historical Society of Michigan. I have utilized many of their wonderful online resources. My knowledge of Detroit's history and my relatives' place in it would not have been possible if not for their generosity in sharing their extensive library online. A special thanks goes to Gail Moreau-DesHarnais for answering my email questions with her wisdom on a specific relative, Mary Mesny. And thanks also to Gail Moreau-DesHarnais, Diane Wolford Sheppard, and Suzanne Boivin Sommerville for their scholarly book in two volumes, *Le Détroit du Lac Érié*, 1701-1710. My copy has numerous sticky notes and highlighted sections. These books have been a great help to me.

Other scholars on French-Canadian history have also been inspirational. I was especially enthralled with the historical books by these authors:

- Faragher, John Mack. *A Great and Noble Scheme, The Tragic Story of the Expulsion of the French Acadians from their American Homeland*. W. W. Norton & Company, New York. 2005.
- Feltoe, Richard. *Redcoated Ploughboys—the Volunteer Battalion of Incorporated Militia of Upper Canada, 1813-1815*. Dundurn Press, 2012.
- Fischer, David Hackett. Champlain's Dream. Simon & Schuster, New York, 2008.
- McNelley, Susan. *Hélène's World, Hélène Desportes of Seventeenth-Century Quebec*. Etta Heritage Press. 2014.

They offered beautiful writing and excellent scholarship as they shared these histories. I didn't know that scholarly books could be so fun to read. I only hope I have done justice to these authors by summarizing pieces of their histories within my stories, and I might, therefore, extend their reach to more readers. Some readers might be inspired to pursue these source materials themselves.

My Ancestry.com DNA cousins have also been a great help. A special thanks goes to Jerry Jasper and Rosalie Duffin, both of whom are descendants of my third great-uncle, Michael Dupee. Jerry reached out to me via Ancestry.com and shared his findings on our third great-grandparents, Norman and Jane Dupee (Norbert Dupuis and Geneviève Leroux), whose history was a big mystery to me. Jerry shared what he had found on Norbert's military history and his land grant in Ontario.

Rosalie also reached out and offered another piece, an e-copy of the land transfer record and a map of the original lots in West Nissouri, Ontario, where I could see Norbert's name. Rosalie shared that, by coincidence, she and her husband own a farm a few plots away from Norbert's original lot. These were valuable pieces of the puzzle for Norbert's story.

I was delighted to meet other cousins online, including Robert Kehrer and William Allor, both of whom are long-time genealogists for the Allor family and have contributed to the expansive foundation for these family trees. I have especially benefitted from the many photos shared on Ancestry.com by William Allor, as they allowed me to "see" relatives I had never met. Robert also offered valuable technical help in dealing with the mechanics of the Family Search genealogy search platform. I have also met fellow Depue relatives on Ancestry.com, such as cousin Sonie Brasile, who has been a busy contributor and sharer of family photos. There are so many other cousins whom I don't know by name but who have shared valuable sources and hints in their online trees.

I want to thank my newly discovered first cousins, Roger Depue and Kathleen (Depue) Ehrhorn, for helping me fill in the missing pieces in my father's story. As our fathers were brothers, we all grew up with ripple effects from the brothers' difficult childhood experiences. Sadly, I had missed out on knowing these cousins earlier.

I am grateful to two of my nieces who have picked up the mantel as family historians: Becky Henderson and Tamara DePue. It is exciting to see their interest grow, and it is reassuring to know another generation will carry on the search. Of course, the search never ends. There are always more discoveries and more stories to tell.

Outside of the genealogy circles, I have benefitted from support for my writing process. I am a member of an ongoing writing group in Attleboro. We are kindred spirits. Everyone in the group benefits from encouragement for the multifaceted writing process. I have read pieces of my book aloud to the group and have benefitted from their constructive feedback, as well as practical information on publishing.

They took me to the next step on how to pitch my work and reach out to publishers. I am very grateful for this.

My close circle of long-time friends—Ellen, Maryalice, Tasha, and Karen—have been cheering me on and shoring up my confidence for decades. We have been through every life milestone together. This book project has been a different type of milestone for me, but one needing their support nonetheless. Since Covid-19, our group has been meeting weekly via Zoom. So I always had a place to report on my progress. And I have always known they have my back, no matter what. Thank you, Ladies!

My publishers at Stillwater River Press, Steve and Dawn Porter, have been excellent teachers and very patient as they have ushered me through the publishing process. This includes the multiple steps of editing, book design, and product distribution. I have felt at ease knowing I have their experience and wisdom as I go down this road. Our relationship will continue with steps ahead, but I am confident in our partnership.

Most importantly, I couldn't have done any of this without the ongoing support of my husband, my best friend and soulmate, Tom Lamonte. He was my first reader, offering his honest feedback and encouragement, chapter by chapter. He put up with my many hours on our laptop computer while I was working on this project. He also shared in reading some of the background histories. And we finally got to go on our trip to Quebec together, twice canceled due to Covid, where we got to see firsthand some of the sites where these ancestors lived. It was more fun to be able to share in this.

Now, as I am wrapping this up, I feel I have grown a little taller in the process. It has been fun doing the research. Genealogy can be addictive. Learning the history and context in which my ancestors have lived has been fascinating. The writing process has been fun while also being a challenge. Writing nonfiction stories, without having been there myself and with only bits of clues to go on for a storyline, is not the kind of writing I imagined when I dreamed of writing a book. But it's been rewarding. I am grateful for the opportunity.

About the Author

JUDY DEPUE, EdD, IS A RETIRED psychologist and Clinical Professor Emerita from Alpert Medical School at Brown University. She knew almost nothing about her father and the distress that led to her parents' divorce when she was an infant. Now, her clinical and research skills are applied to uncover not only her father's story but generations of family. Their strengths and struggles illuminate a French-Canadian cultural identity and their 400-year history in North America. Today, she lives with her husband, Tom Lamonte, in Wrentham, Massachusetts, and today, she can see evidence of a French-Canadian legacy all around.

www.ingramcontent.com/pod-product-compliance
Lightning Source LLC
Chambersburg PA
CBHW052015030426
42335CB00026B/3162